W. STEWART MCCULLOUGH is Professor Emeritus of the Department of Near Eastern Studies at University College, University of Toronto.

The History and Literature of the Palestinian Jews from Cyrus to Herod, 550 BC to 4 BC examines Jewish history against the background of the successive kingdoms which controlled Judea. From the time of Cyrus to the time of Herod, except for a brief period of independence in the second and first centuries BC, it was subservient to either the Persians, the Hellenistic kingdoms, or the Romans. Only in the area of religion did the Jews maintain their freedom almost without interruption. Their greatest tangible achievement in these centuries was in literature. During this period Israel's Scriptures emerged in their final form, summing up a thousand years of Israel's religious history and becoming the foundation of all subsequent Judaism and of early Christianity.

The author discusses the political situation in Judea and the social and economic conditions in so far as we can know them, and the early literary and religious developments. He then moves on to a discussion of the literature of the second and first centuries BC: the scholarly and pietistic traditions, apocalyptic and historical writings, the Dead Sea Scrolls, and the completion of the canon. A brief general bibliography is appended.

The author makes excellent use of the sources available, including the new materials on the Dead Sea Scrolls, and assesses them with a finely critical eye. He writes not only for students of early Judaism, but also for the general reader.

W. STEWART McCULLOUGH

THE HISTORY
AND LITERATURE
OF THE
PALESTINIAN
JEWS
FROM CYRUS
TO HEROD

550 BC TO 4 BC

University of Toronto Press

Toronto and Buffalo

© University of Toronto Press 1975
Toronto and Buffalo
Printed in Canada

Library of Congress Cataloging in Publication Data
McCullough, William Stewart, 1902–
The history and literature of the Palestinian Jews
from Cyrus to Herod, 550 BC to 4 BC
Bibliography: p.
Includes index.
1. Jews–History–586 BC–70 AD I. Title.
DS121.65.M3   933   74-80889
ISBN 0-8020-5317-3

CONTENTS

PART THREE
Literature, 200–4 BC

IX
The Scholarly and Pietistic Literary Traditions
and Early Scriptural Exposition

X
Apocalyptic and historical writings

XI
The Dead Sea Scrolls and the Completion of the Canon

PREFACE

The aim of this volume is to present a general survey of the history and literature of the Palestinian Jews in the last five centuries BC for students and others concerned with the later parts of the Old Testament, the Apocrypha, and early Judaism. The shortness of the bibliography at the end is congruent with the author's purpose, the list being confined to books likely to be accessible to the ordinary reader. These titles can be supplemented by the works mentioned in the notes. In order to keep the study within manageable limits, it is confined to the Jews of Palestine, thereby excluding the Jews of Egypt and of Babylonia, although both of the latter groups had, or were destined to develop, considerable significance in the Jewry of the ancient world.

The importance of the period 550 to 4 BC in Jewish history has long been recognized. It is in this span of time that we witness the completion and consolidation of the literary and religious achievements of ancient Israel. Not only were the Scriptures assembled, but Jewish values and customs, including acceptable expressions of piety, were firmly established, and upon this foundation all subsequent Judaism was to be built. Since the Christian Church was initially the child of the Synagogue, it too stands in debt to these centuries, for much of Israel's legacy was appropriated by the early Christians and became in fact basic for the Christianity of the New Testament.

This book has been published with the help of a grant from the Humanities Research Council of Canada, using funds provided by the Canada Council, and a grant from the Publications Fund of University of Toronto Press. It remains for me to thank Joan Bulger, assistant editor at University of Toronto Press, for her great care in editing the manuscript and seeing it through the process leading to publication.

W.S.McC.
September 1974

ABBREVIATIONS

Abbreviations

IB *Interpreter's Bible*, 12 volumes, New York and Nashville 1952–7

id *idem*, the same

IDB *Interpreter's Dictionary of the Bible*, 4 volumes, New York and Nashville 1962

KJV King James Version of the Bible

Life Josephus, *Life*

lit literally

Loeb *Josephus* in the Loeb Classical Library, 9 volumes, London 1926–65

LXX Septuagint

M Mishnah

Manual Manual of Discipline (DSS)

MS, MSS manuscript, manuscripts

n note

NEB New English Bible

no. number

OT Old Testament

p, pp page, pages

Ps, Pss Psalm, Psalms

rev revised

RSV Revised Standard Version of the Bible

Rule Rule of the Congregation (DSS)

sect section

Thank Pss Thanksgiving Psalms (DSS)

trans translated by

vol, vols volume, volumes

vs, vss verse, verses

War Josephus, *The Jewish War*

War Scroll War of the Sons of Light, etc (DSS)

Z Docs The Zadokite Documents

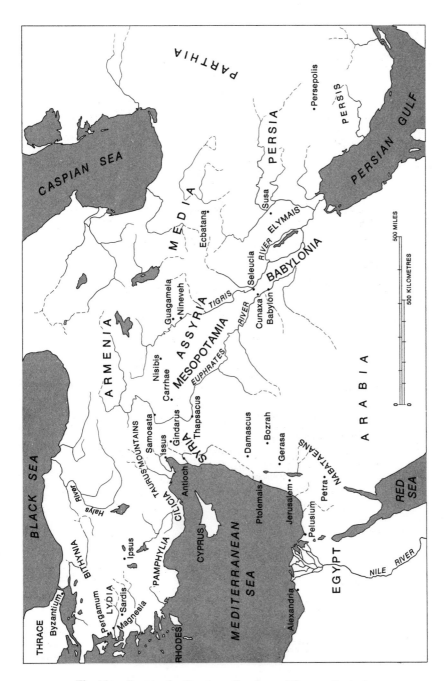

The Near East in the Persian, Greek, and Roman Periods

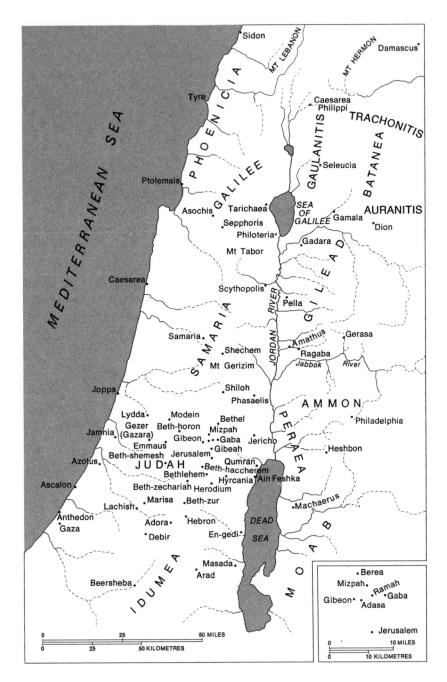

Palestine, Sixth to First Centuries BC

PART ONE

THE LATE BABYLONIAN AND PERSIAN PERIODS

I

JUDAH CIRCA 550 BC

Judah in the sixth century BC was a relatively small state, lying south of Bethel and north of Beer-sheba, with its capital in Jerusalem. To the north was the territory of the former kingdom of Israel (overrun by the Assyrians 724–721 BC), and to the west, along the coast, lay Philistia which did not come under the control of Judah until the second century BC.

The word 'Palestine,' which comes from 'Philistia,' is not a biblical term, and its use by classical writers such as Herodotus and Pliny is imprecise. Herodotus, for instance, refers to Palestine as a part of Syria (I, 105; II, 106). Josephus, too, is often inexact when he employs the word (*Ant* I, 136, 145, etc), but once, in *Ant* xx, 259, he makes Palestine coterminous with the ancestral home of the Jews. It was Christian usage that established Palestine as an acceptable designation of the Holy Land (e.g., Eusebius, *Ecclesiastical History* II, ii, 6; v, xxiii, 3; VII, xiv, 1).

THE POLITICAL SCENE IN WESTERN ASIA

Assyria's power ended with the fall of Nineveh in 612 BC, and thereafter its central and western territories were in the process of coming under the control of a revived Babylon. Shortly after 605 BC the new Babylonian king, Nebuchadrezzar, conquered the Hatti-land (Syria and Palestine), and from this time on, until the fall of Babylon to Cyrus of Persia in 539 BC, Judah was under Babylonian rule. The two ill-advised attempts by the Judeans to throw off Babylonian suzerainty, in 598 and 588–587 BC, were unsuccessful.

In the middle of the sixth century the most arresting development in western Asia was the rise of Persia under Cyrus, properly Cyrus II (559–530 BC),[1] although it is doubtful if the contemporary Babylonian king, Nabonidus (556–539 BC), fully appreciated the impact of the political changes which were taking place. Cyrus had succeeded in 559 BC to a small Persian principality (Anshan and Parsa) which was in fact part of the Median empire, and after consolidating his position at home he proceeded to rebel against Astyages, his Median overlord. This became a three-year struggle, but it ended in victory for Cyrus. The conqueror seems to have been aided by some of the Medes, presumably dissatisfied with Astyages' leadership, and this circumstance helped to ensure full cooperation between Persians and Medes in the new state, whose rulers were to be known as the Achaemenids, after Achaemenes, one of the ancestors of Cyrus. Once his initial wars had accomplished their objectives, Cyrus's aim was to secure peace throughout his realm, and to achieve this he tried to conciliate those he had conquered. Thus in Babylon he took pains to show himself friendly to the cult of Marduk, and he acted to restore the gods whom Nabonidus had earlier brought into the capital to their former places of worship.[2]

THE INTERNAL LIFE OF JUDAH

The secular scene

The evidence for reconstructing the life of Judah in the middle of the sixth century BC is largely inferential. It cannot be denied that the two rebellions against Babylonian rule earlier in the century had dealt a major blow to the life of the community. Towns were devastated and some of the population was exiled to Babylonia. The biblical allusions to the number of people sent into exile range from almost the whole population (as in 2 Kgs 25:21; 2 Chr 36:20) to the more modest figure of 4600 found in Jer 52:28–30. If the Babylonians hoped to extract taxes from Judah, it would hardly have advanced their purpose to exile large numbers of the peasantry; therefore many scholars believe that the exile involved at the most 20,000–30,000 citizens including women and children.[3] If this figure is correct, it means that the great majority of Judeans remained in their homeland throughout the sixth century.

Various biblical references support the view that only a small proportion of the population was exiled: some of the poorest of the land were left to be vinedressers and plowmen (2 Kgs 25:12; Jer 39:10); Gedaliah was appointed over the people who remained in the land of Judah (2 Kgs 25:22; Jer 40:7), or, as it is in Jer 40:5, 'governor of the cities of Judah'; Jeremiah decided to remain in Judah after the fall of Jerusalem (Jer 40:4–6); war refugees, who had sought safety in Moab, Ammon, and Edom, returned to Judah after 587 BC (Jer 40:11–12); some stores of food were available in Samaria (Jer 41:8); those remaining in Judah claimed that they were the true heirs of God's promises (Ezek 11:15; 33:24); the highly poetic language of Lamentations frequently points to those who survived 587 (Lam 1:11; 2:10,12,19; 5:1–5), although it also testifies to restricted food supplies (1:11; 2:12,19; 4:4; but cf Jer 40:10); there is reference in Neh 1:2 to 'the Jews ... who had escaped exile.' One negative piece of evidence about the demographic picture is the absence of any tradition that the Babylonians settled foreign colonists in Judah to replace the exiled natives (cf what happened to Samaria in 722–721 BC, 2 Kgs 17:24). A small augmentation of the existing population would have occurred after 580 BC if the Judeans who fled to Egypt after Gedaliah's murder (Jer 43:1–7) returned to their homes. Since both Jeremiah and his scribe Baruch were taken to Egypt at this time, the survival of the book of Jeremiah suggests that some members of the group eventually came back to Judah.

There is some archaeological evidence pointing to a resumption of normal activity in Judah in the years following the Babylonian wars. Towns such as Gibeah of Saul,[4] Gibeon,[5] and Mizpah[6] seem either to have been continuously occupied throughout these years or to have quickly reestablished themselves after hostilities ended, while the resettlement of other sites such as Beth-zur,[7] Beth-haccherem,[8] En-gedi,[9] and Arad[10] belongs to the early Persian period (i.e., after 539 BC) and possibly earlier. A new settlement near the old city of Jericho may, in view of the natural resources of the area, have begun in the sixth century.[11] We must not, of course, minimize the destruction carried out in Judah by the Babylonians in 598 and 588–587 BC. Jerusalem, with its walls breached and with many of its buildings burned, must have been a shambles (2 Kgs 25:4,9–10; Lam 2:5–6,8–9). We know that Beth-shemesh was so thoroughly devastated that it was never afterwards rebuilt,[12] and this was also the case at Debir or Kiriath-sepher.[13] Nonetheless, since the country's economy was basically agricultural, much of its life must have returned to normal in a short time. In this connection we may note that the Babylonian Talmud records that R. Joseph learnt that the *kormin* ('vinedressers'), said to have been left in Judah by Nebuzaradan (Jer 52:16; cf 2 Kgs 25:12), 'means balsamum gatherers from En-gedi to Ramah' (*Shabbath* 26a).

The Babylonians may have appointed another governor of Judah to take the place of the murdered Gedaliah, but on this point there is no information. Alternatively it is possible that Judah was now placed under the jurisdiction of the governor of Samaria. If this was so, it might elucidate the tradition that the Edomites moved into southern Judah in this century, probably after 587 BC (1 Esd 4:50; *Ant* XI, 61; Ezek 25:12, 35:5; Lam 4:21–2; Obad 10–14; Ps 137:7). A governor based in Samaria might have been less concerned about the Edomite inroads than a governor in Jerusalem.

Sometime in the early part of this century, if not before, the first steps were taken to change Israel's calendar to bring its terminology into line with that used in Babylonia. This may have been encouraged by the exilic Jews of the Euphrates region, but we suspect that the primary motive antedates the Babylonian wars and was in fact convenience in dealing with Babylonian authorities and merchants. Whatever the reason, the Babylonian names for the months began to come into use in Judah, and the older Canaanite names (Abib, Ziv, Ethanim, Bul) began to disappear. The fact that the seven new names for months that occur in the OT (Nisan, Sivan, Elul, Chislev, Tebeth, Shebat, Adar) are used only in post-exilic books (Zech, Ezra, Neh, Est) indicates that by the end of the century the new names were widely accepted. Even in Egypt two of the earliest of the Elephantine papyri, dated respectively 471 and 465 BC, both use the Babylonian names (Elul and Chislev),[14] which may point to more and earlier communication than is commonly supposed between the Jews of Elephantine and those of the homeland. Notwithstanding this innovation, it remains true that the commonest method in the OT of referring to the months is by number, and, despite some evidence that Israel in the monarchical period recognized a New Year in the autumn, the first month is normally placed in the spring.

The religious scene

THE LEGACY FROM EARLIER GENERATIONS

Yahweh (the Lord) was the God of Israel, and these two parties, God and Israel, were believed to be bound together in a covenant relationship, which made Israel the Lord's special people. By the sixth century many Hebrews must have assumed that Yahweh was the only true God, and to that extent they were monotheists, but for others various forms of non-Yahwistic worship, as well as magic, continued to be attractive. Apart from formal worship in the Jerusalem temple, carried out under the direction of priests, the annual religious festivals were the highlights of the religious year. These occasions were Passover (and Unleavened Bread), Weeks (*Shevuoth*), and Booths (*Sukkoth*). The first commemorated the deliverance from Egypt in Moses' time, and the other two were basically agricultural celebrations. There are numerous questions about these feasts (origin, history, mode of celebration, etc), but these cannot be dealt with here. Another side of the religious picture is displayed in the values and customs which were sanctioned by tradition. These ran the gamut of human behaviour, and protected, as we would expect, human life, the marriage relationship, and property rights. Certain social customs such as the circumcision of male children and the observance of certain food laws were undoubtedly in vogue long before the sixth century, but we cannot be sure to what extent the Sabbath was observed as a weekly day of rest.

It was a common Israelite belief that Yahweh had selected certain individuals to serve him in specialized areas. One such group was made up of the priests, whose internal divisions we shall comment on presently, and another of the prophets. Theoretically the latter acted as mouthpieces for Yahweh, and it is evident from the OT that their words on a wide range of subjects carried considerable weight. This was not always so, as is illustrated when a king of Davidic descent, Jehoiakim, felt free in 605 BC to burn the scroll of the prophet Jeremiah (Jer 36).

In addition to those who were professionally religious, there must have been in Judah numerous quiet, God-fearing, ordinary men and women who, through cultic practices or private devotions, found in their belief in Yahweh a refuge and a strength. Many of the Psalms seem to express the hopes and fears, the joys and sorrows, of these godly, pietistic members of the Hebrew community. On the other hand, there were those in Israel who were neither religious professionals nor humble devotees of Yahweh. These are variously described as 'fools,' 'wicked,' 'sinners,' 'insolent' (zedîm), and 'godless' (hanephîm). These terms occur, among other places, in the Psalms and in Proverbs, and they indicate that within the Hebrew community there were those who either treated the religious traditions very lightly or rejected them outright. How large this dissident group was we do not know, but the OT references to them warn us not to exaggerate the piety of the biblical Hebrews. In terms of religious interest and loyalties, Judah was very much a mixed bag.

Another aspect of the religious legacy available to Judah pertains to the nation's literature. Many of the strands that scholars have detected in the later Torah (the Law or Pentateuch, the first five books of the OT), the so-called L, J, and E documents, must have been known in the seventh century. Even the P document, a compendium of priestly views and practices, which in its final form is exilic or post-exilic, preserves numerous pre-exilic laws and traditions, and many of these were probably in written form, especially those concerned with temple procedures. The temple cultus was also responsible for collections of psalms, and these pre-exilic poems were to form the basis for the later Psalter. Another type of literature was the historical chronicle. Three of these documents, none of which is extant, were the Book of the Acts of Solomon (1 Kgs 11:41), the Book of the Chronicles of the Kings of Israel (1 Kgs 14:19), and the Book of the Chronicles of the Kings of Judah (1 Kgs 14:29). These chronicles and sundry other untitled sources (such as the L, J, and E material which some scholars find in 1 and 2 Samuel; the Davidic court memoirs preserved in 2 Sam 9–20; 1 Kgs 1–2; the Elijah and Elisha stories, 1 Kgs 17–19, 21; 2 Kgs 1–13) were at hand for those who wished to present the story of the nation's past.

AFTER THE BABYLONIAN WARS

It must be recognized that, while the rebellion of 588–587 BC resulted in a basic political change in Judah insofar as it ended the rule of the house of David in Jerusalem, no comparable change occurred in the religious sphere. It is true that the fabric of the temple was ruined and that the religious faith of many Judeans must have been sorely tested when Yahweh allowed his sanctuary to be destroyed. Nevertheless, as we shall note below, some form of sacrifice and temple ritual was probably resumed after 587. Even more important was the survival of religious traditions, which were to be found both among 'the people of the land' and in priestly, prophetic, and scholarly circles. It may be that some editing of materials, later to be incorporated into the Scriptures, was carried out by these groups (cf M. Noth's view that the deuteronomistic history was written in Palestine after 587 BC[15]). One indication pointing to the persistence of older practices and values is furnished by Haggai and Zechariah. These prophets addressed Judeans who had not been exiled, and their words show that the fundamental religious framework of Judah in 520 BC was substantially the same as in Jeremiah's time.

It is highly likely that this continuing religious interest expressed itself in temple ritual, necessarily in an attenuated form. The OT references to the destruction of the temple in 587 BC are not precise (2 Kgs 25:9; 2 Chr 36:19; cf Pss 74:4–8; 79:1), but it is a fact that they do not refer to the pulling down of the altar(s), although it may be presumed that any gold or bronze grilles, plating, or ornaments would be removed (cf 1 Kgs 6:22; 8:64; 2 Kgs 16:14–15; Ezek 9:2; 2 Chr 4:1; 2 Kgs 25:13–17). In any case it would be a comparatively simple operation to repair or build some kind of an altar. It is clear from Jer 41:4–8 that the eighty men from the north who came the day after Gedaliah was murdered with offerings 'to present them at the temple of the Lord' must have assumed that some of the temple ceremonies had been resumed. It is probable that the mourning and fasting in the fifth month (cf the burning of the temple in this month in 587 BC, 2 Kgs 25:8–9), which the people of Bethel claimed in 518 BC to have been doing for many years, point to religious observances after 587 BC of which we have no other knowledge (Zech 7:2–3). Any kind of temple activity would demand the availability of priests, and, unless the unlikely hypothesis is assumed that the Babylonians sent every priest in Judah into exile, the priests must have been in attendance. Whatever was done in Jerusalem after 587 BC was undoubtedly a makeshift arrangement, pending some turn of events that would make the complete rebuilding of the temple possible.

In view of the relation of Josiah's religious reforms of 621 BC to a recently discovered 'book of the law' to which the community pledged its loyalty (2 Kgs 22:1 to 23:25), and since it is generally agreed that this book was either Deuteronomy or something closely approximating it, we may assume that in the sixth century Deuteronomy continued to be the operative law in Judah.

An important area in which Deuteronomy seems to have stirred up dissension was with respect to the priesthood. Deuteronomy championed the rights of the Levites (Deut 17:9; etc), whereas since Solomon's time the Zadokites had seemingly dominated the Jerusalem sanctuary (1 Kgs 2:35; 4:2). The records do not permit us to trace the course of the wrangling which must have gone on between the two groups. As the exiles included a number of priests, we suspect mostly from the Jerusalem area (cf the number of priests among returning exiles in Ezra 2:36–9), we may assume that these were Zadokites, and this may account for Ezekiel (whose Babylonian milieu is here accepted) supporting the Zadokites as priests (Ezek 40:46; etc). Priestly tensions were further complicated by the claims advanced for the descendants of Aaron. While the references to Aaronite ancestry in Ezra 7:1–5 and 8:1–2 point to the age of Ezra, it is probable that they conserve a pre-exilic tradition about the superiority of priests of Aaronic lineage.

A more serious internal problem in Judah was the persistence of paganism. However thorough Josiah's reforms were in 621 BC, it is clear from both Jeremiah (2:20–8; 7:5–10,17–18; 7:29 to 8:3) and Ezekiel (8; 9:4; 13:17–23) that non-Yahwistic cults continued to have attractions for some Israelites. Possibly the death of the puritanical Josiah in 609 BC may have resulted in a covert revival of these practices. Deutero-Isaiah's satire on idolatry (Isa 44:9–20) and Trito-Isaiah's references (Isa 57:3–10; 65:2–7,11–12; 66:17) all bear witness to the continuing danger to Yahwism from this quarter.

Literary activity

It is generally supposed that the years following 587 BC were characterized by considerable literary activity. While there is no conclusive evidence about the locale of the writers, we are here positing that much of their work was carried on in Judah. During the Babylonian wars many precious scrolls may have been temporarily secreted in caves, as were the Dead Sea Scrolls of a later age. The availability of skilful and knowledgeable priests and scholars would also have to be assumed. A similar burst of scribal activity occurred in Judea in the late first and the second centuries AD, and for much the same reasons. In both periods the loss of the Hebrew state and the Jerusalem temple seems to have spurred the salvaging of traditions.

In the sixth century BC this interest in the past appears to have expressed itself in three directions. One was in the gathering together of priestly ideas and customs. A second is related to Israel's history in its classical presentation in Joshua-Kings. The growth of these books, some of whose sources have been noted earlier in this chapter, need not detain us here, except to observe that it is commonly thought that the material underwent one or more redactions by Deuteronomists in the seventh or sixth centuries. One result of such editing was that Joshua-Kings, as we now have them, are not a secular chronicle. Rather the secular data tend to be presented in relation to certain fixed religious values, and rulers are judged, not as rulers of a state, but in regard to the cult of Yahweh, a judgment which often reflects Josiah's reforms of 621 BC. The latest addition to Kings is doubtless the account of the pardon extended to Jehoiachin in 561 BC (2 Kgs 25:27–30). Since the return of the Babylonian exiles to Judah and the rebuilding of the temple (520–515 BC) are not recorded in 2 Kings, it is reasonable to conclude that 1 and 2 Kings received final editing not much later than 550 BC.

The third genre of Israel's literary legacy that appears to have been partly collected and edited in the sixth century comprises the writings of or about the prophets. When Zechariah (520–518 BC) referred to 'the former prophets' (Zech 1:4; 7:7,12), his audience must have had some idea of what he was talking about. There understanding may, of course, have rested solely on an oral tradition, but it is more probable that scrolls containing the oracles of earlier prophets were available in the community and that these scrolls supplemented the oral tradition. A careful examination of the extant prophetic writings indicates that they have been extensively edited, although the precise time of this editing can only be conjectured. That some of it was probably done in the sixth century can be illustrated from the book of Amos, for Amos 1:11–12 (about Edom) and 9:11–15 (about the fall of Jerusalem) would appear to come from after 587 BC.

THE BABYLONIAN EXILES

While, strictly speaking, the Babylonian exiles do not belong to our main subject, their Judean derivation seems to call for some notice of them at this point.

Life of the exiles

There is comparatively little information about the life of the Judeans exiled to Babylonia in 598 and 587 BC. Jer 52:30 records a third deportation in 582–581 BC, possibly in reprisal for the murder of Gedaliah. Although Ps 137:3 appears to point to some form of incarceration, it may reflect only the taunts of soldiers towards a defeated enemy, and Isa 42:22 and 52:2 may be but poetic hyberbole. The evidence of Jer 29:5–7 and Ezek 8:1 (cf 14:1; 20:1) suggests that the exiles possessed ordinary civil rights, their only restriction being that they had to remain in Babylonia. The only Judeans under a form of house-arrest appear to have been Jehoiachin and his immediate family. We know from the Babylonian records that over the period 595–570 this royal group received monthly rations of oil from Nebuchadrezzar,[16] and we are told in 2 Kgs 25:27–30 that the new Babylonian king, Amel Marduk

(562–560 BC), released the Judean ruler from confinement but continued his rations. It may be inferred, mostly from data found in Ezekiel, Ezra, Nehemiah, and the P document of the Pentateuch, that the exiles, to protect themselves against absorption by their environment, emphasized certain distinctive practices that could be followed in an alien land and would discourage assimilation, such as dietary habits, sabbath observance, circumcision, marriage customs. These group mores seem to have acquired a new importance in the exilic community, and when, at a later date, some exiled Jews 'returned' to the homeland, they could be counted on to advocate such practices in Judah, as the careers of both Nehemiah and Ezra illustrate.

Literary activity

It is commonly thought that some of the exiles engaged in various forms of prophetic and literary activity. How extensive this was would depend on the number and calibre of the persons involved, and on the number and quality of the available scrolls which initially must have come from Palestine. Jer 29 implies that letters could be received from the homeland, and this arrangement may have permitted scrolls to come as well. One of the earliest of the prophetic writers was Ezekiel. The starting-point of this volume is later than this prophet, but he is extremely important as offering a unique combination of the prophetic and priestly points of view. He is thought to have come to Babylonia among the exiles of 598 BC and to have begun his prophetic ministry 593–592 BC. Whether Ezekiel was active in the compilation of priestly traditions we do not know. The Holiness Code, a collection of cultic prescriptions and moral injunctions in which the concept of holiness is prominent (Lev 17–26), has a number of parallels in content and language with the book of Ezekiel, and this fact has been used to credit the present form of the Holiness Code to Babylonian Jewry and to date it not later than 550 BC.

Deutero-Isaiah

The most striking writer among the exiles was the anonymous author of Isa 40–55, usually known as Deutero-Isaiah. While it is here as-

13

sumed that these chapters are the work of a Judean exile, the Babylonian locale for this part of Isaiah has not been established with any degree of finality. The arguments in favour of a Palestinian origin have much to be said for them. There is less uncertainty about the date because of the following considerations. First, the political background is furnished by the supremacy of Babylon (Isa 47), whose downfall is imminent. As the Neo-Babylonian empire flourished 626–539 BC, the reference just cited must point to a time near the end of this period. Second, the two allusions to Cyrus (44:28; 45:1) must belong sometime in Cyrus's career (559–530 BC). Third, the descriptions of the condition of Judah and Jerusalem reflect a physical disaster such as in fact occurred in 598 and 588–587 BC (44:26; 45:13; 49:8,14,19), and the references to exiles in Babylon must allude to the same wars (45:13; 48:20; 49:9).

The message of Deutero-Isaiah depends, as does that of most of the Hebrew prophets, primarily upon the prophet's idea of God, and secondarily upon the conditions of his age. Of the latter we need say only that the rise of Cyrus created a threat to Babylon and foreshadowed a change in the political climate of western Asia which might be beneficial to Judah. As for the prophet's understanding of God, it is clearly the cap-stone for all the earlier oracles from Israel's seers. The burden of 40:12–17,27–31 is the greatness and goodness of the Lord. Even the creation of darkness and evil is to be attributed to him (45:7). Further, Deutero-Isaiah makes explicit what was probably implicit in the messages of most of the former prophets when he affirms that Yahweh alone is God (44:6; 45:5–6; 46:9). This unqualified monotheism was to be a basic feature of Hebrew thought from this time on. It is because of this conviction that the prophet ridicules all forms of idolatry (40:18–20; 44:9–20; 46:1–7). Finally Deutero-Isaiah takes the older notion of Yahweh having chosen Israel to be his people (Ex 19:5; Deut 7:6; Ps 135:4; etc), and gives it a fresh twist by asserting that Israel is in fact Yahweh's servant (41:8–9).

It is with this conception of Yahweh's nature and purpose guiding him that Deutero-Isaiah delivers his message to his contemporaries. He shares with them his own understanding of God, and he proceeds to assure them that this God is about to comfort his people (40:1–2,9–11; 41:10–13; 43:1–2; 51:3). The exiles will return to their homeland (45:13; 48:20; 49:9–12), and the waste places of Judah will be rebuilt (44:26; 45:13; 49:8,14–21). This whole series of events is spoken of as the Lord's salvation, and, with some poetic license, both heaven and earth are to vanish away (51:5–6,9–11; 52:7–10). A more realistic aspect of this impending change in Judah's fortunes is that Cyrus of Persia, whom Yahweh has raised up, is to be the human instrument that will effect God's purposes (41:1–2; 44:28); in 45:1, an extraordinary verse, Cyrus is even titled 'the Lord's anointed.' The prophet is confident that, as part of this changing picture, Babylon's power will end (47:1–15). One of the best examples of his exuberant hope is chapter 55 in which verse 12 reads (RSV):

> For you shall go out in joy,
>   and be led forth in peace;
> the mountains and the hills before you
>   shall break forth into singing,
>   and all the trees of the field shall clap their hands.

Although Israel enjoyed a special covenant relationship with the Lord (55:3), it is obvious to us, as it was to Deutero-Isaiah that, if monotheism is to be taken seriously, the time must come when all men will acknowledge the one true God. We read in 45:22–3 (RSV):

> Turn to me and be saved,
>   All the ends of the earth!
>   For I am God, and there is no other ...
>   To me every knee shall bow, every tongue shall swear.

The question immediately arises: how is the pagan world to become acquainted with Israel's God? For Deutero-Isaiah's answer we must turn to the Servant Songs.

For a long time four sections of Deutero-Isaiah have been recognized as standing somewhat apart from the rest of his prophecy, although composed by him. These are the Servant Songs, found in 42:1–4; 49:1–6; 50:4–9; 52:13 to 53:12. As their title suggests, these poems relate to the nature and work of a Servant, but the identification of the Servant has been and still is the subject of debate. An old view that the Servant is Israel (conceived of ideally) still enjoys considerable favour (cf the equation of Israel and the Servant in 49:3), but another opinion, that the Servant is one who is to come, a more perfect embodiment of Yahweh's Servant than the Israel of history, also has its champions (cf the distinction between the Servant and Israel in 49:5–6).

The songs indicate that the Servant is to do his work quietly and unsensationally, and that his object is to establish justice in the earth (42:1–4). His task, at times a discouraging one (42:4; 49:4), is to be a light to the Gentiles and to extend the Lord's salvation to the ends of the earth (49:6). It is evident that the Servant's mission involves him in various forms of opposition and oppression (50:6–9), of which the classical description is in the fourth song, especially 53:3–9. Notwithstanding all this, the will of the Lord will prosper at the Servant's hands (53:10–12). These last three verses, as well as 53:4–6, present the thought that in some undefined sense the sufferings of the Servant are for the healing of the nations and constitute part of the means whereby the Servant performs his divinely appointed task.

The poetry of Deutero-Isaiah is among the greatest of the artistic compositions of ancient Israel. The author stands out, not only as the most eminent of the Hebrew prophets, but as a superb literary craftsman, who utilizes with a touch of genius practically all of Israel's poetic traditions to give his words the form in which they come to us. The compassion, urgency, and incisiveness of the message find expression in language peculiarly appropriate to the prophetic word.

II

FROM CYRUS TO MALACHI

THE PERSIAN EMPIRE, 559–330 BC

As we have seen in chapter 1, Cyrus (559–530 BC) laid the foundation of a Persian state, and all the kings who succeeded him traced their descent to the same ancestor, Achaemenes. Cyrus's son and successor, Cambyses (530–522 BC), conquered Egypt in 525 BC, although this was to prove to be a doubtful acquisition, for it involved later Persian kings in putting down repeated Egyptian rebellions. The death of Cambyses gave rise to a political crisis, from which Darius I (an Achaemenid, but from another branch of the family) emerged as sole ruler (522–486 BC). Xerxes I (486–465 BC) and Artaxerxes I (465–424 BC), son and grandson of Darius I, were the next rulers, but the accession of Artaxerxes I by intrigue and murder points to a growing instability in the Persian court.

Cambyses' conquest of Egypt in 525 BC was the last important addition to the Persian empire. The attempt of Darius I to extend his suzerainty into the Greek world failed (Marathon, 490 BC), and a second attempt by Xerxes met with the same result (Salamis, 480 BC, Plataea, 479 BC). It is curious that these stupendous military operations, which must have affected, directly or indirectly, most of Persia's western provinces, and which left their mark on the literature of the Greek world, find no echo in Judah's writings of this period. It was perhaps just as well for Persia that her efforts to get into Europe were unsuccessful. As things were, the Persians had enough trouble maintaining a hold on their Asiatic possessions, which extended from the Indus river on the east to the Aegean on the west. To rule and administer effectively this vast conglomerate of nations, cultures, languages, and religions was an almost impossible task, as the successors of Alexander the Great, who initially controlled virtually the same area, were to discover in the late fourth and early third centuries BC.

Whatever efforts Cyrus may have made to organize his empire, it is generally conceded that it was Darius I who gave it the structure which enabled it to survive until the advent of Alexander the Great. Basic to this organization was the division of the territory into provinces or satrapies, whose numbers and borders varied from time to time. Each satrapy was in the charge of a satrap, and it is clear that, despite various checks and limitations on his power, the satrap everywhere in the empire was an important and powerful person. Herodotus (III, 89–94) furnishes considerable data on the satrapies and the revenues which they brought to the treasury, but this information has to be used cautiously and in conjunction with extant Persian sources.

Very little is known about the religion either of the Achaemenid kings or of their subject people. The historicity of the prophet Zoroaster is commonly assumed and his dates are thought to be 628–551 BC.[1] While the Gathas, poems traditionally ascribed to Zoroaster (and now found in Yasna 28–34, 43–51, 53),[2] give us primary material for reconstructing the prophet's teaching, which was centred in the god Ahura Mazda, the history of early Zoroastrianism is quite obscure. Neither Cyrus nor Cambyses betrays any knowledge of Zoroaster or his god (cf Cambyses' reference to 'the gods of my royal house,' Herodotus III, 65), and it is not until Darius I that Ahura Mazda is publicly acknowledged, as in the Behistun inscription (carved on a high cliff west of Hamadan c 520 BC). Later Persian kings recognize 'the gods,' as well as Ahura Mazda, Anahit, and Mithra specifically, and this would appear to support the conclusion that the Achaemenids accepted a polytheistic world, with Ahura Mazda occupying a prominent place in it. It is possible, therefore, that for most ordinary Iranians some such type of monarchical polytheism furnished the framework for their religious belief. That this kind of religion, which was not notably different from the religions of Egypt, Syria, or Mesopotamia, would have exerted much influence on the development of Judaism in this period is improbable.

It is difficult to generalize about the Achaemenid policy to subject peoples except to observe that, if the populace did not rebel and paid the required tribute, it seems to have been largely left alone. This was also true in the religious sphere, although here our information comes mostly from the Palestinian Jews. The stories of Herodotus about Cambyses' outrageous behaviour in Egypt (III, 27–9, 37) may not be entirely factual, but we have no reason to question the same writer's account of Darius's severity in putting down a rebellion in Babylon (III, 150–9). Xerxes' harsh treatment of the rebellious Egyptians is contrasted by Herodotus with the milder policy of Darius (VII, 7). On the other hand some Persian kings are credited with the virtue of clemency (Cyrus to Croesus, Herodotus I, 86–92; Darius to the Eretrians, Herodotus VI, 119). A possible conclusion from all this is that the Achaemenids settled many of the problems relating to their subjects on a purely empirical basis.

CONDITIONS IN JUDAH IN THE LATE SIXTH AND EARLY FIFTH CENTURIES

Sources

The literary sources for this period of Judah's history have been intensively studied by scholars whose works are readily available, and therefore we shall comment here only on the chief points which have emerged from their study.

An important source is the OT Ezra-Nehemiah, which appears to be part of the work of the Chronicler who has given us 1 and 2 Chronicles (see pp 53–6). As the Chronicler's editorial habits and biases can be detected, at least in part, from the way he handles the earlier biblical material, it is obvious that what he presents to us in Ezra-Nehemiah must be treated cautiously. For the period 538 to 450 BC it is only Ezra 1–6 that can help us. This section of Ezra displays the peculiarity of being partly in Aramaic (4:8 to 6:18). The decree of Cyrus in 1:2–4 (in Hebrew, with an Aramaic version in 6:3–5) and the letters to and from

Artaxerxes (4:8–23) and Darius (5:6–17; 6:6–12) may, in their present form, reflect the hand of the Chronicler, but their substance is probably historical.

A second document related to the canonical Ezra-Nehemiah, 1 Esdras, is examined below. Josephus, another of our sources, seems to have used 1 Esdras, as his account of this period of Jewish history indicates (*Ant* XI, 1–158).[3]

A somewhat different type of source is presented by the prophetic books of Haggai, Zechariah 1–8, and Malachi, each of which is dealt with later in this chapter. Some anonymous prophecy, such as Isa 56–66, also furnishes useful data for this age.

Another kind of material is furnished by the Elephantine Papyri (in Aramaic) which come to us from a Jewish settlement in Elephantine, Egypt, and which are dated 495–400 BC. These give us some incidental information about Palestine in the fifth century BC.[4]

Finally there is 1 Esdras. Although its Greek text probably originated in Egypt c 150 BC, and as such might be thought to lie outside the concern of this chapter, its patent relationship to the biblical Ezra-Nehemiah makes a brief notice of it appropriate here.

The traditions about the revival of Judah in the sixth and fifth centuries are found (apart from the writings of prophets) in three sources: first, in the OT text of Ezra-Nehemiah; second, in the Greek Septuagint, which is a rather literal translation of the foregoing; third, in 1 Esdras, also in Greek. The latter offers a narrative that is generally parallel to 2 Chr 35:1–27; 36:1–21; Ezra 1:1–11; 4:7–24; 2:1 to 4:5; 4:24; 5:1 to 10:44; Neh 7:73; 8:1–13a. 1 Esd 3:1 to 5:6, found nowhere else in the Jewish tradition, is the tale of three bodyguards of Darius who set up a public-speaking contest for themselves on the theme 'the strongest force in society'; the third speaker, identified with the Jew Zerubbabel (4:13), who had espoused two subjects, women and truth, was declared by the king to be the winner. For his reward he requested the king's support for the Jews in reviving life in their homeland and in rebuilding the temple. The conclusion to the story is in 5:1–6, where we read that Darius sent one thousand horsemen to escort the Babylonian refugees back to Judah. This story of the three guards appears to be of foreign origin. The identification of the third guard with Zerubbabel (only once, in 4:13) seems artificial and is doubtless intended to give the tale some apparent relevance to the main theme of 1 Esdras, and perhaps also to enhance the role of Zerubbabel in Judah's life.

When we examine the data furnished by 1 Esdras, particularly the parts corresponding to 2 Chronicles, Ezra, and Nehemiah, we have to conclude that they do not substantially add to what we can glean from the biblical sources. The pietistic comment in 1 Esd 1:23–4 does not really improve 2 Chr 35, and the escort furnished Zerubbabel in 1 Esd 5:2 is probably fanciful (cf Neh 2:9). An inner contradiction in 1 Esdras is related to the vessels taken from the Jewish temple by the Babylonians. In 2:10–15 these are returned in the time of Cyrus (cf Ezra 1:7–11), but in 4:43–6 it is Darius who authorizes their return. A striking feature of the arrangement of the material in 1 Esdras is that the pericope found in Ezra 4:7–24 (dated in the days of Artaxerxes) appears in 1 Esd 2:16–30 as something that happened between the time of Cyrus and the time of Darius.[5] But the most glaring difference between 1 Esdras and Ezra-Nehemiah is that the former completely ignores Nehemiah. As Ben Sira is an independent witness to Nehemiah and his work (49:13), 1 Esdras's silence about the latter is strange. Scholars have noted that the Attarates of 1 Esd 9:49 may be an echo of the Hebrew *tiršatha'* ('governor'), a title applied to Nehemiah in Neh 8:9 and 10:1.

It seems to meet most of the facts if we assume that there were various traditions in circulation about Judah in the early Persian period. One selection of these, put together by the Chronicler, is found in the OT Ezra-Nehemiah. This book was eventually translated into rather pedestrian Greek, perhaps by Theodotion of the second century AD, and it is this translation which is found in the Septuagint. Another selection of these traditions, with numerous parallels to 2 Chronicles, Ezra, and Nehemiah, appears in 1 Esdras, and early in its history it was expanded to include the tale of the three guards. About the middle of the second century BC this was translated, presumably in Egypt, into an idiomatic and almost elegant Greek, to give us 1 Esdras, the book known to Josephus. Whether it was ever longer than it now is, we do not know. We do know that Josephus seems to have used something other than the canonical Ezra-Nehemiah for his presentation of Nehemiah (*Ant* XI, 159–83).

Judah, 540–450 BC

We do not know when Judah was incorporated into the Persian state, except that it must have been after Cyrus's capture of Babylon in 539 BC. We learn from Herodotus (III, 91) that in the time of Darius I Palestine was included in the fifth satrapy, which embraced the territory from Cilicia to Egypt as well as the island of Cyprus, and that its annual tribute was 350 talents ('the tribute of the province from Beyond the River,' Ezra 6:8). What proportion of this amount was extracted from Judah is not known (cf the references to royal taxes in Ezra 4:13,20; 6:8; 7:24), but we learn from Neh 5:4 that there was an impost on fields and vineyards. If the word *hlk* (RSV 'toll') is used in a technical sense in Ezra 4:13,20 and 7:24, it probably means corvée, and indicates that some taskwork was exacted by the authorities.[6]

It is likely that there was some form of military conscription in Persia, although it may have been used only in time of war to supplement the standing army which was drawn mostly from the Persians and Medes. The men of Judah can hardly have escaped such a draft, but the biblical sources say nothing about it. A late parallel is found in the Letter of Aristeas (see pp 28, 87–8, 93–4), which records the tradition that early in the Hellenistic period Ptolemy I of Egypt impressed Jews into his military service (Aristeas 12–14).

Whether there was some expectation in Jewish circles either that God would bring about, or that Persia would allow, the revival of the Davidic monarchy, we do not know. It is clear, however, that for the time being Judah was under the control of a governor. In Ezra 6:7 and Mal 1:8 this personage is nameless, but elsewhere there are references to Sheshbazzar (c 538 BC, Ezra 5:14) and Zerubbabel (c 520 BC, Hag 1:1,14; 2:2,21). The term *phh* (RSV 'governor') is loosely used by biblical writers, and in some cases is applied to the satrap of the fifth satrapy, or to someone closely associated with him, as in Ezra 5:3,6 and 6:6,13. Nothing is known about the duration of a governorship, but it has been conjectured on the basis of Neh 1:1 and 13:6 that the appointment could extend for at least twelve years. During his tenure of office the governor was entitled to a food allowance (Neh 5:14,18). It can be inferred from Ezra 6:7 that he was assisted by a council of elders. Since elders are mentioned elsewhere in Ezra without reference to the governor (5:5,9; 6:8,14; 10:8,14), it seems probable that some of the traditional responsibilities of Israel's eldership (Deut 19:12; 21:2; 22:16; 25:7) were retained under Persian rule. 'Officials' and 'judges' also appear as administrative personnel in Ezra 10:8,14.

Although references in the OT to general economic conditions tend to be incidental or to have a didactic purpose, we can obtain from them a little light on the farming situation in Judah in the period under review.[7] It is Haggai who c 520 BC comments on the depressed state of agriculture (1:6,11; 2:16–17,19), and at that particular time this may have been the case. Other references give a somewhat different picture. Ezra 6:9 indicates the availability of animals and farm produce, as does 7:22, while Mal 3:10 assumes that full tithes can be paid. But the situation could be better, and the prospect of a brighter tomorrow is found in Zech 8:11–12 and Mal 3:10–11. Such trading as was done was probably by barter, although for large transactions small silver and gold ingots were more serviceable. It was Darius I who, taking a cue from Lydia, introduced into his empire a bimetallic coinage of gold darics and silver shekels, but these do not seem to have been accepted everywhere (Greek coinage was often favoured in the western satrapies), and it is probable that the ordinary merchant in Judah would know little about coins (cf the payment in kind to the lumbermen in Ezra 3:7). Some of the Persian satraps had permission to issue their own coins, but not in gold, and it seems likely that the few extant coins of this period with YHD (Judah) stamped on them were authorized by the satrap, but they would have had only a local circulation.[8]

The movement of Jews from Babylonia

If during the years we are now concerned with there was some improvement in living conditions in Judah, this may have been due in part to the migration of exiles from Babylonia. This voluntary movement of Jews to the homeland was, in its beginnings, authorized by Cyrus at the same time that he gave permission in 538 BC to rebuild the Jerusalem temple (see pp 24–5 in this chapter), and the rulers who succeeded Cyrus appear to have acquiesced in the policy he laid down. There were to be no or few restrictions on Babylonian Jews who

wished to move to Palestine. For most of those who took advantage of
Cyrus's clemency, this return would have been a spiritual return, for
only the very oldest could have actually lived in Judah earlier in the
century. How many of the Jewish community in Babylonia chose to go
to Palestine at this time we can only surmise. We get some light on this
problem from the lists of returning exiles found in Ezra and Nehemiah
(Ezra 2:1–67; 8:1–14; Neh 7:5–67; 12:1–26). The relations between
these lists are problematic, although some of the data they furnish
may be sound. It seems reasonable to assume that these lists point to
several migrations of Babylonian Jews to Judah, starting as early as 538
BC, and coming down to Ezra's time (c 398 BC). We may note that
Nehemiah claims to have utilized for census purposes a list available
to him (Neh 7:5–67), and there is nothing intrinsically improbable
about this claim. A striking feature of the lists is the modesty of the
statistics. In Ezra 2:1–67 (virtually identical with Neh 7:5–67) the total
number of returning exiles, possibly over a period of 140 years, is
given as 42,360, in addition to servants and singers. 1 Esd 5:41 claims
that the total excludes children under twelve. Those returning with
Ezra numbered 1514 (Ezra 8:1–14). There can be little doubt that these
periodic infusions of fresh blood into Judah's population were
beneficial to the life of the community. It is possible that political
unrest in Babylonia was a factor in encouraging some Jews there to
migrate to Judah. For instance, Xerxes was faced with a rebellion in
Babylon, but it was only after the defeat of the Persian navy at Salamis
in 480 BC that he was able to turn his attention to the rebels and
suppress them. The great temple of Marduk was destroyed and the
estates of some of the wealthier Babylonians were handed over to
Persians.

THE REBUILDING OF THE TEMPLE

There is no valid reason for questioning the essential reliability of the
tradition recorded in Ezra 1:2–4 (cf Ezra 6:3–5; 1 Esd 2:3–7; 6:24–6)
that it was Cyrus of Persia who in 538 BC authorized the rebuilding of
the Jewish temple in Jerusalem. As Cyrus himself would likely know
nothing about the Jews or their religion, it must be presumed that it

was a group of Babylonian Jews who petitioned Cyrus about this matter, and that their representations were sufficiently persuasive for Cyrus to issue what in modern parlance would be called a building-permit. It is clear also that Cyrus was asked to authorize the emigration from Babylonia of such Jews as wished to go to Judah. It is not improbable that some, if not all, of the temple vessels taken by Nebuchadrezzar in 598 and 587 BC were handed over to the returning exiles to take with them (Ezra 6:5). It is more doubtful that Cyrus contracted to pay for the temple rebuilding (Ezra 6:4; 1 Esd 6:25), and, even if he did, the royal donation may have been considerably diminished by the time it passed through various intervening government agents on the way to its intended recipients.

It was seemingly one Sheshbazzar, described as a leader of Judah (Ezra 1:8,11; 'governor' in 5:14), who headed up the first of the returning exiles in 538 BC, and who brought to Judah the king's permission to rebuild the temple. According to Ezra 5:16 Sheshbazzar laid the foundations of the sanctuary after his arrival in Judah. He may have done this, but we suspect that a great deal of the initial effort must have been expended in clearing the debris from the existing site and in assembling both the artisans and the building materials. These preliminary efforts may have proved too much for the limited resources of the small community, and the work apparently ground to a standstill. Sheshbazzar now disappears from the record.

It is not until some years later, in 520 BC, that there is fresh light on the temple project. At this time two prophets, Haggai and Zechariah, appeared in Judah, and part of the burden of their message was that the temple should be rebuilt (Hag 1:4,9; 2:1–9; Zec 1:16; 6:12–13; 8:9). Curiously neither prophet refers to Cyrus's decree, nor to the earlier work on the temple by Sheshbazzar. Moreover the leaders to whom the prophets point are Zerubbabel the governor and Joshua the high priest (Hag 1:1,12,14; 2:1–5,20–3; Zech 6:9–14), and indeed Zechariah indicates Zerubbabel as the one who laid the foundation of the house (Zech 4:8–10; cf 8:9). Nothing is said by either prophet about the completion of the temple.

It is the Chronicler to whom we must turn for further information about the temple rebuilding. He glosses over Sheshbazzar's work (cf Ezra 5:14–16), notes that cedar timbers had to be brought from Lebanon by sea (Ezra 3:7), describes the laying of the foundation and the attendant ceremonies (Ezra 3:10–13), records Zerubbabel's refusal to let 'the adversaries of Judah and Benjamin' share in the work (Ezra 4:1–3), and gives a detailed account of the efforts of Tattenai and his associates to stop the rebuilding (Ezra 5:3 to 6:12). Tattenai's scheme resulted only in Darius's confirming the earlier decree of Cyrus, including a reiteration of Persia's readiness to pay for the construction costs (Ezra 6:8–10). The work therefore proceeded and finally was finished on the third of Adar, 515 BC (Ezra 6:15), to be followed by an appropriate dedication ceremony (Ezra 6:16–18). About five weeks later the community celebrated Passover and the feast of Unleavened Bread (6:19–22).

The troubles which Zerubbabel had both with individuals and with groups have been variously interpreted. It has been thought that the 'adversaries' of Ezra 4:1–3 were in fact inhabitants of the district of Samaria who, as worshippers of Yahweh, wished to have a share in rebuilding the temple (cf the eighty men from Shechem, Shiloh, and Samaria who came down to Judah after 587 BC to present offerings in the temple, Jer 41:4–8). Zerubbabel did not look upon the offer of assistance from these northerners with favour, and in rebuffing them he may have passed over an opportunity to help heal the old rift between the south (Judah) and the north (Israel). As to the obstructive tactics of Tattenai and his friends (Ezra 5:3 to 6:12), this incident may refer merely to a routine checkup by government officials, or, as Josephus alleges (*Ant* XI, 88–105), it may have been inspired by the leaders in Samaria. In the latter case it may relate to Nehemiah's difficulty in the next century with Sanballat, governor of Samaria (Neh 4; 6). Possibly the jurisdiction of Samaria was likely to be diminished by the revival of Judah, and the northerners were taking such counter-measures as they could. If the primary motive in these incidents was political, religious tension may still have been a secondary factor.

It should be observed that the Chronicler, having taken the position that the Judean population not killed by the Babylonians had been taken into exile (2 Chr 36:20), was obliged to assume that the rebuilding of the temple and the renewal of Judah's life were due to exiles who had returned to Judah after 538 BC (Ezra 2:1–2; 3:8; 6:16,19–21). On the other hand, of the contemporary writers Haggai and Zechariah, only Zechariah (6:10) refers to exiles who have arrived from Babylon, and otherwise both prophets appear to address themselves to those who have always lived in Judah (cf 'the remnant of the people,' Hag 1:12,14; 2:2; Zech 8:6,11–12; 'the people of the land,' Hag 2:4; Zech 7:5).

There is no description in the OT of the second temple except that the Chronicler cites Cyrus's decree as authorizing a structure sixty by sixty cubits, with walls built of three courses of stones and one of timber (Ezra 6:3–4). It is probable that it was similar in size and plan to the first temple, although Josephus preserves the tradition that its height was sixty cubits less than Solomon's temple (*Ant* xv, 385; cf 2 Chr 3:4). The temple area, which was no longer part of a royal complex as in Solomon's time, had its own storage chambers (Neh 10:37–9; 14:5,7–9). Later, when Nehemiah's wall was being built, a 'fortress of the temple' is referred to (Neh 2:8); this probably refers to two towers in the wall, the tower of Hananel and the tower of the hundred (Neh 3:1), which served to guard the north approach to the temple. We suspect that the olivewood cherubim (1 Kgs 6:23–8), the two bronze columns Jachin and Boaz (7:15–22), the bronze sea and the wheeled bronze lavers (7:27–39) were not reproduced in the sixth century BC. On some of the furnishings and utensils see 1 Mac 1:21–3. The ark of the covenant (1 Kgs 6:19), presumed lost in 587 BC (cf 2 Esd 10:21–2), was irreplaceable. It is asserted in the Mishnah (a collection of Jewish traditions compiled about 200 AD) that the ark was not destroyed, but in fact hidden under the pavement near the later wood-store (*Shekalim* 6.1–2). A story found in 2 Bar 6:1–10 tells us that an angel took the ark and various other holy objects and hid them in the earth. A variant of this, with Jeremiah substituted for the angel, is preserved in 2 Mac 2:4–5.

Post-biblical writers do not greatly increase our knowledge of the second temple. The earliest of these is Hecataeus of Abdera who wrote c 300 BC, and who furnishes a brief description of the temple: the sacred enclosure was about five hundred feet long and one hundred and fifty feet wide; the altar, thirty feet square and fifteen feet high, was made of unhewn stones (*Apion* I, 196–9). This reference to an altar of unhewn stones is confirmed in 1 Mac 4:44–7. Ben Sira (c 180 BC), in his panegyric on Simon (50:1–21), waxes eloquent on the sacred service presided over by the high priest, but says little about the temple itself. Simon, Ben Sira reports, repaired the sanctuary and erected some defensive structure, but the details are not clear. The Letter of Aristeas (probably first century BC) contains (83–99) an idealized description of the Jerusalem temple, including its water supply, and of the priestly services, with considerable attention devoted to the vestments of the high priest. Of the few data it gives about the sanctuary itself, we may note that the temple was surrounded by three walls, seventy cubits high, and that in the principal doorway there hung a curtain.

The completion of the temple in 515 BC was an event of great significance for Israel's faith. For the temple was a symbol not only of the reality of Israel's God and of God's special interest in Israel, but of God's presence among his people. In and around the temple there were assembled various cultic traditions, and these, enriched by pageantry and music, were to make the temple procedures of the Jewish religious year, especially on the high festivals, memorable occasions in Jewish life. Since the Lord God of Israel was holy, his temple was holy in a derivative sense, and therefore any ill treatment of the temple by pagan hands was viewed as sacrilege (e.g., the actions of Heliodorus, 2 Mac 3:1–40; and of Antiochus IV, 1 Mac 1:21–3,54,59).

Notwithstanding the unique position which the Jerusalem sanctuary had in the Jewish tradition, it became a fact, as the numbers of Jews living outside of the homeland increased in the Persian, Hellenistic, and Roman eras, that comparatively few Jews participated regularly in the temple rites, and even those from the Diaspora who came to Jerusalem for one of the annual festivals must have been a small proportion of the total Jewish population in the Mediterranean world. Yet loyalty to the Jewish tradition persisted at the local level. The explanation seems to be that many Jews discovered, as Jeremiah had pointed out in the sixth century BC (Jer 29), that God could be sought and prayed to in a foreign land without the benefit of temple ritual. This was made emphatically clear after the destruction of the third temple by the Romans in 70 AD. This loss, which seemed at the time to be catastrophic, was to show that Israel's faith was not dependent upon a temple built with human hands.

PROPHETIC VOICES

It is a sign that Judah's religious life was returning to something like normalcy in the late sixth century when two prophets, Haggai and Zechariah, appeared, both of them claiming that 'the word of the Lord' had come to them. The dates given within these books indicate that the two men were contemporaries, although oddly enough neither one refers to the other in their extant writings.

Haggai

Haggai's ancestry is not recorded, and it is not known whether he was a native Judean or a returned exile. He began to prophesy on the first day of the sixth month in the second year of Darius (520 BC), and his last two dated oracles both come from the twenty-fourth day of the ninth month in the same year (2:10,20). His chief concern is to get the temple rebuilt (1:2–6), and he argues that the drought on the land is an indication of the Lord's displeasure that his house still lies in ruins (1:9–11; cf 2:15–19). This argument, and possibly others that are not recorded, resulted in Zerubbabel the governor and Joshua the high priest, along with 'the remnant of the people,' starting work on the temple (1:12–15). Haggai's account of this is very simple, whereas the Chronicler's version in Ezra 3:8–9 has the construction supervised by priestly and Levitical personnel. It took only about seven weeks for discouragement to set in, so Haggai was moved to speak again, this time a word of encouragement (2:1–9), as he also did about two months later (2:10,15–19). His other two oracles are not related to the temple building. The first, in 2:11–14, seems to have arisen out of a technical discussion with some priests regarding the concepts of holy and unclean. If it had any point for the non-professional, it may have been that the temple ritual would only be acceptable if the people themselves were clean morally. Haggai's last oracle (2:20–23) is unique in that it is a personal word from the Lord to Zerubbabel. It points to an imminent worldwide cataclysm, and on that day, the prophet says, the Lord will make Zerubbabel like a signet ring. The latter prediction suggests that Zerubbabel was destined for some leadership role other than that of governor. In any case nothing came of this prediction, and if the prophet thereby lost his credibility, this may explain why we hear nothing more about him.

Zechariah

The book of Zechariah consists of fourteen chapters, of which 1–8 are clearly a unity, dealing as they do with a prophet named Zechariah and with a recognizable situation in Judah in the sixth century. Chapters 9–14 (discussed more fully in this work in chapter 5) appear to belong to a much later period, for Zechariah is nowhere mentioned, and in 9:1–8 there is an apparent reference to Alexander the Great. This treatment of Zechariah will therefore be based only on chapters 1–8.

Zechariah is described as the son of Berechiah, son of Iddo (1:1), and in Ezra 5:1 as the son of Iddo, which may mean a descendant of Iddo, although it is hardly likely that the latter is the tenth-century prophet of that name (cf 2 Chr 12:15; 13:22). In Neh 12:4 Iddo appears in a list of priests who returned from Babylon, and if this points to our prophet's family, it would mean that he was of priestly lineage. He began his prophetic work in the eighth month of the second year of Darius, and his latest dated oracle (7:1) comes from the ninth month of the fourth year of Darius (518 BC). He nowhere refers to the completion of the temple, but parts of chapter 8 (such as vss 1–8, 14–23) may belong to the years immediately after 515 BC.

Zechariah's prophetic techniques are not greatly different from those of Amos. Like Amos he uses the familiar formulae, 'Thus says the Lord,' or 'the word of the Lord came to Zechariah' (1:1; 4:8; 6:9; 7:1,4,8; 8:1,4,6; etc). Also, like Amos, he utilizes visions (1:8–17,18–21; 2:1–5; 3:1–10; etc). What marks off Zechariah's visions from those of Amos is that Zechariah does not converse directly with the Lord. A nameless interpreting angel appears in each of the visions (usually 'the angel who talked with me'), and in some cases two angels appear (as in 2:3; 3:1; in the latter verse Satan as an accusing angel is one of the two). In 1:14; 2:3; 3:6; 4:6 it is the angel who instructs Zechariah regarding what he is to proclaim. From all this it might be concluded that Zechariah represents a shift in prophetic procedure and even in prophetic experience. A vital awareness of God's presence, even for a prophet, may have been less common than it once was. It is probable, too, that Judah's greatly reduced political stature, as well as new literary conventions such as are found in Ezekiel, were factors in the changes now becoming apparent in prophetic circles.

Although Zechariah stands in the line of the old prophetic tradition, reminding Judah of her past waywardness and of the punishment which came her way (7:8–14) and calling her to repentance (1:1–6), the general tenor of both his visions and his oracles is somewhat reminiscent of Deutero-Isaiah. He gives some attention to the rebuilding of the temple (1:16; 4:7–10; 6:12–15; 8:9), but much of his effort is intended to comfort and build up hope in his fellow countrymen. Exiles still in Babylon are urged to come to Zion (2:6–13; cf 8:7–8) and share in the temple reconstruction (6:15). Israel's God will be established as sovereign over all nations (6:1–8), and Israel will be free from political foes (1:18–21). The Lord is returning to Jerusalem (1:16; 8:3), and the city will henceforth need no walls of defence (2:1–5). All manner of evil will be obliterated (5:1–10; 8:16–17). Parts of chapter 8 are almost lyrical in their portrayal of the blessings of the future (vss 3–8, 11–15). An attractive aspect of this picture is the hope that the Gentile world will share in the worship of Israel's God (2:11; 8:20–3).

A somewhat different side of Zechariah is revealed in his concern for Joshua the high priest and Zerubbabel the civil governor. We do not know enough about the background of these oracles to be able to elucidate them with complete satisfaction. Verses 4:1–6a,10b–14 present a very obscure vision, but it may be intended to enhance the stature of Judah's two leaders. Verses 3:1–10 imply that Joshua was accused of some sin and that subsequently the alleged iniquity was removed. This would in effect confirm his position in the community. As for Zerubbabel, the Persian authorities doubtless looked upon him merely as a person appointed to govern Judah, but there were those in Judah who interpreted his appointment differently and saw in him a civil leader who would prove to be the righteous branch of whom

Jeremiah had spoken (Jer 23:5). Zechariah seemingly shared in this hope (3:8; 4:11–14; 6:9–14). At this point speculation takes over. As nothing more is heard of the governor, it is tempting to suppose that the Persians got wind of these aspirations centring on Zerubbabel and promptly removed him from office.

Anonymous prophecy

After the appearance in Israel of a long series of men acknowledged to be authentic prophets, it is notable that in the sixth century BC this tradition began to change, and what we are presented with is a considerable amount of prophetic material whose authors remain nameless, and whose precise dates and settings are often impossible to recover. As this newer prophetic writing has become part of the canonical prophets, we have to assume that there were circles in Judah – and we cannot exclude the possibility of similar groups among the Babylonian Jewry – which made it their business to preserve prophetic writings, edit them in some acceptable way, and add to them, from time to time, such additional material as seemed appropriate. One example of this, the addition to the book of Amos in 9:11–15, has earlier been referred to. The best illustration is the book of Isaiah. This book as we now have it would appear to come from an Isaianic coterie (perhaps going back to Isaiah's disciples, Isa 8:16), which preserved not only the utterances of the eighth-century prophet, but the spoken and written oracles of others who were considered to belong to the Isaianic tradition. The additions which were made to the original Isaiah are now found principally in chapters 24–7, 34–5, and 40–66 of our present book of Isaiah, and what impresses the reader is the wide spectrum of ideas, hopes, and eschatological notions which this material displays. It is also evident that the obligation to write anonymously reduced neither the vigour of the style nor the felicity of the language in which the prophetic word was expressed.

Trito-Isaiah (Isa 56–66) is a specific example of anonymous prophecy, probably to be dated in the late sixth century. This part of Isaiah is a collection of poems seemingly from more than one author. The last eight verses (66:17–24) are a prose addition probably contributed by some editor. The absence of allusions to concrete historical events makes the determination of the date of these oracles almost impossible. It is commonly thought that the language betrays the influence of Deutero-Isaiah. If this is a valid observation, it would support a date for the poems in question about, or later than, 550 BC. The reference in 64:8–12 (cf 58:12) to the desolation of Jerusalem and the ruined temple must be later than 587 and earlier than 520 BC. Verses 62:10–12 may reflect Cyrus's decree of 538 BC. Verse 66:1 seems to show familiarity with a plan to rebuild the temple, which indicates the period 538–520 BC. These various considerations favour a date around, or even prior to, the age of Haggai and Zechariah.

In at least four passages there are references to the speaker or writer, but it is uncertain whether he is the same individual in all instances. In 58:1 God's call to the prophet is alluded to; 61:1–11 describes the anointment for his task and outlines his message; in 62:1–5 the speaker states the gist of his proclamation; and in 63:7 to 64:12 there is his long intercessory prayer which presently changes into a lament.

These chapters follow prophetic usage in both exhortation and admonishment. On the one hand the doing of justice and the keeping of the Sabbath are commended (56:2,4,6; 58:6–7,13; 61:8), and on the other hand idolatry and paganism (57:3–10; 65:3–4,7,11; 66:3,17), false fasting (58:3–9a), the corruption of leaders (56:9–12), indifference to the sufferings of the righteous (57:1–2), disregard of food restrictions (65:4; 66:17), false worship (66:1–4), and internal enemies (66:5) are condemned.

The most distinctive aspect of these chapters is their eschatology.[9] Despite the prophetic admonishments just noted, and despite the prospect that the future will include an awesome judgment (63:1–6; 65:11–15; 66:15–16), the descriptions of what lies ahead for Judah and Jerusalem are intended to extend encouragement to, and build hope in, 'those who mourn in Zion.' Yahweh is going to intervene in history (59:16–20); the exiles will return (56:8; 60:4,8–9; 66:20); the new Jerusalem here on earth will enjoy peace, prosperity, and felicity (58:9b–14; 60:5–7,10–11,15–22; 62:6–12; 65:8–10,17–25; 66:7–14). All this will come to pass because, behind the Lord's chastisement of those who have erred, there is a persistent graciousness which will comfort and heal Israel. God will renew his covenant with them, and they will be known as 'a people whom the Lord has blessed' (61:8–9).

There is some ambivalence in Trito-Isaiah's eschatology in respect to the Gentiles. In some passages foreigners are to have a very negative share in Israel's future blessedness (60:10–14; 61:5), whereas in others Gentile proselytes will participate in Israel's life (56:3–4,6–7; 60:3; 66:22–3). Verse 66:21 is somewhat ambiguous: one interpretation is that it points to proselytes serving as the Lord's priests.

These chapters of Isaiah clearly come from a group of sensitive writers who fully understood the conventions of traditional Hebrew poetry. In structure, imagery, and rhetorical devices some of these poems (e.g., 61:1–11; 65:17–25) are superb examples of prophetic literary style and match the best found anywhere in the OT.

Malachi

This book, whose title means 'my messenger,' may be anonymous, but for convenience its author will be referred to as Malachi. His date can be established only roughly. The references to an operating sanctuary and altar (1:7,10; 2:3,11–13) indicate a time after 515 BC. As the age of Nehemiah and Ezra seems still to lie in the future, it is probable that the prophet lived prior to 450 BC. A reference to 'your governor' in 1:8 points vaguely to the Persian period.

Malachi is not exactly a cheerful soul. Perhaps he could not be otherwise, for he found very little to hearten him in his immediate environment. The tirade against Edom in 1:2–5 may indicate some current dispute with Judah's southern neighbour. Within Judah itself agriculture was not in a healthy state (3:11), and this was true of much of the country's social and religious life. There were those who feared the Lord (3:16–18; 4:2), but Malachi was much more concerned with those who did not. Among these were scoffers (2:17; 3:13–15), not unlike those whom the psalmists allude to (Pss 1:1; 14:1; 42:3; 73:11; etc); there were those who proved faithless to their Jewish wives and married Gentile women (2:10–11,14–16); there was a general disregard of kindness, honesty, and justice (3:5). But what really agitated Malachi were cultic irregularities. In 1:6–14 the priests are accused of offering imperfect animals as sacrifices (cf 3:3), and in 3:8–11 tithing procedures are faulted. The priesthood is specifically blamed in 2:1–3, and, after a laudatory word for the Lord's covenant with Levi (2:4–7), the hierarchy is again belaboured in 2:8–9. These criticisms of the cult personnel are somewhat confusing, for we cannot be sure whether Malachi is following a Deuteronomic tradition or what came to be called the P document.

Although Malachi leaves some room for repentance (3:6–7), his real hope appears to lie in the future. He speaks confidently of the appearance of the Lord in judgment (cf the 'book of remembrance' in 3:16), an event to be preceded by the coming of a messenger (3:1–5,16–18; 4:1–3). The reference to Elijah in 4:5–6, in which that prophet is to come before 'the great and terrible day of the Lord,' seems to be the result of a later editor's effort to identify Elijah with the messenger of 3:1. The one really remarkable verse in Malachi is 1:11, where a degree of true religion, in the sense of the tacit recognition of Israel's God, is attributed to worship in the pagan world (cf Peter's words in Acts 10:34–5).

III

THE AGE OF
NEHEMIAH AND EZRA

It is indicative of the political isolation of Judah and the provincialism of the Jews that the larger events of the Persian world are almost completely ignored by the Jewish sources of this period. The latter, which are basically the books of Ezra and Nehemiah, are concerned only with matters pertaining directly to Judah.

The last century of the Persian empire was marked by recurrent plots over the accession to the throne, and this weakness was combined with an increasing amount of trouble with rebellious satrapies. It is typical of what was happening that only the murder of Xerxes cleared the way for the accession of Artaxerxes I in 465 BC, and that within five years the new king had to deal with serious rebellions in Bactria and Egypt. It is of interest that, while five of the dated Elephantine Papyri (Cowley, texts 7–11) come from the period of the Egyptian rebellion (460–454 BC), they make no allusion to the current political unrest. Following the death of Artaxerxes I in 424 BC it required a year's time and two murders before Darius II became the legitimate king in 423 BC. His son, Artaxerxes II, succeeded him in 404 BC, only to fall heir to a rebellion in Egypt which by 401 BC had secured Egypt's independence under Amyrtaeus (Twenty-Eighth Dynasty). In this same year the king had to face a challenge to his authority from his brother Cyrus, who earlier had been appointed satrap of Lydia. This rebellion was put down in the summer of 401 BC (battle of Cunaxa), and, while the whole episode received classical treatment in Xenephon's *Anabasis*, no echo of it is to be found in the OT, although Cunaxa is only about fifty miles north of Babylon. Artaxerxes' troubles were not confined to his brother. The whole of Asia Minor west of the Halys River seems to have been in a constant state of turmoil. The accession of Artaxerxes III in 359 BC appeared at first to bring stability to the Persian world. The king was able to suppress revolts in Syria and Phoenicia, and, after earlier unsuccessful attempts, he finally ended Egypt's independence c 343–342 BC. The subsequent history of western Asia might have been different if Artaxerxes had not been poisoned in 338 BC. Two years elapsed before Darius III became king in 336 BC, but it was his misfortune to have to meet a challenge from Europe in the form of an army of Macedonians and Greeks led by Alexander of Macedon. The forces of Persia crumbled before Alexander (Granicus, 334 BC; Issus, 333 BC; and Guagamela, 331 BC), and the Achaemenid dynasty came to an end. These political changes in Asia, which were in fact the harbingers of the Hellenistic Age, seemed to be unknown to the Jews or, if known, were thought to be irrelevant to Judah's life. The one biblical book which may reflect the beginning of this period is Zechariah 9–14 (see chapter 5).

TROUBLES IN JUDAH PRIOR TO NEHEMIAH'S TIME

The Chronicler has preserved in Ezra 4:6–23 two pericopes which appear to throw some light on conditions in Judah in the fifth century prior to the age of Nehemiah. One is a single verse (Ezra 4:6) describing some trouble at the beginning of the reign of Xerxes. Apparently the northern Israelites filed a complaint (the nature of which is not stated) with the king against Judah. The longer extract, Ezra 4:7–23, is dated in the days of Artaxerxes, presumably Artaxerxes I. It is presented as coming from the people of Samaria, Rehum the commander and Shimshai the scribe being their spokesmen. Their accusation is that Jerusalem, which has a history of rebellion, is being rebuilt, including its walls, and that, if this is allowed to continue, the royal revenues from this area will be diminished. The king, having looked into the matter, ordered the rebuilding of the city to stop until he decreed otherwise. Rehum and his associates then went to Jerusalem and 'by force and power' had the work stopped. The phraseology may indicate some physical struggle connected with the enforcement of the king's decree.

NEHEMIAH

Sources

The only biblical sources for this period are the books of Ezra and Nehemiah, although these can be supplemented by data derived from the Elephantine Papyri. The fifth-century Herodotus, who has a penchant for the unusual and the anecdotal, says nothing about the Jews, Judah, Jerusalem, or the Jewish temple. He does refer to 'the part of Syria called Palestine' (I, 105), and he notes that the Phoenicians and the Syrians of Palestine practise circumcision, a custom which they claim to have learned from the Egyptians (II, 104). Herodotus knows about Ashkelon (I, 105), but whether he himself ever journeyed that far south is doubtful. Since he does not mention the Lebanon, the Jordan River, or Damascus, it can be inferred that his acquaintance with the interior of Syria was negligible.

The Memoirs of Nehemiah come to us from the Chronicler, but they are found interfused with other material which the Chronicler felt it necessary to preserve. His presentation of the memoirs is further complicated by his view that Ezra preceded Nehemiah in coming to Judah, and that the two men were for a time contemporaries. All this creates a literary problem, and to deal with it in such a way as to isolate the facts from improbable traditions is not easy. The discussion which follows assumes that the basic texts for reconstructing Nehemiah's career (arranged in chronological order) are Neh 1–2; 3 (this may not come from Nehemiah, but its topographic data are useful); 4; 6; 7:1–4; 11:1–2; 12:27–43; 5:14–19; 13:4–31; 10:28–37a; 5:1–13.

Nehemiah's career: First governorship

Nehemiah, son of an otherwise unknown Hacaliah and a member of the Babylonian community of Jews, had entered government service, and when we first meet him, 445–444 BC, he is in Susa, the administrative capital of Persia. His role is that of a cup-bearer[1] to king Artaxerxes (presumed to be Artaxerxes I, 465–424 BC). Since he has access to the queen (Neh 2:6), it is probable that he is a eunuch.[2] In Neh 1:1–3 some men who have just come from Judah bring Nehemiah word that the Jews in the homeland are in great trouble. Apparently some disaster has struck Jerusalem, but because of our ignorance of Palestine's history in this period it is impossible to say what actually happened (cf the comments on Ezra 4:6–23, pp 37–8 above). Nehemiah is greatly distressed over this, and, when Artaxerxes notes the change in his servant's mood, he explains to the king the cause of his sadness and then asks his royal master to send him to Judah 'that I may rebuild it.' Nehemiah's position in the court, while a minor one, is such that this request is not an unreasonable one, and the king accedes to it. It is only as the narrative develops that we are told in Neh 5:14 that Nehemiah's status in Judah is that of governor. We have to assume that the office had recently become vacant and that Nehemiah timed his request with a view to this circumstance. The governor-designate then sets out for Judah with a military escort and with the necessary documentation, including authorization to draw upon the local building resources. There is no information about the journey, although Josephus claims that Nehemiah picked up some Jews in Babylon who wished to migrate to Judah (*Ant* xi, 168).

Whatever the duration of the original leave of absence from his court duties (Neh 2:6), it is evident from Neh 5:14 that Nehemiah served for twelve years as governor (from c 445–444 to 433–432 BC). Some details of his domestic arrangements during this time are in Neh 5:14–18. In 433–432 BC he returned to Susa, and subsequently he came back to Judah (Artaxerxes I was still king), but for how long is not stated (Neh 13:6–7). We learn from one of the Elephantine papyri (Cowley, text 30, line 1) that Bigvai (or Bagohi) was governor of Judah in 408 BC, and this year must therefore be a terminal date for Nehemiah's term of office.

Josephus, in summing up Nehemiah's career, wrote that 'he left the walls of Jerusalem as his eternal monument' (*Ant* xi, 183), and there can be no doubt that his supervision of the rebuilding of the walls was one of his great services to Judah. After some initial inspection of the situation and considerable organization of the human resources, Nehemiah got the work on the walls started shortly after his arrival in Judah. The building proceeded despite various efforts to stop it on the part of Sanballat the Horonite, Tobiah the Ammonite, and Geshem the Arab. Sanballat is connected with Samaria in Neh 4:2; in an Elephantine papyrus of 408 BC one Sanballat appears as the governor of Samaria,[3] but he is never referred to in this way by Nehemiah. Tobiah the Ammonite is described in Neh 2:19 as 'the servant'; this is probably a technical term and may indicate some official position in Ammon. Geshem probably had a similar post in Edom. In Neh 4:7 the Ashdodites are included among Nehemiah's opponents, which means that virtually all of Judah's neighbours were lined up against Nehemiah's efforts. As long as the opposition was merely vocal, it could be tolerated, but when it developed into a threat of physical violence, it became necessary for Nehemiah to post guards and to be prepared to meet force with force. No such confrontation ever occurred (Neh 4:1–20), although Josephus claims that it did and that many Jews were killed (*Ant* xi, 174). Attempts to trap Nehemiah into a meeting which might have ended in an outrage to himself were unsuccessful, as was the effort to compromise the governor by getting him to seek refuge from an alleged assassin by fleeing to the temple (Neh 6:1–14). In the end the wall was completed and dedicated; the ceremonies are described in Neh 12:27–43. Neh 6:15 states that the wall was finished in fifty-two days, whereas Josephus says that the rebuilding took two years and four months (*Ant* xi, 179). We do not know either the condition of the wall when the work began (cf Ezra 4:12) or the human skills and material resources at the governor's disposal, and we cannot therefore determine whether Neh 6:15 or Josephus is likely to be correct. The data on the building of the wall recorded in Neh 3:1–32 are not such that, even when used with the findings of modern archaeologists, we can be sure how extensive Nehemiah's Jerusalem was, nor can we always locate exactly the various gates, towers, etc mentioned in the biblical narrative. The primary value of the wall was psychological. By its visible existence it assured Judah that its former life was now fully reestablished. In practical terms life within Jerusalem was now more secure, and the gates enabled the local authorities to control the movements of people, animals, and merchandise in and out of the city.

Neh 11:1–2 appears to be a fragment from the memoirs relating to an effort to increase the population of Jerusalem. Some Jews volunteered to change their habitat and move into the city, while at the same time a process of lot-casting brought one-tenth of the people within the walls. The social and economic problems created by these newcomers can readily be imagined. Both Ben Sira (49:13) and Josephus (*Ant* xi, 181–2) record traditions of Nehemiah's house-building in Jerusalem, doubtless in response to the increased population.

Nehemiah's second governorship

Nehemiah's second period as governor began under the same Artaxerxes who had appointed him in the first place, and the date can therefore not be later than 424 BC. Most of our information comes from Neh 13, and it has often been noted that Nehemiah here appears, in contrast to his earlier activities, to be concerned with the internal life of Judah, particularly with matters relating to the temple cult.

We are told in Neh 13:4–9 that during Nehemiah's absence the priest Eliashib (presumably the high priest of Neh 3:1) had put one of the store-rooms of the temple at the disposal of Tobiah with whom he was connected (in what way is not clear), and that this Tobiah, thought to be the Ammonite of Neh 2:19, had stored there some household effects. As the Deuternonomic law (23:3) was very cool towards Ammonites, and as Nehemiah had little reason to consider Tobiah a friend, Eliashib's action outraged the governor. Tobiah's furniture was thrown out of the temple, the room was purified, and it reverted to being a store-room for sundry things used in the temple services.

In Neh 13:10–14 it is related that Nehemiah discovered that the Levites had not been given their tithes (the basis of their livelihood, Num 18:21–4; Neh 10:37–9), and that they had abandoned the service of the temple and gone back to their villages. Earlier in the century Malachi (3:8–10) had been confronted with the same situation. Presumably such things happened partly because of economic conditions and partly because of the people's indifference to the traditional claims of the Levites. Nehemiah took remedial action by reorganizing the tithing arrangements, and this made the reestablishment of the Levites in the cult comparatively easy.

Nehemiah was evidently devoted to sabbath observance, although this is not referred to in connection with the building of the wall. In 13:15–22 we learn that over the summer season he had noted Jewish farmers working on the Sabbath and transporting farm produce to Jerusalem on the Sabbath and selling it. Phoenician merchants were also active in Jerusalem on the Sabbath. Nehemiah complained to the city officials about these matters, but, when nothing was done, Nehemiah himself acted. He had the city gates closed for the whole of the Sabbath, and when some merchants tried to do business on the Sabbath outside the gates, this was stopped.

Nehemiah, like other Jewish leaders before and after him, was very sensitive to the intermarriage question, for intermarriages on a large scale could easily wreck the religious values of Israel's life. Malachi (2:11) was aware of this problem, but Nehemiah does not seem to have found it a pressing issue until his second governorship (Neh 13:23–9). It now came to his attention that Jews had married non-Jewish women (of Ashdod, Ammon, and Moab), and that their children could not understand Hebrew. After administering some minor physical punishment to the men concerned, he made them take an oath not to arrange marriages with foreigners for their children. Nothing is said about breaking up the marriages already contracted.

In Neh 13:28 one specific instance of intermarriage is cited: a male member (unnamed) of the high priest's family, a son of Jehoiada, had married the daughter of Sanballat. When Nehemiah learned of this, he banished the man from Jerusalem. Josephus seems to preserve a variant of this: he gives Manasseh as the name of the man and Nikaso as that of the woman, but he dates the episode in the time of Darius III, 336–330 BC (*Ant* XI, 302–3, 306–12).

The covenant which the Jewish community entered into in Neh 10:28–37 seems to be out of place in its present context, and various scholars have suggested that it belongs after Neh 13. Nehemiah, whose name heads the list of signatories in Neh 10:1, may well have played a leading role on this occasion. The people pledged themselves to avoid mixed marriages, to observe the Sabbath and the sabbatical year, to pay one-third of a shekel annually for the support of the temple (probably in weight equal to the half-shekel of Ex 30:11−16),[4] to cast lots for the bringing of the wood supply to the temple,[5] and to bring in first fruits and sundry other donations to the temple.

The pericope in Neh 5:1−13 appears to have no connection with the building of Jerusalem's walls. It presupposes a long drought, but there is little to indicate its date or milieu. Its general tone is not dissimilar to Neh 13, and therefore it is here tentatively being assigned to the period of Nehemiah's second governorship. It describes an unhappy development in Judah's life: family property and even children had been mortgaged to buy food or pay taxes, and interest was being charged on the money loaned (cf Deut 23:20). Nehemiah and his friends not only made loans to the needy, but the wealthier members of the community were forced to return agricultural holdings being kept as surety (the text of verses 10−11 is obscure), and in the presence of priests the verbal agreement covering this was sealed by an oath.

Nehemiah appears throughout his memoirs in a very favourable light. Much of his strength came from his simple but sincere piety (Neh 2:4,20; 4:9,14,20; 5:13,19; etc). His realism taught him what things were possible in Judah of the fifth century, and within these limits he worked for the community's welfare. Josephus said of him: 'He was a man of kind and just nature, and most anxious to serve his countrymen' (*Ant* xi, 183).

EZRA

Chronology and sources

As in the case of Nehemiah, our information about Ezra is derived almost entirely from the books of Ezra and Nehemiah (cf 1 Esd 8−9; *Ant* xi, 120−58). The Chronicler, who edited these books, found in his sources the name of only one Persian king, Artaxerxes, who could be related to Ezra and Nehemiah, and his presentation of the material was therefore based on the assumption that the two men were contemporaries. A careful examination of the data, however, makes it clear that the two Jewish leaders worked independently of each other. As the work of Nehemiah appears to precede that of Ezra, we are obliged to do something about the Chronicler's scheme which makes Ezra come to Judah in the seventh year of Artaxerxes (i.e., c 458 BC), and Nehemiah about fourteen years later. Various solutions for this problem have been advanced. One, for instance, is that Ezra 7:7–8 should read 'thirty-seven' instead of 'seven,' which would bring Ezra to Judah c 427 BC. Another theory, which in this writer's opinion has the most to be said for it, is the supposition that Ezra is to be placed in the time of Artaxerxes II (404–359 BC), and it is this hypothesis which will be assumed in what follows.

Ezra's early life

Comparatively little is known about Ezra's life. He was a priest, the son of Seraiah, a member of the Jewish community in Babylonia. We are not told where he lived, but, as he had some access to the Persian court, his home may not have been in Babylonia at all, but in Susa in Susiana (Elam). He is also described as a scribe, skilled in the law of Moses. It is possible that he had some post in the court secretariat, for he was in a position to make a request of the king (Ezra 7:6,28), although the nature of his petition can only be inferred from the letter which Artaxerxes wrote (Ezra 7:11–26). This document, whose basic phraseology may have been supplied by Ezra himself, has been embroidered by the Chronicler, which makes the evaluation of the text difficult. We may infer from verses 14 and 25–6 that Ezra was authorized to investigate the extent to which Jewish law was in force in Judah and to appoint magistrates to secure its observance. Presumably Ezra must have argued that a community governed by traditional Jewish law would be a stable political unit in the empire and would strengthen Persia's hold on this strategic region. The letter, in addition, sanctions the emigration of Jews to Jerusalem (vs 13), the taking of various gifts for the Jewish temple (vss 15–19), the payment out of the state's resources of certain stipulated amounts of silver and farm produce for the service of the temple, and the exemption of all the temple staff from government imposts (vss 20–4). It is curious that, as the Ezra narrative now stands, there is no specific evidence to indicate that Ezra at any time drew upon the Persian treasury for any of the potential gifts put at his disposal in verses 20–3 (cf Ezra 8:36).

Ezra, armed with his royal letter, proceeded to gather from Babylonian Jewry those who wished to emigrate to Palestine. Josephus has a tradition that Ezra invited the Jews of Media (northern Israelites who settled there after the fall of Samaria, 2 Kgs 17:6) to join his expedition and that some of them did (*Ant* xi, 131–2). In Ezra 8:1–14 there is a list of those accompanying Ezra, totalling about 1500, but only the 18 leaders are named. Some priests were in the expedition (vss 2,24), but most were laymen. When the caravan was being assembled beside the canal leading to Ahava (not identified), Ezra noted the absence of Levites, who may have found secular life in Babylonia more attractive than temple service in Jerusalem, and he had to make a special effort to round up 38 Levites as well as 220 temple servants (Ezra 8:15–20). This done, and with a propitiatory fast observed and the treasures placed in the keeping of responsible persons, the expedition set out. It was Ezra's decision that it would not have a Persian escort. The four-month journey was made without incident (Ezra 8:31 may imply that ambushes were effectively dealt with). It required three days to demobilize the caravan and to make arrangements to incorporate the newcomers into Judah's life. Then the various treasures were delivered to the temple and appropriate offerings were made (Ezra 8:32–5).

Ezra in Judah

Ezra's subsequent career in Judah was concerned with two issues: the publicizing of a code of Jewish law, followed by the observance of the feast of Booths; and the mixed marriage problem. This is the probable chronological sequence, and it is the order in which these will be discussed below.

THE CODE OF LAW

The material dealing with a book of law and the celebration of the feast of Booths is found in Neh 7:73b to 8:18 (in 8:9 'Nehemiah' appears to be an addition to the text). The time reference in 7:73b ('when the seventh month had come') is not very helpful, for the year is not indicated. If we assume that Ezra's primary purpose in coming to Judah was related to an investigation of Jewish law, we might expect him to set about this part of his work as soon as it was feasible. In this case the seventh month could refer to the year when Ezra reached Jerusalem (398 BC). We cannot be sure how much importance at this time was attached to the beginning of the seventh month, except that as a new moon day it was a Sabbath (cf Amos 8:5), and that as the seventh new moon day it rated special sacrifices in the temple (cf Num 29:1–6). It was at a later date to become the Jewish New Year's Day.

On this day an assembly of people, principally citizens of Jerusalem, were gathered in the square before the Water Gate, and they told Ezra the scribe 'to bring the scroll of the law of Moses' (Neh 8:1). This implies that Ezra had been giving the scroll some publicity, and perhaps he had suggested that on a suitable occasion, such as the next new moon day, he would be glad to expound it to an audience. Ezra accordingly brought the scroll and read from it for the whole forenoon. Neh 8:7–8 implies that, in a manner that is not perfectly clear, certain Levites who may have had a prior knowledge of the scroll helped the people to understand what had been read, perhaps through a form of group instruction. Some of the people reacted to all this by mourning and weeping (Josephus says because of repentance for past sins, Ant XI, 155), but Ezra urged that it was a time for joy, not sadness. The next day a smaller group of priests, Levites, and family heads met again to study the scroll.

Various attempts have been made to identify Ezra's scroll, but, owing to the paucity of reliable data, none has gained general acceptance. If, as has been earlier claimed, some form of Deuteronomy furnished the operative religious law in Judah from 621 BC on, Ezra may have presented a slightly revised form of Deuteronomy, to which selections from the priestly code (the P document) were prefaced. Or if Ezra and some fellow priests had been working on a definitive collection of priestly traditions, it may have been this collection (the P document) which was introduced to Judah at this time. It is less likely that the scroll was the whole of the Pentateuch, although a scholar like Eissfeldt espouses this view (Eissfeldt, p 557).

Whatever Ezra's law book was, its presentation to the Jewish community may very well have been followed by some kind of public ceremony pledging the loyalty of the group to the new scroll. At critical times in the past Judah had entered into a formal commitment regarding some matter at issue, as in Asa's time (2 Chr 15:12–15), in Hezekiah's reign (2 Chr 29:1–36, especially vs 10), and in 621 BC in connection with the finding of the book of the law in the temple (2 Kgs 23:1–3). It therefore would be consonant with past practice for Ezra and his contemporaries to have had a ceremony of dedication to what from now on would be the public law of Judah. Neh 9:38, a verse not closely related to its context, may be an echo of such an agreement.

The P document, which may have some connection with Ezra, is generally conceded to be the latest strand which can be identified in the Torah. Like the earlier Pentateuchal sources it is a narrative document, starting off with the magnificent account of the creation in Gen 1. But in its total structure the narration of events tends to be subordinate to its main interest, which is the preservation and inculcation of various priestly procedures, ordinances, and values. Most of the laws of P are relatively old, but others must in their present form (e.g., the Day of Atonement regulations in Lev 16) be relatively new. Insofar as its cultic observances are the most developed of those now found in the Pentateuch, P in its present form would appear to be a late work. That it takes a single sanctuary for granted suggests that it comes after Deuteronomy, and since it does not seem to have influenced Haggai, Zechariah, or Malachi, it can hardly have been known to these prophets. It is generally thought, therefore, that the priestly narratives, laws, and traditions which came to constitute the P document were brought together over a period of time, from 550 to 400 BC. The work may have been jointly undertaken by priests in both Judah and Babylonia.

Neh 8:13–18 contains a description of the celebration of the feast of Booths (*Sukkoth*). As this was an old agricultural festival, it must have been kept in some form every year (Deut 16:13–15). If there was any novelty about its observance in Ezra's time (Neh 8:17), it could have been in some matters of detail. The account in Nehemiah implies that the feast began on the second or third of the month (no date is specified in Ex 34:22; Deut 16:13), whereas the priestly tradition of Lev 23:39–43 stipulates that it should start on the fifteenth of the seventh month. During the eight-day celebration there was further reading from Ezra's scroll.

The mixed marriage problem is dealt with in Ezra 9–10 and Neh 9:1–5a. This issue had confronted both Malachi (2:11, 14–16) and more recently Nehemiah (13:23–9), but the measures they had taken had not proved effective. Whether Ezra knew of the prevalence of mixed marriages in Judah before he left Babylonia is uncertain, but it is clear that he became aware of it within a few months of his arrival in Jerusalem through the complaints of local officials (Ezra 9:1). Ezra's response to what he learned is described in Ezra 9:3–15 (mourning, fasting, praying); he viewed the situation, not as a social phenomenon, but as a great sin against Israel's God. The popular reaction to Ezra's public prayer was the gathering in the temple area of a crowd of Jerusalemites of all ages. It was one of the bystanders, Shecaniah, who suggested to Ezra that the way to right this wrong would be to divorce the foreign wives. Ezra approved this proposal, and he had the leaders who surrounded him, including priests, Levites, and laymen, take an oath that they would carry it out. This was followed by the calling of a public assembly (absentees were subject to penalties) in the ninth month, probably in the year of Ezra's arrival, 398 BC. At this gathering the details of what should be done were worked out. A divorce court was set up, and at appointed times those who had taken foreign wives were to appear before it, after preliminary local hearings in the villages and towns. The court sat for three months (or four, if there was an intercalated month in 397 BC), and by April 397 BC its work was finished. Ezra 10:18–44 provides a list of those who had taken foreign wives: it includes 17 priests, 4 of whom were from the high priestly family of Joshua, 6 Levites, 1 singer, 3 gatekeepers, and 84 laymen, a total of 111 persons. The last verse (44) is obscure, but 1 Esd 9:36 is probably correct in suggesting that the men concerned put away both their wives and their children (cf *Ant* xi, 152). It is possible that there was some formal adjournment of the special court, and that the Levites played a distinctive role on this occasion (Neh 9:1–5a).

Ezra's strong stand on the matter of mixed marriages helped Judah to establish a community tradition unfavourable to such unions, and without such a tradition it is hard to see how Judaism would have survived in the Graeco-Roman world. On the other hand there is a less positive side to the picture. If Ezra 10:44 means that the foreign women and their children were put away, it may be presumed that they returned to their homes. It is not difficult to see that, apart from the hardships to the women and children concerned, these divorces must have created a great deal of resentment among Judah's neighbors. This separateness of the Jews, designed primarily to safeguard Israel's religion from pagan contamination, must have looked to many Gentiles like a form of social exclusiveness, and it was undoubtedly a factor in creating animosity to the Jews in the ancient world.

In the OT Ezra stands out as an individual less sharply than Nehemiah. Josephus's account of Ezra's accomplishments is essentially the biblical one, although he adds the detail that Ezra died an old man in Jerusalem (*Ant* xi, 158). It is 2 (4) Esdras, which comes from about the same time as Josephus, that casts Ezra in the role of a restorer of the law burned in 587 BC (14:21). That Ezra and his five assistants produced twenty-four scrolls for the public (five of which would constitute the Torah), in addition to seventy which were to be reserved for the learned, is an indication of the growth of an Ezra legend in which Ezra is a virtual second Moses. Another line of Jewish tradition is that the law, coming originally from Moses, was transmitted via Joshua, the elders, and the prophets (the last of whom were Haggai, Zechariah, and Malachi) to the men of the Great Synagogue (more accurately 'Great Assembly'), and that Ezra was one of the leading members of this assembly.[6]

IV

THE FOURTH CENTURY
TO 330 BC

GENERAL HISTORY

As we have seen in the preceding chapter, the fourth century was a troubled one for Persia. In two areas close to Judah, Egypt and Phoenicia, Artaxerxes III (359–338 BC) had to wage war, in the case of Egypt to end the independence it had enjoyed for fifty years, and in the case of Phoenicia to put down a revolt begun c 351 BC. Sidon was taken in 345 BC, and Egypt was finally reconquered 343–342 BC. It is unlikely that Judah was involved directly in the Phoenician uprising,[1] although it must have been affected to some degree by the military activities so close to its borders.

Of the governors of Judah we know almost nothing. Bigvai (Bagohi), as we have seen, was governor in 408 BC,[2] but how long he was in office after this we do not know. Excavations at Ramat Raḥel (Beth-haccherem) have unearthed fourth-century stamped seals, two of which have the inscriptions 'Judah, Jehoazar the governor' and 'belonging to Ahiyo the governor.'[3] These seals, therefore, give us the names of two additional governors. A seal impression from Jericho with the inscription *yhud urio* and a coin from Beth Zur with *yhzqyhw yhd*, both from this century and both using names that could be priestly, have been thought to indicate that the governorship of Judah was now in the hands of the high priest. Urio may be the same name as Uriah of Neh 3:4, and Hezekiah may be the chief priest of this name referred to by Josephus as in office c 312 BC (*Apion* I, 187).[4] It is difficult, however, to fit these alleged high priestly names into the list of high priests supplied by the Chronicler in Neh 12:10. This list gives us Eliashib, as high priest throughout Nehemiah's career (Neh 3:1; 13:4); Joiada (Jodas of *Ant* XI, 297); Jonathan (an error for Jehohanan, cf Ezra 10:6), identical with Joannes of *Ant* XI, 297, who, according to Cowley (text 30, line 18), was high priest in Jerusalem c 411 BC, and who was in this position in Ezra's time (Ezra 10:6); Jaddua (probably the Jaddus of *Ant* XI, 306–12, who held office in the time of Darius III, 336–330 BC). The Chronicler's list implies that Jehohanan and Jaddua between them served for over seventy years, which is improbable but not impossible. A rather sad commentary on the high priesthood is found in a story recorded by Josephus. He informs us that in the time of Jehohanan, and in the reign of the second Artaxerxes (probably Artaxerxes II, 404–359), the governor of Judah, Bagoses (Bigvai), imposed for seven years a heavy fee for the daily burnt offerings in the temple. The reason for this was that Jehohanan had murdered his own brother Yeshua in the temple (*Ant* XI, 297–301).

LITERARY AND CULTIC DEVELOPMENTS

It should be observed that evidence for the precise dating of most of the books to be dealt with below is almost completely lacking. To squeeze them into a seventy-year period in the fourth century is to some extent arbitrary, and largely a matter of convenience for the presentation of the subject. Some books may be later, others earlier, than the title of this chapter suggests.

The Law (Torah or Pentateuch)

The Law, which was to become the foundation stone of all later Judaism, appears to have received its definitive form early in the fourth century. Ever since the promulgation of Deuteronomy in 621 BC, and in view of the influence which this scroll exerted, it was becoming more and more evident that the will of Israel's God could be most effectively presented through the written word. Further, the extinction of the Hebrew monarchy and the realization that Judah must reconcile itself to life under an alien power doubtless encouraged the collection and preservation of all extant documents and traditions. The end result of all these factors was, among other things, the emergence of the Torah. Whether Ezra had anything to do with the final stages of its compilation we do not know. What scholars are quite certain about is that the Torah is the outcome of a long process of accumulation and redaction.

The contents of the Torah embrace a wide range of myth, legend, history, tradition, cultic practice, legal procedures, and moral law. The earliest parts (Eissfeldt's L document) appear to come from the time of David or shortly thereafter, the J and E documents belong to the period of the monarchy, probably before 700 BC, and its latest strand, the P document (commented on in chapter 3), is dated in its present form, 550–400 BC. When the final stages in the redaction of all this material were reached, the L, J, and E traditions, which may have been previously combined, were incorporated into P, the latter serving as a kind of backing for the whole. Deuteronomy, seventh century BC, could not be fitted into P's framework, and was therefore appended to the end as an extensive conclusion. Since Moses was in a sense the father of Israel as a nation, and since some of Israel's basic laws were attributed to him (e.g., Ex 34:1–28, in the J document), Moses could be thought of as the father of Israel's law, just as Solomon was considered to be the father of Israel's wisdom. Hence, by extension, all the laws of Israel were attributed to him, and the Torah became the Law of Moses. The Law was Israel's first Scripture, and even when at a later date other writings came to be associated with it to complete Judaism's Bible, the Torah remained Scripture *par excellence*. Its individual laws (613 by Jewish reckoning) were to shape Israel's thought, values, and life from that day to this.

No matter what view of the origin of the Pentateuch is held,[5] this work stands out as a remarkable literary achievement of the ancient Near East. If we disregard its understandable concern for religious ritual and the minutiae of temple practice, its narratives about the patriarchs, about Jacob's descendants, and about Moses and the exodus are vivid tales which by common consent are recognized as literary classics of the ancient world. But much more than this the Torah is based upon a religious philosophy, an interpretation of Israel's early history, and a set of moral values which subsequent Judaism acknowledged to be fundamental to its very existence. That the Christian Church also appropriated both the view of the world which the Torah expounds and its non-ritualistic religious code is a tribute to the wisdom and insight of those Jewish scholars to whose devoted work the Torah is a memorial.

The Torah as a written document could be of service to the Jewish community only insofar as it was known to the people. Even in Ezra's time we are told that a group of Levites helped the Jerusalemites to understand the law which Ezra had read (Neh 8:7–8), and on the following day priests, Levites, and community leaders came together to study the words of the law (Neh 8:13). While the scribe in the sense of a professional writer or scrivener was an established feature of Israel's life (cf 'secretary,' 2 Sam 8:17; 1 Kgs 4:3; Baruch, the scribe whom Jeremiah employed, Jer 36:32), the scribes who now emerge in Judah's life were not merely writers; they were scholars who were familiar with the community's traditions and who had some competence in the exposition of the Law. Their prototype was Ezra himself (Ezra 7:6). Many of them were in fact Levites (2 Chr 34:13; cf Neh 8:13), and they came to be an important human factor in the development of Judaism. In a very real sense their work was a form of divine service, a supplement to the temple cult. When the latter ceased in 70 AD, the activities of these scholars proved to be the salvation of the Jewish tradition.

The Chronicler

The Chronicler, who has given us 1 and 2 Chronicles as well as Ezra-Nehemiah, apparently worked in this period. As his narrative stops with Ezra's career, he must have written after 398 BC. To account for his confusion in the sequence of Nehemiah and Ezra we should perhaps let fifty years pass, which would being him down to c 350 BC. In 1 Chr 3 the list of David's descendants after Jeconiah (Jehoiachin), exiled in 597 BC, runs to eight generations, which takes us to the fourth century, as does the list of high priests in Neh 12:10–11. Hence it seems reasonable to date the Chronicler 350–300 BC.

The Chronicler covers the biblical story from Adam to Ezra. His main sources were those available to us, from Genesis to Kings, but in addition he used other documents and traditions, one of which appears to have been a Midrash (RSV 'commentary'; on Midrash see note 12, p 242) on Kings (2 Chr 24:27). The pericope describing Manasseh's temporary imprisonment in Babylon (2 Chr 33:10–13) must come from one of these extra-biblical sources. The biblical writings are used very selectively, and material unfavourable to the Chronicler's subject tends to be suppressed (e.g., in the David narrative nothing is said about the Bath Sheba incident). The idealization of David accounts for his being credited with preparations for the building of the temple (1 Chr 22:2–19), as well as with giving Solomon the architectural plan for the temple (1 Chr 28:11–19).

The Chronicler shares in a general way the views and theological ideas of the priestly tradition as reflected in the P document of the Torah. He assumes that God intervenes in Israel's history, and that in this world a process of retributive justice is working itself out. But in one respect the Chronicler's position is somewhat different from that of P. He lays a great deal of stress on the rights and duties of the Levites: in Chronicles-Ezra-Nehemiah the word 'Levites' occurs 158 times ('priests' 144 times), whereas in the historical books (Joshua to Kings) it is found 17 times, and 'priests' 74 times. It seems evident that the Chronicler deemed it important in the fourth century to stress the role and status of the Levites.

A major concern of the Chronicler was the cultus in the Jerusalem temple. In his time the public services appear to have acquired a structure and form which are not provided for in the Torah. It may be presumed that the fourth-century arrangements rest upon earlier practices, but the details of the latter have not survived. Levites are now divided into 22 (or 23) classes, possibly originally 24 (1 Chr 23:6–23; 24 in *Ant* VII, 367), and the priests into 24 classes (1 Chr 24:1–19; cf *Life* 2). Another side of the Chronicler's cultic interest is seen in his prescriptions for temple music. In 1 Chr 15:16–24 (cf 2 Chr

7:6) David's musical arrangements connected with the bringing of the ark to Jerusalem are undoubtedly an antedating of the fourth-century situation. Similarly the use in 1 Chr 16:4–42 of parts of Pss 105; 96; 106 must indicate that we have here a contemporary liturgical tradition (cf 2 Chr 5:12–13; 29:25–30). Levites, described as 'singers,' from certain stated families are assigned either vocal parts (1 Chr 16:4) or various musical instruments (1 Chr 15:16–22; 16:5–6), but more precise details are lacking. In 1 Chr 25 we are given the 24 courses into which the singers were divided. In verses 1–3 the use of the verb nb' ('to prophesy') has been thought to indicate that some singers served as cult prophets, but this is doubtful. It is indicative of the Chronicler's interest in this matter that the word 'singers' appears 33 times in Chronicles-Ezra-Nehemiah, and only 5 times elsewhere in the OT. It is clear from Neh 12:27–9 that the same personnel and musical instruments were available for non-temple use, in this case for the dedication of Jerusalem's wall. Other illustrations of the strong cultic interest of the Chronicler are seen in his accounts of the purification of the temple in Hezekiah's time (2 Chr 29:3–36), and also Hezekiah's arrangements for the organization and support of the priests and Levites (2 Chr 31:2–19).

Another aspect of the Chronicler's thought is reflected in what he says, and does not say, about northern Israel. After dealing with David and Solomon (1 Chr 10 to 2 Chr 9), and after noting the separation from Judah of northern Israel at the beginning of the reign of Rehoboam (2 Chr 10), the Chronicler proceeds to concentrate upon the history of Judah and to ignore the northern kingdom except when its history impinges on that of Judah. Hoshea, the last of Israel's kings, is not even mentioned, nor is the fall of Samaria to the Assyrians in 722–721 BC. The Chronicler's estimate of the northerners is implicit when he asserts in 2 Chr 13:10 that the Lord is Judah's God, and in 2 Chr 25:7 that 'the Lord is not with Israel.' In 2 Chr 19:2 the Israelites are dubbed 'the wicked,' who have sinned against the Lord (2 Chr 28:10), and the priests who serve the northerners are dismissed as illegitimate (2 Chr 11:14–15; 13:9), as they are in 1 Kgs 12:31. This hard line towards Israel is slightly softened in the account of Hezekiah's reign. That king invited all Israel to come to Jerusalem for the Passover, but his messengers were mostly derided in the north (2 Chr 30:1–11). It is a reasonable conclusion from all this that the Chronicler had a decidedly negative view of the people who in his day were still living in northern Israel.

The Priesthood

The tensions within priestly circles in the seventh to sixth centuries, to which allusion was made in chapter 1, seem to have been largely resolved by the fourth century. The Zadokites, who had come to control the Jerusalem temple (as in Hezekiah's time, 2 Chr 31:10), and whose rights were championed by Ezekiel (40:46; 43:19; 44:15), appear to have jousted with other priests whose claim to legitimacy rested upon their Aaronic descent. The rights of the latter are assumed in the P document (Ex 31:10; 35:19; etc). It remained for the Chronicler to supply Zadok with a genealogy which traced his descent back to Aaron, through one of the latter's sons, Eleazar (1 Chr 6:1–8). Another son, Ithamar (Lev 10:16), was the ancestor of the non-Zadokite priests. In 1 Chr 24:1–19, 16 of the 24 courses into which the Aaronite priesthood was divided are made up of the descendants of Eleazar (i.e., the Zadokites), whereas only 8 are descended from Ithamar. We may deduce from this that in the Chronicler's time the Zadokites had managed to retain a somewhat superior status among Israel's clergy.

Although there are comparatively few references to the high priest in the historical books (2 Kgs 12:11; 22:4–8; 23:4), it is difficult to imagine that the Jerusalem temple could have operated without someone in charge of priestly affairs. The P document is therefore on defensible ground when it assumes the early existence of such a functionary (Num 35:25), although we suspect that the regulations governing the high priest, now found in Lev 21:10–15, may have taken shape only gradually. In the post-exilic period the absence of a king in Jerusalem may have added to the lustre of the high priest, but as long as there was a strong secular governor this can hardly have affected the actual power which the high priest exercised. It has been thought that P's anointing of the high priest (Ex 29:4–9) may be an example of the transference to the high priesthood of what was basically a royal rite (cf 1 Kgs 1:45; 19:15–16; 2 Kgs 11:12; 23:30). As late as 408 BC, as we know from an Elephantine papyrus,[6] there was still (or at least in 411 BC) an influential governor (Bigvai/Bagohi) in Jerusalem as well as a high priest (Johanan). It is clear, however, that if political circumstances reduced the power of the civil governor, or even led to his non-appointment, the high priest as a leading Jewish personage was in a position to profit from such a situation.

Prophecy

RUTH AND JONAH

The Hebrew short stories of Ruth and Jonah cannot be precisely dated, but their occasional use of Aramaic and their broad and generous attitude to the non-Hebrew world strongly suggest that in their present form they were written in the post-exilic period, possibly during or shortly after the time of Ezra. Their preservation in Judah and their eventual inclusion in the canon of Scripture indicate that, in contrast to the provincialism of Nehemiah and Ezra, there were those in the Jewish community who championed less restrictive views.

Ruth[7] / This is an exceptionally well-told tale, often looked upon as a textbook example of the Hebrew short story. The simplicity of the narrative, the delineation of the characters, and the economy of the prose style have combined to produce a vignette of life in ancient Israel which has intrigued readers of every generation. If the story has a factual basis, there can be little doubt that in the course of its oral transmission the facts were somewhat embellished. Some have argued that the section relating to David's ancestry (4:17b–22) is secondary and quite unhistorical. This may be so, although one answer to such an argument is to ask: if there was no valid tradition that one of David's great-grandmothers was a Moabitess, would anyone in the post-exilic age have advanced such an idea?

Some have looked upon this book as a pamphlet designed to counter the strict marriage regulations associated with Nehemiah and Ezra. This may have been the author's intent, although it must be admitted that his little book displays no polemic interest and no animus towards any one. It seems best to take the tale at its face value, as voicing views which may well have antedated Deutero-Isaiah. Genuine human kindness transcends ethnic origins and national boundaries, and when a foreigner, in this case Ruth, shows interest in the worship of Yahweh, she is to be welcomed with warmth and affection. If 4:17b–22 is taken as part of the original story, then these verses demonstrate how even a Moabite ancestor had, in the economy of God, her small share in preparing Israel for the advent of the great king David.

Jonah / In 2 Kgs 14:25 there is reference to an eighth-century prophet, Jonah the son of Amittai, who gave moral support to the expansionist policy of Jeroboam II, king in Samaria. This Jonah was presumably a good nationalist, and he was chosen by the author of our book of Jonah as a suitable figure around whom he could weave his own little didactic tale. The latter seems to be based, in part, upon two legends, one of a man being saved after being swallowed by a great fish, and the other of a plant whose growth was accelerated by the word of the Lord God. Wherever he got this material, our author used it skilfully for his own purposes, and he produced a story of a Hebrew prophet that is unique in Israel's literature.

If we set aside as patently untenable the view that the book of Jonah is a record of historical events, we are left with two alternative modes of interpretation. One takes the book to be an allegory, with Jonah representing Israel and the sojourn in the fish's belly the Babylonian exile. The meaning of the other elements of the story, as in most allegories, would then depend upon the imaginative ingenuity of the interpreter. The second way is to take it as a parable. This permits one to look for the main thrust of the book without being obliged to attach meaning to its incidental details.

Whether the story is viewed as allegory or parable, the author's intent is quite clear. In his view Israel's God is concerned with Nineveh, so concerned in fact that he sends a prophet from his own people to bring about Nineveh's repentance. If this is an echo from the teaching of Deutero-Isaiah (e.g., Isa 42:1–4; 45:22–3), then we have the earliest date for the book of Jonah. Our author intimates that some Jews did not see things as did Deutero-Isaiah, and had no desire to share their religious beliefs with the Gentile world. This is shown, first, by Jonah's unsuccessful attempt to avoid going to Nineveh, and secondly, when he finally reached the Assyrian capital and was instrumental in bringing about the repentance of the whole population, by his displeasure at the success of his mission. The reactions of Jonah, which the book describes, must be a caricature of the attitudes of some of the author's contemporaries.

It is usually assumed that the psalm which Jonah uttered in the fish's belly (2:2–9) is a psalm of thanksgiving and not an integral part of the book. Admittedly its inclusion or omission makes no difference to the flow of the narrative. Someone, however, evidently thought it was appropriate in its present position; if this was the author of the book, he may have used it to emphasize his point that a really devout man, as the words of the psalm imply Jonah was, can be blind to some of the demands of God.

JOEL

Nothing is known about Joel's life, but his interest in temple matters (1:13; 2:15,17) gives some support to the view that he was a prophet attached to the Jerusalem sanctuary. Despite his place in the Scriptures among eighth-century prophets, it is generally agreed that he flourished in the early fourth century BC.

Joel's initial prophetic words seem to have been inspired by a plague of locusts, accompanied by drought, which he interpreted as an intimation that the Day of the Lord (cf Amos 5:18–20) was near (Joel 1:2–20; 2:1–11). He calls the people to repentance (2:12–17), and promises a restoration of fertility to Judah (2:18–27). His most distinctive oracles, however, are of an eschatological character. At some undefined time after the aforementioned restoration has been accomplished, the Lord will pour out his spirit upon Israel (2:28–9); portents will appear in heaven and on earth (2:30–2); the nations will be summoned to a final battle (3:9–11); and there will be a judgment of the Gentiles in the valley of Jehoshaphat because of what they have done to Israel (3:1–3,12–16a), with special treatment for Phoenicia and Philistia (3:4–8; cf Egypt and Edom in 3:19). The prophecy ends with a picture of Judah's future blessings, with the Lord dwelling in Zion (3:16b–21).

THE END OF TRADITIONAL PROPHECY

Prophets in one form or another appeared among the Israelites from Moses to Malachi, and then in the fifth to fourth centuries BC the whole prophetic movement died out. Even anonymous prophecy seems to have been finished by this time, although Zech 9–14 may come from the late fourth or early third century (see chapter 5). While it lasted, prophecy served as the human channel whereby the word of the Lord was directed to particular situations in Israel's life, and as such it was one of the means for moulding Israel into a holy people.

We may suspect, however, that in the age after Moses there was always a certain reserve towards prophets, especially on the part of priests. The claims of the prophets were to some extent subjective, and the appearance of 'false prophets' tended to undermine the acceptability of all prophets. The only test of true prophecy that Deuteronomy can suggest is whether a sign or word given by a prophet actually comes to pass (Deut 13:1–5; 18:15–22). But this test covers solely the predictive element in prophecy, which was frequently only a part of the message of a given prophet.

It is probable that the public acceptance of the Deuteronomic code in 621 BC, with its guidelines for almost every aspect of Hebrew life, created a situation in which the ministry of prophets became more and more superfluous. Further, the glorification of Moses, which is part of the Deuteronomic tradition (cf Deut 34:10–12), did make it almost impossible for any would-be prophet to do more than reiterate what Moses had earlier said. It is interesting that the P document, which was taking shape in the sixth and fifth centuries BC, has no real place for anything like charismatic prophecy (cf Num 11:24–9; 12:6, where the text presents difficulties). In the later work of the Chronicler the musical talents of the temple orchestra are represented as a form of 'prophesying' (1 Chr 25:1), and in 2 Chr 20:14–19 a temple singer, Jahaziel, actually speaks in a prophetic role.

The wisdom literature

THE WISDOM MOVEMENT

In the OT 'wisdom' and 'wise' sometimes refer to technical and artistic skill (e.g., Exod 28:3; 35:10; 1 Kgs 7:14; Isa 40:20; Jer 10:9), but in the literature under review wisdom designates a quality of mind and heart whereby an individual is able both to cope with the problems of life and to give good counsel to others. Tribal leaders were expected to be wise (Deut 1:15), and we may assume that Israel's elders, who probably constituted the local government at the village and town levels, and who had various duties to perform (Deut 19:12; 21:2,19; 22:15; 25:7; cf Ezek 7:26), were, in their way, wise men. Further, certain individuals for one reason or another were reputed to be wise, such as the unnamed wise women in David's time (2 Sam 14:2; 20:16) and Agur (Pro 30:1). But the outstanding figure of this sort, in the biblical tradition, is Solomon (1 Kgs 3; 4:29–34; 5:7,12; 10:1–10,23–4), and there is no reason for questioning the view that in some respects Solomon was a shrewd ruler, with a gift for epigram. Later ages came to look upon him as the father of Hebrew wisdom.

Another level of wisdom is found in the recorders, scribes (secretaries), and counsellors whom we meet in the royal court (e.g., 2 Sam 8:16–17; 15:12; 20:24; 1 Kgs 4:3; 2 Kgs 12:10; 18:18; etc). It is probable that the reference in Jeremiah to the wise, as a group distinct from priests and prophets (Jer 18:18), designates these professional counsellors who served the king (cf Jer 9:23).

It was the confluence of these various traditions, issuing from the elders, sages, scribes, and counsellors, which ultimately produced the wisdom movement, whose workers were most commonly known as wise men (ḥakam, plural ḥᵃkamîm). This word was to endure into later Judaism as a common term for a scholar. Those making up the group were in fact Israel's learned men, the intelligentsia. The wisdom movement in Israel was inevitably influenced, mostly in minor ways, by parallel developments in the ancient Near East, notably in Egypt and Mesopotamia, but the details of such influence cannot be spelled out here.[8]

The practitioners of wisdom must not be thought of as a compact watertight group within Hebrew society. They were involved in many facets of Jewish life, and, as we see from Ben Sira (c 180 BC), they could be counted on to give their support to the temple and the priesthood. It is possible that with the priests they had a hand in gathering and arranging the traditions that ultimately became Israel's Torah. But their real claim to our attention is their own distinctive literature, of which we shall here notice only the books of Proverbs, Job, and the Song of Solomon.[9]

THE BOOK OF PROVERBS

Proverbs is a collection of precepts, epigrams, and moral essays, all in poetic form. Its structure is indicated below.

1:1–7: Introduction

1:8 to 9:18: This section is made up mostly of short moral essays, each of which deals with one theme. Two of these are concerned with wisdom, which is virtually personified (1:20–33; 8:1–36).

10:1 to 22:16: This section, entitled 'The Proverbs of Solomon,' consists mostly of couplets. Those in 10–15 usually display contrasting parallelism, whereas those in 16–22 rarely do so. The couplets are self-contained and appear in random sequence, so that if their present order were altered, no essential change would be effected.

22:17 to 24:22, to which 24:23–34 seems to be an appendix: This section, 'the words of the wise' (22:17), is unique in that 22:17 to 23:14 (some take it to be longer) seems to be related to an Egyptian document of about 1000 B.C., written by Amen-em-ope, 'Teaching for Life and Instruction for Prosperity.'[10] The ideological and verbal resemblances between the two suggest either that the Hebrew scribe actually had a copy of the Egyptian writing before him (in a translation), or that he recalled with considerable accuracy some earlier exposure to its contents.

25:1 to 29:7: This has as its heading, 'These are the proverbs of Solomon which the men of Hezekiah, king of Judah, copied.'

30–31: Four sections, constituting an appendix to the preceding material: 30:1–14, the words of Agur; 30:15–31, a series of five numerical sayings, the opening verse of each constituting a kind of riddle (verses 32–3 seem to be at loose ends); 31:1–9, the words of Lemuel; 31:10–31, an acrostic poem on the virtues of a good wife.

It is clear from this analysis that Proverbs, as we have it, is a combination of materials which at one time existed independently. The dates at which these several sections were compiled and the date at which they were brought together can only be surmised. The political and social background of most of the proverbs is so vague that they cannot be dated with any exactitude. The references to kings (14:28; 16:10,13; 20:2,8,26,28; etc) are probably to Israel's kings, which indicates a date prior to 587 BC. In 25:1 there is a reference to some proverbs being copied out in Hezekiah's time (c 700 BC). There is nothing inherently improbable in this statement, which suggests that some of our proverbs had attained their present form in the late eighth century BC. The use of the phrase, 'The Proverbs of Solomon' (1:1; 10:1; 25:1), betokens a tradition that some epigrams were composed or collected by Solomon, which, if Solomon was an astute king (cf 1 Kgs 3:5–14,16–28; 4:29–34; etc), is not difficult to believe, although to identify his contributions in the book of Proverbs is quite impossible. Further, the personalization of Wisdom as the first creation of the Lord (8:22–31) is a concept of considerable religious importance, yet it is not found in the oracles of the prophets. This leads us to conclude that this view of Wisdom can hardly be earlier than 600 BC, and is probably later. Finally, if the references to the law in 28:4,7,9 and 29:18 are to a recognized body of religious teaching, they must be dated sometime after Josiah's reformation of 621 BC. The conclusion of the matter is that we have very little concrete evidence for dating the various parts of Proverbs. It is probably safest to say that these sayings represent all stages of Hebrew life in Palestine, and that the book took its present form c 400 BC.

The contents of Proverbs cannot be adequately summarized, for they cover almost the whole range of human conduct. The acceptance of parental advice, the value of wealth, solicitude for the poor, intemperance, sex (within and without the marriage relationship), controlling the temper and the tongue, pride, cheerfulness – these are some of the subjects dealt with. While the book contains some inconsequential material, on the whole it presents a very sensible treatment of some recurring human problems, a kind of guide to right living within the Jewish tradition. Many of the maxims are humanistic and prudential, but others find their motivation and sanction in the recognition of God ('God' occurs 7 times in the book, and 'Lord' 86 times). In the words attributed to Agur there is actually a short prayer to the Lord (30:7–9).

It has long been noticed that the righteousness and justice with which Proverbs is concerned (e.g. 1:2–4) are not conspicuously associated with conformity to cult and ritual, but are apparent in the quality of daily life. This seeming indifference to the cult is not absolute: sacrifices and offerings are alluded to in 3:9; 7:14; 15:8; 21:3,27. Nevertheless the absence of references to the temple, the altar, priests, Levites, the festivals, the Sabbath must mean that the authors of Proverbs, while not against these things and persons, believed that other matters were of greater importance. It is probably the same sense of values which makes Proverbs solicitous for man as a human being, rather than for man as a member of the Hebrew community. The words 'Israel' and 'Judah' each occur only once in these chapters (in historical notes, 1:1; 25:1), and key terms such as 'Jerusalem,' 'Moses,' 'covenant' do not occur at all. It is of course evident that the writers of Proverbs were Israelites, but it is also clear that their concern with human conduct extended beyond the borders of Israel.

To the question of how this book or its antecedents were used in ancient Israel only a conjectural answer can be given. It is usually assumed, mostly on analogy with Egyptian practice, that from Solomon's time on some methods of educating well-to-do youths were available in ancient Israel. It is further supposed that, to whatever other use it was put, a book such as Proverbs served as an instructional text in dealing with the young. The frequent 'my son' (1:8,10,15; 2:1; 3:1,11; etc) may have come originally from a father-son relationship, but in Proverbs it usually seems best to take it as a teacher's address to a pupil. Learning would be by rote (cf Isa 29:13), and it is conceivable that at a certain stage in the learning process the couplet, so common in Proverbs, was used, with the instructor reciting the first line and the pupil responding with the second. If Proverbs played a role in the training of the young, who would be mostly from the influential and affluent sections of Hebrew society, this would explain why much of the book is oriented to Israel's upper classes (e.g., 3:9–10; 7:1–27; 10:15; 11:4,28; 13:8,11,22; etc). In this connection it is instructive that the impressive poem on a virtuous wife with which the book ends (31:10–31) extols the virtues, not of a peasant woman, but of a well-to-do patrician lady.

THE BOOK OF JOB

Job is the most speculative as well as the most profound book produced by the wisdom school, and it is often grouped with the Psalms and the Prophets as constituting the vital core of the literature of ancient Israel. If we assume that the author was a Hebrew, we have to admit that his work is strangely indifferent to his fellow-countrymen, as well as to the covenant idea of Israel as the people of God. The book's main theme appears to be the suffering of Job, a blameless and upright man, and this becomes a theological issue when it is viewed, as Job himself views it, in the context of a belief in a just and compassionate God. This problem is in fact part of the larger problem of why evil exists in a world created and sustained by such a God, but, as the book offers no answer to this latter question, we may assume that the author realized that it was not within his power to deal with this matter definitively.

A number of scholars have found the book's intent in another direction. The dialogue reveals that Job's three friends share the view (found, for instance, in Deut 28; Ps 1) that righteousness brings prosperity in this world, and sinfulness misfortune. There is a measure of truth in this position, but if it is made an absolute dogma, it is flatly contradicted by the facts of life. It is theorized that one motive behind the writing of Job was to refute this doctrine, the first stage of the refutation being in the prologue, wherein Job is made to suffer even though he is 'blameless and upright.'

The question of foreign influences on the author of Job has been carefully studied ever since the recovery of the literatures of the ancient Near East has made such study feasible. Parallels, both remote and close, to the story of Job have been found in Egypt and Mesopotamia. In Egypt, for instance, 'The Tale of the Eloquent Peasant' and in Babylonia the Babylonian Job ('I will praise the Lord of

Wisdom') have various contacts with Job, but both are markedly different from it. The conclusion seems to be that, while the author of Job may have known about these and other similar writings, it is impossible to demonstrate that he was dependent on them directly. About the most we can say is that Israel's wisdom writers faced a world full of human problems, that these problems were given literary treatment in various parts of the ancient Near East, and that in subtle and devious ways the latter may have affected the author of Job as well as other writers in Israel.

The structure of Job is quite straightforward.

1–2: The prologue, seemingly part of an old folk tale, describes a series of misfortunes which befall the saintly Job. These troubles are due to the action of Satan, one of the heavenly entourage, who is sceptical of the genuineness of Job's piety, and who is authorized by God to afflict Job in sundry ways. Job emerges from these tests most creditably.

3–31: These chapters, which are the core of the book, are a kind of symposium in which Job and the three friends who have come to comfort him speak in turn. The resulting dialogue does not display any real progress in the argumentation, for each speaker presents his own case with little reference to the person preceding him. The original plan of the book, apparently, was to have three cycles of speeches. Two of these are intact, 3–14 and 15–21, but the third, 22–7, is imperfectly preserved: Bildad's speech (25) consists of only six verses, and Zophar's is entirely missing. The various efforts to remedy what may be a dislocated text cannot be discussed here, although we may note that some scholars find Zophar's lost speech in 27:7–23. It is generally agreed that 28, whose subject is wisdom, is an independent poem, unrelated to the general theme of the book, but possibly by the same author. Job's peroration is in 29–31.

32–37: This section, comprising four speeches by Elihu, a younger man, is commonly thought to be a later addition to the book. It reiterates, and slightly expands, points made earlier by Job's three older friends.

38:1 to 42:6: This can well be considered the most important part of the book. 38:1 to 40:2 and 40:6 to 41:34 are two speeches addressed to Job by the Lord. Job's responses are in 40:3–5 and 42:1–6. Two sections in the Lord's second speech, 40:15-24 (on Behemoth, probably a hippopotamus) and 41:1-34 (on Leviathan, probably a crocodile), are believed by most scholars to be later accretions to the text. Debate on the Lord's speeches has revolved around two points: whether there was originally one speech or two, and whether these speeches are original to the book or secondary additions. Many scholars are of the opinion that it is a literary and dramatic necessity that the Lord should speak at least once at the end of the dialogue, and that Job's final words are 42:2,3b,5-6.

42:7-17: This is clearly the conclusion of the tale, the first part of which now appears in 1-2. In these verses the Lord is represented as rebuffing the three friends and approving what Job has spoken (vs 17). The section ends with Job once more enjoying until the end of his long life health, prosperity, and happiness.[11]

Any reconstruction of the literary history of the book of Job is necessarily conjectural. One view is that a member of the wisdom school, a man of unusual literary gifts, decided to present in poetic form a treatment of the old thorny problem of the prosperity of the wicked and the misfortunes of the righteous (cf Jer 12:1-2; 20:14-18; Pss 3; 10; 22; etc). Taking the folk-tale of Job as his starting-point, he used this known pious figure as a mouthpiece for a righteous man who has to endure suffering, and he created the three friends as foils for Job's words. In trying to represent different points of view our author was doubtless reflecting differences expressed by his contemporaries on the matters at issue. We would expect him to put his most careful thought into the utterances he ascribed to the Lord. His use of the conclusion of the folk-tale, which cannot be said to contribute much to his main purpose, may have been an embarrassing necessity dictated by the popularity of the story. The date when all this was done has been variously placed between 550 and 300 BC. The secondary material may have been added within fifty years of the original composition.

The discussion on human suffering which is presented in the poems in 3-31 is somewhat inconclusive, partly because all four speakers proceed from the same assumption – that the Lord rewards the righteous and punishes the wicked. Job's principal difference with his friends is over his own moral character: his position is that his past behaviour sheds no light on his present sufferings, and in support of his basic integrity he takes, as his final utterance, the oath of innocence (or clearance) in 31. On the other hand Job's three 'comforters' (16:2) insinuate that his misfortunes are the result of his past sins, but this is something Job cannot concede. The friends, nevertheless, keep harping on this theme. In his first speech Zophar claims that God exacts of Job less than his guilt deserves (11:6), and Eliphaz, who started out in 4–5 in a most conciliatory mood, ends in 22 by accusing Job of various moral sins (vss 5–11), and appeals to him to return to the ways of God (vss 21–30).

Confronted by these biting attacks from his well-meaning friends, it is a tribute to Job's inner resources that he stands his ground. It is true that he wishes he had never been born (3:1–19), or that God would put an end to him (7:8–13). Although he feels in 19:7–12 that he has been abandoned by God (cf 7:17–18; 12:4) and given into the hands of the ungodly (16:6–17), he never loses his conviction that God is real, that he has a witness in heaven who will vouch for him (16:16–22; the witness of vs 19 must be either God himself or a member of the heavenly entourage), and that his redeemer lives (19:25a; the rest of this passage, vss 25b–26, is obscure). Whatever else may lie behind 16 and 19, Job's faith that he will ultimately be vindicated here finds expression. His last formal utterance (31) is made in the context of a moral order sanctioned by God; his fervent desire is not to be 'false to God above' (vs 28).

Twice in his speeches (13:22; 31:35) Job had asked the Lord to answer him, but he had heard no voice save the voices of his friends. But now in 38 God breaks his silence and speaks. This is the acid test for our poet. What words and thoughts can he ascribe to God by way of shedding light upon the predicament in which Job finds himself? In 38–40 the author makes the point, possibly with too much use of irony, that Job over against God is a very finite creature, with restricted vision, power, and understanding. The Lord's suggestion in 40:10–14 that Job should assume the moral supervision of the world merely points to Job's utter incapacity for such a task. It is clear that Job, being human and of limited capability, has spoken without knowledge regarding God and his ways; he is in fact in a weak position to cast reflections on the manner in which the Lord arranges the life of the world. This, in essence, is what Job himself now realizes in 40:4; 42:2,3b,5–6. Two factors implicit in God's speeches encouraged Job to come to this realization. One was that God should even speak to him after all that he, Job, had said. Clearly God was still friendly towards him. The second was that God, except for telling him that in speaking of some matters he was grossly ignorant (38:2), did not endorse the accusations of the three friends (cf 42:7). Thus Job's basic belief in God's friendliness (cf Immanuel, 'God is with us,' in Isa 7:14) and his grasp of God's moral demands were now confirmed. The awareness of this, or of something akin to it, must lie behind Job's assertion in 42:5b that '... now my eye sees thee.' All this is a somewhat indirect answer to Job's difficulties, but it is sufficient insofar as Job now realizes that some of the points he had raised are really not as important as he had thought. Our author may have felt that this was the only light which he could shed on the perplexities of God's ways with man. He may have shared the view of a later Jewish scholar, R. Yannai of the third century AD, who said, 'It is not in our power to explain the well-being of the wicked or the sorrows of the righteous' (M, Aboth 4.15).

As literature the book of Job ranks with the best in the OT. The author's vocabulary is richer than that of any other ancient Hebrew writer, and he uses it to produce many poems of unmatched beauty. While there were earlier samples of dialogue for him to follow (Gen 23:3–16; 1 Kgs 22:3–28; Isa 6:1–8; Jer 1:4–19; etc), he went far beyond such models in producing both the heavenly conversation between God and Satan (1–2) and the speeches of Job, his friends, and the Lord in 3:1 to 42:6. He was well versed in the standard literary forms which the prophets and psalmists used: laments appear in 3:3–26; 6:1 to 7:21; 9:13 to 10:22; etc., and hymns in 5:8–16; 9:4–12; 11:7–11; 12:13–25; etc. These technical devices were employed by our poet for his own purposes, and the result is a work of rare genius which has stirred the human soul in every age.

THE SONG OF SOLOMON

The Song of Solomon (hereafter the Song), the first verse of which is 'The Song of Songs which is Solomon's,' shares with the book of Esther the distinction of being very secular, for, like Esther, it nowhere mentions the name of God. Although by the seventh to eighth centuries AD it was being used liturgically in the celebration of Passover,[12] we do not know to what use the Song was put in the period covered by this volume. We do know that in the second century AD there were Jewish scholars who questioned the propriety of including it in the Holy Scriptures.[13] In opposition to such men R. Akiba put forward an astonishing endorsement of the Song: 'All the ages are not worth the day on which the Song of Songs was given to Israel: for all the Writings [i.e., the Hagiographa] are holy, but the Song of Songs is the Holy of Holies.'[14]

The reason why some Jews had reservations about the Song is quite clear. The plain reading of its text reveals that it comprises a number of lyrics whose general theme is human love. The Jewish community had no objection to love as such, and indeed Judaism's general attitude to sex can only be described as extraordinarily sensible; but the problem was, and is, that, since this book is in a canon of Scripture, what religious value can be discerned in it?

The answers, ancient and modern, to this question fall roughly into three categories. The first takes the Song as an allegory: the lover is the Lord and the beloved is Israel. This became the standard Jewish interpretation; it is reflected in the Targum on the Song. Another approach, which in fact is a sophisticated version of the first, looks at the Song as the literary residue of a Hebrew adaptation of a pagan liturgy, such as the Babylonian ritual associated with Tammuz and Ishtar. Apart from the facts that Yahweh is nowhere alluded to, that there are no known liturgical terms in the book, and that the biblical and Mishnaic data leave no room for the incorporation of the Song into the Jewish festivals, it seems improbable that a work allegedly in-debted to pagan sources could so successfully mask its origin as to become accepted in the Jewish community.

The second general category of interpretation sees the Song as drama. The Song is taken to be a dramatic poem, and the material is then divided among two or three leading characters and a chorus (or choruses). This theory suffers from the fact that, starting with the same text, there is little agreement among scholars on how it is to be apportioned among the speakers. Further, a work with no story or plot and no plausible characterization can hardly be described as drama.

The third line of interpretation, which in its basic premises is very old, appears to many moderns to be the most satisfactory. It takes the Song to be a collection of love lyrics dealing candidly but poetically with human love in some of its manifestations. This view of the Song was known in Jewish circles in the second century AD, for R. Akiba condemned those who sang snatches from the Song in the wine-shops.[15] Scholars who interpret the Song in this way find in it an anthology of twenty-five or so separate lyrics or fragments of lyrics, some of which may have been recited or sung in wedding ceremonies. For instance, while we do not know enough about ancient Jewish weddings to speak about their celebration with any degree of confidence, it is possible to take 3:6–11 as a nuptial song, possibly going back to Solomon's time. Ps 45 indicates that rhetorical exaggeration was considered appropriate on such an occasion. The lyrics comprising the Song make no attempt to conceal the basic sensuousness of their subject, but they treat it, nonetheless, with restraint and a remarkable freshness. Even the references to nature, as in 2:8–17; 4:12–15; 6:11; 7:11–13, avoid the didacticism to which most Hebrew writers were prone, and reflect a rapport with the natural world unusual in the OT.

The factors relevant to the date and locale of the Song are too detailed to be presented here. They favour the general conclusion that, while the songs are of varied dates, and while some of them are probably from northern Israel, in their present form they come from a Judean compiler of the fifth or fourth century BC.

The tradition that these songs are Solomon's (1:1) is more difficult to explain. Solomon, as we have earlier noted, was considered the father of Hebrew wisdom, but the Song is a far cry from those writings termed Israel's wisdom literature. It can be argued that the Song is poetry, that the creation of any kind of poetry demanded technical skill on the part of the poet, and that such skill might be called a kind of wisdom (cf Jer 9:17, where mourning women are said to be 'wise'), but if this argument is pressed, all the psalmists would be members of the wisdom fraternity. In 1 Kgs 4:32 Solomon is credited with writing 1005 songs, and it must have been supposed that the Song was one of these.

The nearest the Song comes to formal wisdom is in 8:6–7, where the speaker affirms that

> Love is strong as death ...
> Many waters cannot quench love,
>   neither can floods drown it.

The Psalms

The one hundred and fifty poems which constitute the Psalter are a collection of prayers and hymns, the great majority of which are addressed directly to God. A small number refer to God in the third person (e.g., 19:1–6; 100; 103), and an even smaller number contain responses by God, presumably uttered on appropriate occasions by members of the temple staff (e.g., 12:5; 91:14–16). All of these poems acknowledge the sovereignty of God, and their use in the temple cult or outside of it is a way of honouring God. Hence the Jewish designation of the collection as *Tehillim*, 'songs of praise.'

The work of many scholars, of whom J. Begrich, H. Gunkel, and S. Mowinckel are the most outstanding, has led to the general acceptance of the view that the Psalms can best be understood as poems used in the ceremonies of the Jerusalem temple. The clearest examples are 24; 68; 118; 132, but the numerous other references to sacrifices (27:6; 43:4; 50:14; 54:6; 56:12; etc), sacred processions (42:4), communal praise (30:4), temple music (33:2–3; 43:4; 47:5–6; etc) give substantial support to the theory that the Psalms have a cultic origin. As we do not know very much about temple procedures in ancient Israel, except what can be deduced from the prescriptions in the Pentateuch, we cannot say precisely how psalms were used in the ritual. It is thought that temple personnel, particularly the singers, supplied the requisite vocal and instrumental skills.

The fact that the Psalms rest upon a common theology and employ a common vocabulary tends to obscure their very real differences. These differences have long been noted by scholars, but it is only in the present century that there has emerged some measure of consensus on the types of psalms to be found in the Psalter. What follows presents only the principal results of this scholarly investigation.

THE CULTIC PSALMS

The song or ballad is one of the oldest forms of human speech, and in Israel, as in other areas of the ancient Near East, it was associated with such occasions as harvest, marriage, the burial of the dead, etc. Its greatest development in Israel appears to have taken place in conjunction with the temple cultus. The chief types of psalms noted below were initially connected with temple procedures. It should be observed that, while it is tolerably easy to classify most psalms, some appear to be of a mixed type (e.g., 103), while others are ill-fitted for any of the main categories posited here.

The royal psalms / From Saul's time (late eleventh century BC) to 587 BC the king was a very important person in Israel's life, and in a very real sense his well-being and the nation's went hand in hand. Prayers for him, as one anointed for his office, became part of the ritual in Solomon's temple, although how often and on what particular occasions we can only surmise)except that one royal psalm, 45, appears to be for a king's wedding). Psalms 2; 20; 21; 72 are representative of this category.

Hymns of the community / These psalms, such as 8; 19:1–6; 24; 29; 33; etc, extol the glory and greatness of God. A subclass of the hymns (called by some the 'enthronement psalms') praise the Lord as king, and may have been associated with an annual renewal of the Mosaic covenant. Psalms 47; 93; 96–9 are in this subgroup.

Community songs of thanksgiving / Closely akin to the hymns, these are seen in 67; 124; 129; 136.

Songs of thanksgiving for individuals / Usually songs of thanksgiving for deliverance from danger, distress, or illness, these are found in 30; 32; 34; and elsewhere. It is this type of song that is represented in the thanksgiving psalms found at Qumran.

Community songs of trust / A variation of the hymn, these are illustrated by 103 and 125.

Songs of trust for individuals / These are seen in 11; 23; 27:1–6; 62; 91.

Community lamentations / These arose out of distressful national situations. In these psalms the troubles are described and God's help is sought, as in 12; 44; 74; 79; 80; 83.

The lamentation of an individual / An anguished cry to God, this is the commonest type of psalm; it may be seen in 3; 5; 6; 7; 13; 17; etc. The 'evil-doers' or 'workers of evil,' used sixteen times in the Psalter, are probably impious Israelites (cf the wicked, sinners, and scoffers mentioned in 1:1).

THE NON-CULTIC POEMS

While the great majority of the psalms are clearly cultic in origin, the Psalter contains a number of poems, some quite didactic (often called wisdom psalms), which are unlikely to have played a role in the ordinary temple procedures. These include 1; 19:7–14; 34; 37; 49; 78; 105; etc. It is also possible that some psalms which may originally have had a place in temple worship became detached from the cult and ended up as aids in private devotions (e.g., 23).

The question of what dates are to be given to individual psalms can be answered only in the most general terms. The royal psalms must belong to the period of the Hebrew monarchy, and therefore they antedate 587 BC. Two of the community lamentations, 74 and 79, reflect the sixth-century destruction of Jerusalem by the Babylonians, and 137 ('By the waters of Babylon') must be exilic or post-exilic. Those psalms that refer to the Law (1; 19:7–14; 119; cf 78:5; 94:12) presuppose the existence of an accepted body of law. This may be Deuteronomy, but if it is the Torah, these psalms are among the latest in the Psalter. In short, the psalms range in date from the period of the monarchy down to possibly the early fourth century BC.

It is commonly agreed that the Psalter as it now stands is the result of combining various earlier collections of poetry. The note at the end of

72:20, 'The prayers of David, the son of Jesse, are ended,' suggests that this psalm once stood at the end of a collection of Davidic psalms,[16] either 3–41 (the absence of 'David' from the titles of 10 and 33 can be satisfactorily accounted for), or 3–41; 51–65; 68–70. This collection appears to include some of the oldest psalms. The Korah psalms (42; 44–9; 84–5; 87–8) probably at one time had a separate existence, as did the Asaph ones (50; 73–83). Both Korah and Asaph appear to designate guilds of temple singers (1 Chr 15:19; 2 Chr 29:30; Ezra 2:41). Psalms 120–34, each titled 'A Song of Ascents' (RSV), were most likely used for one of the festivals. It is impossible to determine what principles governed either the arrangement of psalms within the smaller collections, or the sequence of psalms in the final Psalter. In the latter the Davidic psalms were probably placed first because of David's traditional connection with the whole cultic organization (1 Chr 22:2 to 29:5), and because it was thought that he had originated the use of psalms in the temple services.

If the creation of the Psalter arose out of the needs and usage of the temple, we would expect the priests and Levites to have had a considerable share in this compilation. If so, they worked unobtrusively, for the temple clergy are referred to in the psalms quite infrequently: 'Levites' is not found at all; 'priest' appears in 110:4; 'priests' in 132:9,16 (cf 78:64; 99:6); and 'singers' in 68:25; 87:7. However, in view of the fact that the first psalm is a wisdom psalm, and since most of the non-cultic psalms referred to earlier may also have come from wisdom circles, it can be theorized that the scholars of Judah were partners with the clergy in putting the finishing touches on what became the accepted collection of Israel's temple poetry. This process was likely concluded by 350 BC. The fact that the Chronicler in 1 Chr 16:8–36a utilized parts of three psalms (105:1–15; 96:1b–13a; 106:47–8) appears to support this date.

These poems, assembled in the fourth century, had a history of long usage behind them, and they were doubtless intended to be what in fact they became, the standard psalm book for the second temple. This book was the literary record of the rich and varied religious experiences of Israel's saints over a period of some hundreds of years, and its idiom and ideology were to shape Jewish devotional life and liturgical practice throughout all subsequent centuries.

In retrospect

As we look back on the fourth century, it is clear that it and the preceding century constituted an era of great consequence for the Jewish community. The fruits of the earlier centuries were now becoming visible: the Law was firmly embedded in Jewish life and its study and teaching were becoming increasingly important; other writings were being associated with the Torah, and these presently would be forming an expanded Scripture; the cultic practices of the Jerusalem temple were being regularized. These features of Jewish religious practice and thought were to determine the lines along which Judaism was to develop in the future.

THE SAMARITANS: PART I

The emergence of the people living in central Palestine as a distinct Hebrew sect (referred to as 'Samaritans' only once in the OT, 2 Kgs 17:29) must be understood as a long process, being in part the result of a very old and deep-seated antagonism, reinforced by certain religious antipathies, between the Hebrew tribes of the north (Israel) and the one and a half tribes living in the south (Judah). This situation worsened with the fall of Samaria, 722–721 BC, for the Assyrian settlement of various foreign groups in northern Israel (1 Kgs 17:1–6,24) gave the southern Jews grounds for asserting that, while Yahwism persisted up north (1 Kgs 17:26–8,32–3), various forms of paganism also flourished (1 Kgs 17:29–34a). In 2 Kgs 23:19–20 Josiah is reported, as part of his religious reformation, to have destroyed various 'high places; in the cities of Samaria (which Assyria, in its death throes, no longer controlled), and this leads one to speculate whether a sanctuary on Mount Gerizim might have suffered at this time. Despite the rather unfavourable Judean stance towards them some northerners seem to have favoured worship in the Jerusalem temple, as an incident in Jeremiah's time illustrates (Jer 41:4–9). Moreover there were voices in Judah that looked forward to the day when all of Israel, south and north, would be united in the worship of their common God (e.g., Jer 31:2–6; Ezek 37:15–28).

We cannot deal in detail with the Samaritan view of their early history.[17] The essential points in their tradition are that Gerizim is God's holy mountain and that a sanctuary was built there as early as the time of Joshua; that the only legitimate priesthood in Israel is that which served the Gerizim temple, the priests being descended from Aaron through Eleazar and Phinehas (cf 1 Chr 6:49–53); that their ancestors were sent into exile in Haran by the Assyrians (722–721 BC), but that later (the date does not seem to be known) they were permitted to return and worship on Mount Gerizim once more.

It was in the late sixth and the fifth centuries that the relationship between Judeans and Samaritans appears to have further deteriorated. An early sign of this is seen in Ezra 4:1–3, where the Jews turn down an offer from the Samaritans (described as 'the adversaries of Judah and Benjamin') to assist in the rebuilding of the Jerusalem temple. About this time (520 BC) there was some official investigation of the building operation by one Tattenai, an official of the satrapy, and his associates, but, when he communicated with Darius, Tattenai was instructed to allow the work to proceed (Ezra 5:3 to 6:13). There is nothing in the biblical text to suggest that this was more than an official check of a building project. Josephus, however, maintains that the Samaritans provoked Tattenai's investigation in an attempt to harass the Jews (Ant XI, 88–105). Somewhat later, in the reign of Artaxerxes I (465–424 BC), Rehum and Shimshai, Persian bureaucrats, evidently spurred by various groups in Samaria (Ezra 4:9–10,17), were instrumental in having the rebuilding of Jerusalem, including its walls, stopped by royal decree (Ezra 4:8–23). Incidents such as these were bound to make friendly relations between Jews and Samaritans very difficult.

Nehemiah's troubles with Sanballat of Samaria (Neh 4; 6) may have been partly political, for the appointment of a Jewish governor in Jerusalem may have been part of an administrative change which curtailed Sanballat's authority in that area. In any case the friction between the two men probably affected their respective constituencies. Later on, when Nehemiah was bent on discouraging Jews from marrying foreign women (Neh 13:23–7), he was outraged by the marriage of a son of the Jewish high priest to Sanballat's daughter, and expelled the man (and presumably his wife) from Jerusalem (Neh 13:28). This must have had unpleasant repercussions in Samaria.

On the more positive side of Jewish-Samaritan relationships, it must be noted, first, that when Yedoniah and his friends of Elephantine wrote to Palestine in 408 BC to obtain permission to rebuild their temple, which had recently been destroyed, their letters were sent to Bigvai, governor of Judea, and Delaiah and Shelemiah, sons of Sanballat, governor of Samaria.[18] The Elephantine Jews seem to have had less than an orthodox grasp of Israel's religious practices, and their understanding of conditions in the homeland may also have been defective, but apparently they had no reservations about appealing to both Jerusalem and Samaria as centres likely to be sympathetic to their plea. The reply from Bigvai and Delaiah (Cowley, text 32) is of interest because it indicated both that the two men concerned did not intend to give the Elephantine Jews more than sympathy, and that on the matter in question Jerusalem and Samaria were as one.

Another indication of some degree of fraternization between the two communities relates to the Pentateuch. While, as we have seen, the latter was put together in Judah sometime after 400 BC, copies of it soon came into Samaritan hands, and there is every reason to believe that this definitive edition of Israel's Torah was as warmly welcomed in Samaria as it was in Jerusalem. Many of the traditions which went into its making are believed by modern scholars to have had a northern Israelite provenance, such as those of the E document, as well as most of Deuteronomy, and their presence in the final Torah could hardly do anything but commend the work to the Samaritans. We can assume that the text of the Torah accepted in the fourth century by both communities was identical.

The erection of a Samaritan temple on Mount Gerizim, probably in the late fourth century, a temple which the Samaritans claimed was the only legitimate one in which to worship Israel's God, was undoubtedly a sore vexation to the Jews. Solid facts, however, related to the building of this sanctuary are hard to find. Its existence in 167 BC is alluded to in 2 Mac 6:2. Josephus reports that there was such a temple 'built after the model of the sanctuary at Jerusalem,' and that it was

destroyed after two hundred years by the Jewish leader John Hyrcanus in 128 BC (*Ant* XIII, 254–6; cf *War* I, 63). Excavations at Tell
er-Râs on Mount Gerizim (1962, 1964, 1966) have revealed a temple of
the Roman period, thought to be one erected by the Emperior Hadrian
(117–38 AD), and underneath this an earlier building (building B),
built on bedrock, 68 × 65 feet. This may be the Samaritan temple.[19]

It is Josephus who gives us our only account of how and when the
Samaritan temple was built. He claims that Sanballat of Samaria, in
order to keep intact his daughter's marriage with Manasseh of the
high priestly family of Jerusalem, offered to build his son-in-law a
temple on Mount Gerizim where he could exercise his priestly func-
tions. This would presumably have had to be approved by the Persian
king, Darius III (336–330 BC). The latter's defeat at Issus (333 BC) by
Alexander made it necessary for Sanballat to change his political
allegiance, which he did by going over to Alexander at Tyre (332 BC).
In doing so he asked the Macedonian king to sanction the building of a
temple in which Manasseh could officiate. Alexander consented, and
the temple was subsequently built (*Ant* XI, 306–24). Josephus's source
apparently did not record the length of time required to complete the
structure.

There is little that is incredible about the substance of this tradition
in Josephus, although we would not expect the concern for a
son-in-law's career to be the sole reason for Sanballat's willingness to
erect a temple on Gerizim. It may be that after Ezra's time the orthodox
Jewish views on marriage offended many Samaritans, and that the
same brand of orthodoxy may have discouraged Samaritans from
participating in the ceremonies of the Jewish temple. Moreover the
Torah which the Samaritans shared with the Jews could be used to
point to Gerizim, of ancient sanctity (Deut 11:29; 27:12; cf Josh 8:33),
as 'the place which the Lord your God will choose to make his name
dwell there' (Deut 12:11).

The long-felt difficulty about reconciling Nehemiah's reference to
Sanballat's daughter (Neh 13:28) with Josephus's reference to Manasseh and Nikaso (*Ant* XI, 309) may be partly cleared up by the Samaria
papyri.[20] These fragmentary documents, whose dates range from 375
to 335 BC, support hypothetically the following sequence in Samaria's
governors:

Sanballat I (Nehemiah's contemporary)
Delaiah, son of Sanballat I (Cowley, text 30, line 29)
Sanballat II, son of Delaiah
Hananiah, son of Sanballat II (c 354 BC)
Sanballat III, son of Hananiah

F.M. Cross claims that it was Sanballat III who figures in Josephus's narrative as the father-in-law of Manasseh. If this is so, then it appears that Josephus has telescoped events and confused Sanballat I and Sanballat III.

PART TWO

THE HELLENISTIC AGE AND THE
BEGINNING OF ROMAN RULE

V

THE BEGINNINGS OF
THE HELLENISTIC AGE:
FROM ALEXANDER THE GREAT
TO 200 BC

THE HISTORY OF THE NEAR EAST
AS IT RELATES TO PALESTINE

Alexander the Great's defeat of the forces of Darius III (336–330 BC) not only ended the hegemony of Achaemenid Persia in western Asia and Egypt, but introduced Europeans – Greeks and Macedonians – to the seats of political power in these regions. More importantly the culture of the rulers, which was basically Greek, had an opportunity to spread into the non-Greek world on a scale not hitherto possible. The result was that Hellenism in one form or another became from this point on an ingredient in the total life of western Asia. Not that the native cultures were ever entirely superseded by that of the new rulers, but the fact that the latter in some sense represented the Greek tradition gave Hellenism a prestige that paved the way for its gradual dissemination. This circumstance naturally affected the life of the Palestinian Jews.

Alexander the Great died in Babylon in 323 BC, leaving behind a vast territory, from the Greek mainland on the west to northwestern India on the east, which was under the military control of the Macedonians and Greeks. Within a year such unity as this empire had was broken when ambitious generals began to assert themselves, and so commenced a twenty-year period of fratricidal fighting. The battle of Ipsus in 301 BC resolved most of the issues and determined the main political divisions of the ensuing Hellenistic Age. One of the participants in this turmoil was the Macedonian general Ptolemy, son of Lagus.

Ptolemy, who belonged to the lesser nobility of Macedon, had served Alexander with distinction in his Asiatic campaign. When his master died, and when the council of generals was allotting areas of responsibility, Ptolemy contrived to have himself appointed satrap of Egypt. He came to Egypt in 323 BC, and in the 'wars of the successors' he managed to retain his satrapy. In 305 BC he declared himself to be king, and he thus became the founder of the Ptolemaic dynasty, which lasted until 30 BC.

Ptolemy and his immediate successors had various territorial interests outside the land of the Nile, one of which was Coele-Syria, which embraced southern Syria and Palestine. This region was important to Egypt for strategic and economic reasons. But another of Alexander's generals, Seleucus, the founder of the Seleucid dynasty which initially controlled northern Syria, parts of Asia Minor, and most of Mesopotamia and Iran, also coveted this area, and the stage was therefore set for strife. In the years 320–301 three attempts by Ptolemy to occupy Coele-Syria were thwarted by Antigonus (since 321 BC commander of the Macedonian and Greek forces in all of Asia) and his son Demetrius. Then the leading generals, who included Ptolemy and Seleucus, united against Antigonus and defeated and killed him at Ipsus (in Phrygia) in 301 BC. Seleucus claimed that the coalition had agreed that, once Antigonus was out of the way, he should get Coele-Syria. But Ptolemy disregarded this claim and proceeded for the fourth time to take over this region. This was not a happy omen for the future. Beneath the surface, tension between Ptolemy and Seleucus, and later between their successors, was to plague the history of this area for years to come.

For a hundred years the Ptolemies ruled Coele-Syria, their administrative centre being in southern Phoenicia at Akka (Acre), renamed Ptolemais. It was an important area economically, both because of the taxes extracted from it and because of its exports to Egypt. Some first-hand data on this trade are supplied by papyrus documents, notably by the Zenon Papyri.[1] Zenon was in the service of Apollonius, the *dioiketes* (a kind of vizier) of Egypt in the time of Ptolemy II (283–245 BC), and c 259 BC he spent a year in Palestine. The Zenon Papyri (from the files of Zenon) are mostly related to matters in Egypt, but some furnish various details about commerce with southern Syria. We learn, for instance, that slaves were purchased in Idumea, and that the incense trade was centred in Gaza. Wheat and olive oil were other exports to Egypt. Nothing is said in these documents about Palestine's imports from Egypt.

Another aspect of Ptolemaic rule in Palestine was the establishment of the so-called Greek cities. These towns were usually old sites which were given new names, and some of them may have been set up before the Ptolemaic period began. Places such as Gerasa, Pella, and Dion may be pre-Ptolemaic, while others like Ptolemais, Philoteria, Philadelphia, and Scythopolis appear to be Ptolemaic. We know little about the internal polity of these centres, but for a brief survey of them, including some that are later than the Ptolemies, see the chapter on 'The Greek Towns of Palestine' in Tcherikover's book (pp 90–116), cited in note 1 (p 237). These cities were primarily garrison towns for the Ptolemaic authorities, but they also served as economic centres. They doubtless helped to diffuse some knowledge of the Greek language, but merchants and conscripted or mercenary soldiers would have little or no knowledge of Greek culture, and their role in the dissemination of Hellenism must not be exaggerated. Incidentally, as Tcherikover notes (p 114), there is no evidence of the establishment of any Greek city within the traditional borders of Judea.

The third century BC was marked by the so-called Syrian wars (begun in 276, 260, and 246 BC) between the Ptolemies and the Seleucids.[2] These wars, despite their name, had ramifications far beyond Syria. The third one (referred to in Dan 11:7–8) was in fact a great expedition led by Ptolemy III (247–261 BC) into Seleucid territory as far as Seleuceia on the Tigris, but, apart from instigating a Seleucid counter-attack, which culminated in a peace in 241 BC, it accomplished nothing. A much more serious political development was the accession in 223 BC of a new Seleucid king, Antiochus III, who was determined to assert Seleucid rule wherever it had any legitimate claim. In 221 BC he attacked Ptolemaic positions in Lebanon, and in 219 he took Ptolemais, and in 218 most of Palestine. But in the spring of 217 Ptolemy IV (221–203 BC) led a well-trained army into Palestine and defeated Antiochus at Raphia, southwest of Gaza (cf Dan 11:10b–12). In 3 Maccabees there is a fantastic Jewish tale relating to this victory. Fifteen years later Antiochus tried once more. His attack began in 202 BC, and in the autumn of 201 Gaza fell. Scopas, an Aetolian condottiere employed by Egypt, proceeded to counter-attack, and to retake parts of Palestine, including Jerusalem. But when in 200 BC he pushed northwards, he was met by the Seleucid army under Antiochus at Panion (Paneas), east of Tyre, and defeated. He and his army sought refuge in Sidon where they were besieged until their surrender in the spring of 199 BC. This defeat of Scopas ended Ptolemaic rule in Coele-Syria, and the long-held ambition of the Seleucids to control the area was now realized. This change in political rulers was to have important consequences for the Palestinian Jews.

THE HISTORY OF JUDEA[3] FROM ALEXANDER TO 200 BC

Sources for the history of this period are almost non-existent. Palestine, and especially Judea, was still so isolated that, except for tax-collectors and merchants, it received little attention from the outside world, and if any chronicles were kept by the Jews themselves, they did not survive the hurly-burly of the age. The wars in and around Judah, and the armies so frequently on the march on the fringes of its territory (as in 332–1, 320, 315, 312–311, 302–300, 276, after 261, after 247, 221–217, 202–200 BC), must have greatly handicapped any attempt to chronicle the history of the times.

332–301 BC

From the sieges of Tyre and Gaza in 332 BC Alexander proceeded directly to Egypt. In the spring of 331 he returned to Syria, taking the coast route as far as Tyre, and then turning east and north to cross the Euphrates at Thapsacus. He never appeared in or near Palestine again. The story preserved by Josephus (*Ant* XI, 317–19, 325–39) that Alexander visited Jerusalem after the siege of Tyre is usually thought to be apocryphal, although if the Jewish temple had been a better-known shrine, the essence of the story could not so easily be dismissed, for Alexander tended to recognize such gods as he encountered. On there being some Jews in Alexander's army, presumably in the auxiliary forces, see *Apion* I, 192–3.

Almost nothing is known of Alexander's improvised administration of Coele-Syria. In 332 BC Parmenion, Alexander's second-in-command, was sent to take over Damascus, which he did (as well as acquiring very considerable booty), and it can perhaps be assumed that Damascus or Sidon served temporarily as an administrative centre of this area. Alexander's subsequent arrangements in Egypt for collecting taxes indicate that he was aware of the need both to obtain regular revenues and to protect the peasantry against extortion, and it is probable that a similar scheme was worked out in Syria. There would have been, as elsewhere, a financial superintendent for the area, who would be under Harpalus, the head of the whole civil service.[4] By the time Alexander returned to Susa from India in 324 BC, Harpalus had turned out to be a rogue, and to escape Alexander's wrath he had fled to Greece. We can only imagine what corruption was rampant in Coele-Syria between 330 and 324 BC.

After the deaths of Alexander (323 BC) and Perdiccas, commander of the army in Asia (321 BC), the Macedonian generals, meeting at Triparadisus, appointed Laomedon governor of Syria and Phoenicia. Ptolemy disregarded this appointment and occupied the country for the first time in 320 BC. His later reoccupation in 312 BC, the two occupations of Antigonus in 315 and 312–311 BC, and the final occupation by Ptolemy in 302–300 BC, with their attendant wars, could only have been disastrous for the daily life of both Jews and Samaritans. Josephus preserves the account (based on Agatharchides, a second-century BC Greek writer) that Ptolemy entered Jerusalem on the Sabbath day, and that since the Jews would not take up arms on this day, he was able to take the city without a struggle (*Ant* XII, 4–6; *Apion* I, 208–11). This, presumably, was in 320 BC. The Letter of Aristeas (12–21), which seems to have been used by Josephus (*Ant* XII, 7–8), adds that Ptolemy took 100,000 Jewish prisoners to Egypt, 30,000 of whom were placed in the auxiliary forces of the army, and the remainder, claimed by his own soldiers to be war booty, sold as slaves. The letter further states that at a later date Ptolemy II was prevailed upon to redeem the surviving Jewish slaves at the state's expense. If there is a kernel of fact behind this extravagant tale, it may relate to Ptolemy's second occupation of Palestine in 312 BC, after the battle of Gaza. The army of Demetrius may have had some Jewish and Samaritan conscripts in it (Demetrius and his father had ruled Palestine since 315 BC), and such of these as were captured by Ptolemy would likely have suffered the fate which Aristeas describes.

301–200 BC

We must presume that the Ptolemies, as was their practice elsewhere, administered Coele-Syria through a military governor (*strategos*) whose headquarters were in Ptolemais. Whether there were lesser officials in other parts of the region, as in Jerusalem, we do not know. The Ptolemies were experts in extracting taxes from their subjects, and, while it is unlikely that their tax system in Syria was as complicated as in Egypt itself, it was doubtless sufficient for their purpose. In addition to the usual taxes on agricultural products there were customs dues at such ports as Sidon, Ptolemais, and Gaza. It is improbable that the poll-tax levied on the whole Egyptian population, with some exceptions, was imposed on Coele-Syria. Josephus gives the total tax from Coele-Syria, Phoenicia, Judea, and Samaria as 8,000 talents (*Ant* XII, 175), but this seems much too high a figure.[5] Most taxes were collected by tax farmers who made bids at the tax auctions held periodically in Alexandria. Josephus's account of a successful tax farmer (*Ant* XII, 160–185, 224) is thought to be an essentially accurate picture of the times. In this instance the person is Joseph the Tobiad (or the son of Tobias), an inhabitant of Jerusalem, related through his mother to the Jewish high priest Onias (probably Onias II). He went to Alexandria where he gained the favour of Ptolemy (probably Ptolemy III, 247–221 BC), and obtained the tax-collecting rights for Coele-Syria. On his return to Palestine, and with his authority bolstered by 2,000 soldiers, his brutal treatment of the leading men at both Ascalon and Scythopolis persuaded people to pay his levy, and for twenty-two years he exercised his tax-collecting privileges, becoming very wealthy in the process.

The role of the Jewish high priest in the Ptolemaic administration of Palestine is uncertain.[6] Josephus, in his narrative about Joseph the tax collector, relates that Onias the high priest had withheld the money on account of which 'he had received the chief magistracy (*prostasia*) and had obtained the high-priestly office' (*Ant* XII, 161). Earlier Josephus, speaking of the same Onias, refers to the latter's withholding 'the tribute (*phoros*) of twenty talents of silver which his fathers had paid to the kings out of their own revenues' (*Ant* XII, 158). These references may indicate that the high priest was recognized by the Ptolemies as the governor of Judah as well as its religious head, and that on his accession to office he paid his royal overlord twenty silver talents. It seems likely that the high priest was assisted by a council of elders, the forerunner of the later Sanhedrin, although the evidence for such a council or senate pertains to the Seleucid period (1 Mac 7:33; 12:6; etc; *Ant* XII, 138).

The century of Ptolemaic rule in Judea was, apart from the disturbances to civilian life caused by the recurring wars, relatively quiet in the sense that the relations between the Jews and the Ptolemaic authorities were unmarred by overt strife. Josephus even records that Ptolemy III, after the third Syrian war, came to Jerusalem to offer sacrifices and to present votive offerings for his recent victory (*Apion* II, 48). While this story, for which Josephus is the sole authority, may be apocryphal, its very existence points to a degree of mutual tolerance between the two parties. The same conclusion can be drawn from the synoptic view of Hellenistic history presented in Daniel 11. Verses 5–9 of this chapter, which cover the Ptolemaic period down to the rise of Antiochus III of Syria, have nothing negative to report as far as Judea is concerned.

Hellenism and the Jews

Earlier in this chapter we observed that Alexander and his successors created a political situation that favoured the extension of certain aspects of Hellenism into areas which hitherto had known little about it. While the Ptolemies had a share in this, as is illustrated by their founding and fostering the Museum in Alexandria as a seat of learning, they were the least aggressive culturally of all the Hellenistic dynasties. This was perhaps fortunate for Judea, for it meant that the Hellenism to which the Palestinian Jews were exposed for about one hundred years was a relatively mild type. This is shown by what happened at the old Israelite site of Mareshah (Josh 15:44; 2 Chr 11:8), where about 257 BC an official of Ptolemy II established a colony of Sidonians, the place being named Marisa (Marissa); this is reckoned by Josephus to be in Idumaea (*War* I, 63). The limited excavations of the site indicate that its culture was highly syncretistic.[7]

Only two aspects of this Hellenism require comment here. One is the expanded use of the Greek language. Greek must have been known to some people in Jerusalem long before the time of Alexander, but increasingly after Alexander Greek came into wider use. Any Jew having government or foreign-business connections would perforce have to know some Greek, and those Jews who were intellectually curious would now find it easier to explore the Greek literary tradition. The effects of this exposure to Hellenism on Jewish writers are hard to assess, as is shown by the inconclusiveness of the attempts to find Greek influence in Ecclesiastes.

Another side of Hellenism, pertinent to our present inquiry, is religion. The Greeks sponsored codes of conduct that were essentially humanistic, and views of the world ranging from monism and polytheism to atheism, and these therefore presented a world view which was in formal or practical opposition to that held by the Jews. A feature of this culture that grated upon the pious Jew was the deification of human beings, a practice known in both the Greek and Egyptian worlds before the time of Alexander. In the Hellenistic Age the deifying of kings was usually associated with a public cultus, and participation in the ceremony was in effect a political gesture indicative of loyalty to the king in question. Further, the Hellenistic centuries lifted certain Egyptian and Asiatic gods and goddesses, with strong fertility cults, out of their homelands and made them almost universally known, as witness Serapis, Isis, Cybele, and Atargatis. This whole mélange of gods and goddesses, of deified kings and queens, of novelties in philosophy and ethics, constituted a world of religious ideology and practice utterly foreign to Judaism, and much more subtle than the old Canaanite paganism. If there was some good in parts of this tradition, Judaism tended to take a jaundiced view of it all. It was, in most Jewish eyes, sheer idolatry, and references in Jewish literature from 300 BC onwards indicate the Jewish abhorrence of the prevalent heathen cults (Dan 3; 6; Jub 12:1–8; Lett Jer; 1 Mac 1:43; 3 Mac 4:16; 2 Enoch 10:6; Wisd Sol 13:10–19; 14:12–21). This attitude is further illustrated in one of the sections (tractates) of the Mishnah entitled *Abodah Zarah* ('idolatry'). This very interesting document shows the pains which Jews would take to avoid aiding or abetting any form of pagan religion.

LITERARY AND RELIGIOUS DEVELOPMENTS

The canonization of the Prophets

The Prologue to Ben Sira indicates that by 132 BC the Prophets had become associated with the Law, and the two formed, along with other works described as 'the other books of our fathers,' an authoritative corpus of Jewish writings. The reference in 2 Mac 15:9 to 'the law and the prophets' may be an echo of the time when the Scriptures comprised these two sections only (cf Matt 5:17). If, however, we try to establish the probable date when the association of the Prophets with the Law was first recognized, we find the evidence very elusive.

The references in Ben Sira, and the order in which they are made, to Isaiah, Jeremiah, Ezekiel, and 'the twelve prophets' (Ben S 48:22–5; 49:6–10), attest to a group of prophetic writings identical with the Latter Prophets in the Hebrew canon, and Ben Sira (c 180 BC) therefore furnishes the latest date for this collection. Ben Sira's allusions to persons and events in Joshua-Kings (46:1 to 49:6) indicate that these historical works, to be known at a later date as the Former Prophets, were available to him. Since Daniel, composed about 166 BC, was never included in the Prophets, it is presumed that this was because the prophetic collection was firmly established before it was written. This appears to suppport the terminal date, derived from Ben Sira, for the canonization of the Prophets.

For the earliest date we have to turn to Samaritan history. The latter is an uncertain subject, and any conclusions based upon it are to some extent conjectural. If, however, we assume that the building of the temple on Mount Gerizim occurred in the last third of the fourth century BC (see pp 76–80), this can only have been an irritant to the Jewish community, and it must have made anything like a normal relationship between Jews and Samaritans almost impossible. The Samaritans had, of course, the Torah, to whose traditions they had as much claim as the Jews. But, even before the Gerizim sanctuary was built, they may have looked suspiciously at any attempt to put the writings of the old prophets, who were mostly Judeans, into a definitive collection that could be used to supplement the Torah. If such a collection had been available before the building of the Gerizim temple, the Samaritans might have appropriated it and edited it (as they later did the Torah) in accordance with their own views. The fact that the Samaritans never adopted the prophets may be due simply to the circumstance that such a prophetic corpus was not fully determined at the time the Samaritan temple was built. If this argument, admittedly hypothetical, can be accepted, it points to 330–300 BC as the earliest date for the collection of prophetic writings. Drawing these various considerations together, and having regard to the latest date suggested earlier, we can posit that the canon of the Prophets was settled by c 250 BC.

Whatever precise date we assign to their formal compilation, the assembling of the prophetic oracles must have been a process that extended over a considerable period of time, and in its earlier stages it may have been concurrent with the movement that led to the compilation of the Pentateuch. It is likely that the creation of the Torah and its ascription to Moses stimulated an interest in the prophets who, by hypothesis, had the Torah, and who were concerned with its application to Israel's life. Perhaps the most compelling motive for turning to the old prophets was the hope that Israel, now without any living prophetic voices, would find in these old oracles strength and insight for an era when the people of God were facing all the problems and challenges of the Hellenistic Age. That the literary records of the prophets were thus saved for Israel's immediate comfort and instruction also meant that they were to be available for future generations. Not only the Jews, but later the Christian community, were to find in these works an almost boundless source of spiritual refreshment, a perennial challenge to all forms of injustice and inhumanity, and a reservoir of hope for the future.

Judea's share in the creation of the Septuagint

The Septuagint is the Greek translation of Israel's Scriptures and of other Jewish writings mostly from the pre-Christian period.

While the main concern of this volume is the Jews of Palestine, we cannot overlook the fact that during the Ptolemaic rule in Egypt numbers of Jews from Palestine were brought, or went of their own accord, to Egypt (*Ant* XII, 7–9), and in consequence there was established there, mostly in Alexandria, a large Jewish settlement. This is the basic background of the Letter of Aristeas. This extravagant tale describes how Ptolemy II (283–245 BC) wrote to Eleazar, the high priest of Jerusalem, asking him to send some bilingual scholars to Egypt to translate the Jewish Law from Hebrew into Greek for the royal library. Subsequently 72 competent Jews were sent to Ptolemy, and, after an elaborate reception (including a great banquet) in Alexandria, they were housed on an island (probably Pharos) where they worked at the translation, which in fact they finished in 72 days (cf Latin *septuaginta*, seventy). The translators then returned to Judea with munificent presents from the king. This letter is thought to be largely fictitious and to be a piece of Jewish propaganda of c 100 BC. It is conceivable, however, that behind the story there may be some solid facts, such as the following.

1 / That a translation of the Hebrew Torah into Greek was made in Alexandria about the middle of the third century BC, and that it was intended, initially, not for the Museum's library, but for the Jews of Alexandria. This was, in fact, the beginning of the Septuagint.

2 / That some biblical scholars from Jerusalem may have assisted in the work. Most of these would have been experts in both Hebrew and Greek, although the likelihood of this depends upon the state of Greek learning in Jerusalem at the time, a subject on which we have no knowledge.

3 / That an authoritative Hebrew text may have been procured from Jerusalem (cf Aristeas 46, 176–7). Some Alexandrian Jews who had been exposed to the traditions of the Museum may have been con-

scious of the need to use a reliable Hebrew text, and they may have looked to Jerusalem to supply it. This possibility, thanks to the MS discoveries at Qumran (the Dead Sea Scrolls), is not as remote as it once was. To summarize a very complicated problem in textual criticism, the fragments of the Hebrew text of Samuel found in cave 4 (4Q Sam^a, 4Q Sam^b) point to a Palestinian text similar or related to the Hebrew text in Alexandria that lies behind, or leads up to, the Septuagint.[8] If Jerusalem and Alexandria had identical or similar texts of the Former Prophets, it is likely that they shared other texts as well. In the third century BC, when both Jewish communities were under the same Ptolemaic overlord, exchanges of goods, personnel, and even sacred manuscripts between the two groups must not have been uncommon.

Varieties of religious practice and thought

PIETY

The temple cultus / Jewish piety expressed itself in various ways, of which one of the more impressive was the maintenance of, and participation in, the temple cultus. The latter was under the direction of the priests, who carried out the provisions of the Torah in accordance with tradition. The temple was a busy place, for there were daily sacrifices, morning and evening, as well as special offerings on the Sabbath, on new moon days (the one at the beginning of the seventh month was very special), and of course at the great festivals, Passover, Weeks, and Booths. On most of these occasions only the citizens of Jerusalem and its vicinity could hope to be present, but the annual feasts, particularly Passover, attracted thousands of Jews from the remoter parts of Judea as well as from the Diaspora.

Since the temple procedures were performed on behalf of all Israel, it was thought important that the laity should be represented when these were carried out. By the first century AD, as the Mishnah testifies (*Bikkurim* 3.2; *Taanith* 4.1–4), an arrangement had been effected whereby groups of laymen (singular *maamad*) were selected to attend the temple ceremonies for one week at a time, twice a year. Thus the whole Jewish people was represented, theoretically, in the cultus by both priests and laity. We do not know how the members of a *maamad* were chosen, nor how far back into the pre-Christian period this practice goes.

Ben Sira gives us a picture of a temple ceremony, in 50:5–21, in which the leading participant was Simon the high priest, and, while this evidence belongs to the early second century BC, there is every reason to believe that such temple ritual was performed with equal zeal in the third century. The burning of the sacrifice, the pouring of the wine at the base of the altar, the shouts of the priests, the blasts of the trumpets, the voices of the singers, the people's participation in the prayers, the prostration of the worshippers at appropriate times, the priestly benediction – all these acts added up to an experience of worship which confirmed Israel in its ancient faith.

Tobit / Piety of a more individual type is reflected in some of the stories which probably originated in the third century, one of which is the well-constructed tale about Tobit and his son Tobias. Father and son are portrayed as God-fearing Jews, given to prayer, solicitous for the wage-earner and the poor, eschewing immorality, drunkenness, and marriage with foreigners, and following the golden rule in its negative form (4:15). This characteristic set of Jewish virtues is supplemented by a belief in angels (11:14), which permits the author to introduce Raphael as the angel who brings men's prayers before God (12:12,15), and is further enlarged by the hope that the heathen will eventually recognize the God of Israel (13:11; 14:6–7). A vignette of Jerusalem's future glory is found in 13:15–18. All in all, this little book presents a very attractive, and doubtless a very faithful, picture of the pious Jew of this period.

Daniel 1–6 / Of the same literary genre as Tobit, but reflecting less placid political circumstances, are the narratives in Dan 1–6. Daniel himself does not appear in 3, but it is being included here because it relates to his three friends mentioned in 1. It seems that in Jewish circles a number of stories had collected around the figure of Daniel. The latter must go back ultimately to the Ugaritic Dan'el, the dispenser of fertility,[9] but in one Hebrew tradition he has become an ancient personage to be associated with Noah and Job as a figure of the righteous man (Ezek 14:14). Later, as in Ezek 28:3, Daniel appears as a proverbially wise person. It is from this mélange of Daniel material that Dan 1–6 appears to be drawn. These chapters show no connection with the age of Antiochus IV, and are probably to be dated in the third century. While there are allusions to Jewish food habits (1:5–16) and to the practice of personal prayer (6:10), their main thrust is theological. History is a succession of man-made empires (2, 5), but in the end God will establish his everlasting kingdom (2:44–5). In the meantime Jews must be faithful to their God, and must not participate in any of the current forms of paganism, even when these are supported by the secular power (3; 6). This was a counsel of perfection, for in the Hellenistic Age it could not always have been easy for Jews to stand up and say, 'Be it known to you, O king, that we will not serve or worship the golden image which you have set up' (3:18).

The Letter of Jeremiah / The so-called Letter of Jeremiah is variously placed in different versions of the Apocrypha. In some Greek MSS, as well as in the Vulgate, it is attached to the book of Baruch (1 Baruch) as chapter 6. Since, however, the letter has nothing to do with Baruch, it is now generally treated, as in the RSV, as a separate composition.

The letter purports to be one dispatched by Jeremiah to his fellow Jews in Judah who were about to be sent into captivity in Babylon (either in 598 or 587 BC). It differs, therefore, from the letter in Jer 29:1–23, which the prophet directed to Jews already in exile in Babylonia. The letter under consideration can best be described as a rather rambling polemical sermon whose aim is to hold Babylonian idolatry up to ridicule and to urge the Jews, when they reach Babylon, not to fear its entrenched paganism. Its view of non-Hebrew religion is essentially the same as that found in Isa 40:19–20; 44:9–20; 46:5–7; Jer 10:1–16 (non-Jeremaic); Hab 2:18–19; Ps 115:4–8; Dan 3; 5:23; Bel; and much later, although in a more sophisticated form, in Wisd Sol 13:10 to 15:17. Neither in the letter nor in the other sources just quoted does there seem to be any appreciation on the part of Jewish writers of the fact that religions which use images generally look on them as symbols and do not confuse the symbol with the reality for which it stands.

It is probable that the letter was written either in Aramaic or in Hebrew, although it is extant only in a Greek translation. The writer may have been a member of Babylonian Jewry (cf Babylonian references in vss 41–3; cf Herodotus I, 199), and the reference to a seven-generation stay in Babylon (vs 3) may date him about 300 BC. It is also possible that the whole Babylonian setting for the letter is fictitious, and that the author, who may have been in Palestine, had in mind the aggressive paganism which surrounded all Jews, wherever they were, in the Hellenistic Age.

SCEPTICISM AS REFLECTED IN ECCLESIASTES (QOHELETH)

Qoheleth (the Preacher, RSV) is a short work by a Jewish scholar living in Palestine in the third century BC. We shall refer to both book and author as Qoheleth. The internal evidence does not support more precise dating, although a few scholars take 4:13–16 to be a reference to Ptolemy v of Egypt, who became king in 203 BC at the age of six. At one time it was thought that this little book had been extensively interpolated, but the current view is that it is substantially as Qoheleth wrote it, with only a few later additions to the text, such as 12:9–14.

Qoheleth cannot be described as a systematic treatise. Rather it is essentially a small notebook in which the author has recorded such thoughts as have occurred to him along life's way. The work is very loosely presented, as well as repetitious, and there is no development in its thought. The general mood is that of a sceptic, and, while earlier Hebrew writers had struggled with theism's problem of evil (Jer 12:1–2; Job 9:22–3; 21:7–15; Pss 38:21–2; 74:22–3; 83:1–2), in no other book in the OT is this mood so prominent.

Vanity of vanities! All is vanity. (1:2)

I considered all that my hands had done ... and behold, all was vanity and a striving after wind. (2:11)

For the fate of the sons of men and the fate of beasts is the same; as one dies, so dies the other. (3:19)

Be not righteous overmuch, and do not make yourself overwise; why should you destroy yourself? Be not wicked overmuch, neither be a fool; why should you die before your time? (7:16–17)

One fate comes to all, to the righteous and the wicked, to the good and the evil. (9:2)

Despite these and other similar sentiments, Qoheleth never suggests suicide as a way out. Probably there were two factors that made him stick with life. One was his conviction that, whatever else might be the case, life was to be enjoyed:

I know that there is nothing better for them (the sons of men) than to be happy and enjoy themselves as long as they live. (3:12)

Go, eat your bread with enjoyment and drink your wine with a merry heart. (9:7)

Enjoy life with the wife whom you love. (9:9)

The second steadying factor in Qoheleth's thinking was his belief in God. God is the inscrutable Giver (God is the subject of 'give' in seven instances), whom men must fear ('fear,' in this sense, appears five times). Qoheleth's God is not the intimate God of Ps 23. He is a Power before whom, and especially in whose temple, it is wise to be circumspect (5:1–2,4–6). Oddly this faith in God is not overtly associated with Israel's traditions. 'Law,' 'prophets,' 'priests,' 'Levites' do not occur in these chapters, and, apart from a reference to the house of God (5:1) and to religious vows (5:4–5), Israel's religious institutions are ignored, as is its history (except for 'the son of David, king in Jerusalem' in 1–2). Qoheleth may have been basically an egoist, which would throw light upon his seeming indifference to the mores and claims of the community to which he belonged.

In view of Qoheleth's negativism and his unconcern with Israel and its traditions it seems surprising that his book came to be included in the Jewish Scriptures. Its attribution to Solomon (deduced from 1:1) was undoubtedly a factor that led to its acceptance, although the Mishnah records that there was considerable debate about the canonicity of the book (*Yadaim* 3.5). It is not at all improbable that an unstated reason for its inclusion was the recognition that Qoheleth represented a minority point of view within the whole Jewish community. We know from Judaism's toleration of sects (Pharisees, Sadducees, Essenes), and from the Mishnah's practice of preserving in its text the opinions of dissident rabbis, that the Jewish community accepted differences of opinion within Israel's fold. Qoheleth's words may have been looked upon as a minimal, but acceptable, acknowledgment of his Jewish heritage.

ANONYMOUS PROPHECY (ZECHARIAH 9–14)

Anonymous prophecy, to which reference was made in chapter 2, seems to have continued to be written in the fourth and early third centuries. Attempts to date such prophecies are beset with much uncertainty, for the evidence available is usually ambiguous. If the date suggested earlier in this chapter, c 250 BC, for the closing of the collection of the prophetic writings is accepted, it follows that additions were unlikely to be made to the prophetic corpus after this date.

One of the latest of the anonymous writings is found in Zech 9–14. These chapters, which probably come from two or three different hands, are thought to date from early in the Greek period, possibly 330–275 BC. This material contains some of the most enigmatic passages in the OT, as, e.g., 11:4–17; 12:10–14; 13:7–9, which seem to describe historical incidents that we cannot identify with any confidence.

After what is generally interpreted as a reference to Alexander the Great's campaigns in Phoenicia and Philistia (9:1–8), the hope is expressed that Zion's king is about to appear (9:9–10), as is the Lord himself, which will result in Zion's triumph over the Greek world (9:11–17). Verses 10:3–12 and 11:1–3 may be a variation of this theme, if the word 'shepherds' of 10:3 and 11:3 refers to Ptolemaic officials in Judea.

In 12–14 we have further eschatology. 12:1–9 elaborates the subject of 9:11–17: Judah and Jerusalem will repel an attack by all the nations of the earth. In 13:1–6, possibly the aftermath of the preceding, Judah will be purified of idolatry, and coupled with this there is in verses 3–6 a curious denunciation of prophets. In 14 the theme of an attack by the nations against Jerusalem is resumed. The city will be taken and half the population sent into exile. Then the Lord will come and fight against the nations, the Mount of Olives will be split in two, and there will be other astonishing changes in nature (vss 4–8,10–11). The Lord's participation in the fighting will bring a plague affecting men and beasts (vss 12,15). The Gentiles who survive will be won over to the worship of the Lord, and will celebrate the feast of Booths (vs 16), although it may be necessary to put pressure upon some of them to do so (vss 17–19). The prophecy ends on a somewhat minor, earth-centred note about the sacredness of ordinary objects (typified by horse-bells and pots) in the Jerusalem of the future (vss 20–1).

THE BEGINNINGS OF APOCALYPTIC

It has long been recognized that Israel's apocalyptic movement had its beginnings in Hebrew prophecy. The latter was based on the experience of revelation, either something heard ('Then the Lord said to me,' Isa 8:1), or something seen ('Then the Lord God showed me,' Amos 7:1). Apocalyptic, then, in its simplest form is essentially a perpetuation into the post-prophetic period of these fundamental aspects of Israel's prophetic religion. Further, most of the classical prophets were concerned with the consequences, both immediate and more remote, of Israel's religious behaviour, i.e., there was an incipient eschatology in their oracles. It was these two features of prophecy, revelation (apocalypse) and eschatology, which were picked up and developed by the later apocalyptists. This writer's principal reservation about S.B. Frost's definition of apocalyptic as 'the mythologizing of eschatology'[10] is that the apocalyptists, in addition to using a mythologized eschatology, claimed explicitly or implicitly to bring some kind of revelation.

When authentic prophets ceased to appear in the post-exilic period, and when the standard collection of prophetic writings was more or less closed by c 250 BC, thereby ruling out further anonymous additions to it, the prophetic impulse was by no means squelched. What happened was that it was forced to take new forms, and in doing so it produced what was in effect a new genre of Jewish literature: apocalyptic. One of its most striking characteristics was that the writers nearly always wrote under a pseudonym, and this pen-name, more often than not, was that of some worthy of the past, chosen perhaps in the hope that it would give additional credibility to the message. Despite this use of pseudonymity we must give the apocalyptists credit for believing that they had a message from the Lord God for Israel. If their presentation of this message seems at times to be bizarre and fantastic, the fact remains that most of the basic features of their writings can be paralleled, in less extravagant forms, in the records of the earlier prophets. Even their surveys of history are not in principle different from those found in the OT, as, for example, those in Neh 9:6–37; Pss 78; 106. The chief novelties in their works, apart from pseudonymity, are trends towards a dualistic cosmology, concern with the final judgment and its consequences, and calculations of times and seasons.

O. Plüger, in a study entitled *Theocracy and Eschatology* (Oxford 1968), suggests that there was some tension in the post-exilic Jewish community between the priestly circles, so concerned with the theocratic ideal in the present world that there was no need of eschatological expectations, and other groups who maintained an interest in the older eschatological traditions of the prophets and who speculated freely about them. Our so-called apocalyptic literature has come largely from members of these latter groups. Whether these apocalyptists were influenced by Iranian ideas, as Plüger assumes, is doubtful.[11]

THE BOOK OF NOAH

As an example of an early apocalyptic work, although a rather poor example, we shall look at the Book of Noah. This writing seems to be referred to in Jub 10:13; 21:10, and fragments of it are thought to be found in Enoch 6–11; 54:7 to 55:2; 60; 65:1 to 69:25; 106–7.[12] It would appear to be pre-Maccabean, and it presumably must belong between 250 and 175 BC. The greater part of it is a highly imaginative elaboration of scriptural traditions or myths, and it therefore belongs to the same genre as the later Jewish midrashim (explanations of, or stories about, biblical texts). What external forces or ideas helped to shape this elaboration it is difficult to say.

The principal topics which these fragments deal with, or touch on, are the following.

1 / The birth of Noah (106; cf Gen 5:28–32; 6:8–10), and the Flood story (54:7 to 55:2; 65 to 67:3; cf Gen 6:11 to 8:22).

2 / A proliferated body of angels, some of whom are named: Michael, Uriel, Raphael, and Gabriel; the latter's role is to bring men's prayers to God (9:1–3; cf Raphael in Tobit, 5:4; 12:11–21). On the heavenly retinue of Israel's God, see Deut 33:2; 1 Kgs 22:19; Isa 6:1–7; Job 1:6; 2:1; and on special angels, see Gen 3:24; Josh 5:14; Isa 63:9.

3 / An expansion of the myth of Gen 6:1–4. We learn that two hundred angels were involved in this incident, and the names of their nineteen leaders are given (Enoch 6:1–8; cf 69:1–12). Azazel, who does not appear in 6, turns out, in 9:6 and 10:4, to be the chief culprit. In 10 we have an account of the wayward angels, who are to be bound until the day of the great judgment (not elaborated), when they will be cast into the abyss of fire for ever (cf 67:4–13).

4 / An incipient dualism. The sinful angels involved in Gen 6:1–4 are in fact now cast in a role that is antagonistic to the purposes of God. Azazel, earlier known in Lev 16:8–10,21–2 as a desert demon, here becomes the teacher of all unrighteousness on earth (Enoch 9:6; 10:8), although elsewhere Samjaza (Semiazaz) is the leader of the sinful angels (6:3; 10:11; 69:2).

5 / A rather simple eschatology which does not go beyond the sketches found in the OT prophets. It is an earth-centred hope, embracing the conversion of the Gentiles (10:16 to 11:2). There is one reference (60:8) to 'the garden where the elect and righteous dwell,' but this is not further described.

6 / The secrets of the physical universe (60:11–23). The data thus divulged turn out to be essentially a presentation of earlier traditions, as in Gen 1:14–19; Pss 18:13–15; 81:7; 135:7; 148:8; Job 28:25–6; 38:22–5,28–9,34–6. This passage in Enoch is of interest as an early Jewish attempt to describe the natural world. A more sophisticated presentation is found in Enoch 72–82.

THE SAMARITANS: PART II

In chapter 4 we left the Samaritans in possession (along with the Jews) of the Pentateuch as a holy book, and with their cultic worship of the

Lord God centred in a recently built temple on Mount Gerizim. The existence of this Samaritan sanctuary was to mar Samaritan-Jewish relationships for two hundred years, as is illustrated by Josephus's account of an attack on Judea by the Samaritans in the late third century (*Ant* XII, 156).[13] Early in the second century BC Ben Sira refers to the Samaritans as 'the foolish people that dwell in Shechem' (50:25–6). These mutual ill-feelings were carried over to Alexandria, where there were settlements of both Jews and Samaritans (*Ant* XI, 7, 10; XIII, 74–9).

We should here note two developments that occurred in Samaria early in the Hellenistic period. One was a punitive treatment of the city of Samaria by Alexander the Great in 331 BC, because of the murder of his governor, and the settlement of a Macedonian colony in the city either by Alexander in this same year or later by his general Perdiccas (died 321 BC). Samaria revived with the new settlers, and, while their numbers are unknown, their presence must have changed somewhat the character of the city. The cave in the Wâdi Dâliyeh (north of old Jericho), excavated in 1963, brought to light the Samaria papyri, as well as skeletal and other remains, indicating that the cave was a hiding-place for refugees fleeing from Samaria at the time of Alexander's reprisal. The second development of this period, as archaeology now informs us, was that in the late fourth century BC Shechem (Balâṭah) was rebuilt and resettled, presumably by Samaritans disgruntled with conditions in Samaria.[14] This ancient site, hallowed in Samaritan history in connection with Joshua's administration,[15] lay at the foot of Mount Gerizim, and its contiguity to the temple meant that the Samaritans now had a strong centre for the preservation and development of their traditions.

It is probable, in view of the strained relations between the Jews and the Samaritans, that in the third century BC a beginning was made by the Samaritans at editing the Palestinian text of the Pentateuch, which they shared with the Jews, to bring it into line with traditions which the Samaritans considered to be authentic. These alterations in the text have long been identified: one of the better-known is the substitution of 'has chosen' (*bḥr*) for 'will choose' (*ybḥr*) 21 times in Deuteronomy (regarding God's choice of a place for his altar). It is likely that these Samaritan changes in the Pentateuchal text took some time to work out before they reached a final and acceptable form. When this process was completed we do not know. J.D. Purvis argues that the destruction of the Samaritan temple and the devastation of Shechem by the Jews in 128 BC created an internal crisis among the Samaritans, and that out of this came their revision of the Pentateuch, a revision that made it clear that they, and not the Jews, were the true Israel.[16] P.W. Skehan claims that the Samaritan amendment of the Torah 'was complete in all its essentials by the beginning of the second century BC at the latest.'[17]

VI

PALESTINE UNDER THE
SELEUCIDS
200–143 BC

Antiochus III

The vast area in Asia, stretching from western Asia Minor to eastern Iran, which Seleucus I controlled at his death in 281 BC, was destined in the ensuing decades to be whittled away by various political forces. The chief of these in Iran was Parthia, whose beginnings go back to the second half of the third century BC. When Antiochus III succeeded to the Seleucid throne in 223 BC, he was determined to arrest this contraction of Seleucid territory. While his expeditions into Parthia and Bactria could show only limited gains (211–206 BC), his effort to bring Coele-Syria under his control was, as we have seen earlier (pp 85–6), eventually quite successful. His decision to extend his kingdom to Thrace and Greece brought him into a disastrous conflict with Rome. The Romans drove him out of Greece (Thermopylae, 191 BC), and followed him to Asia where they defeated him again (Magnesia, 190 BC). The peace treaty of Apamea, 188 BC, obliged Antiochus to give up all claims to territory in Asia Minor west of the Taurus Mountains and the Halys River, which ended any hopes the Seleucids may have entertained of getting back into Europe. The enormous war indemnity which Antiochus agreed to pay to Rome was to keep his kingdom impoverished for the next twelve years.[1] Antiochus met his death in 187 BC in Elymais, when he tried to seize the treasury of a temple, doubtless in an effort to bolster the resources of his harried kingdom.

Seleucus IV

Seleucus IV, who succeeded his father, ruled from 187 to 175 BC. He avoided military adventures and concentrated on raising the annual payments due to Rome. His chief minister, Heliodorus, who seems to have been charged with economic matters, assassinated the king in 175 BC.

Antiochus IV (Epiphanes)

Antiochus, the brother of Seleucus IV, was living in Athens at the time of the latter's murder, but he determined to seize the Seleucid throne, although his two nephews (Demetrius, a hostage in Rome, and Antiochus, a child in Syria) had prior claim to it. He succeeded in this move, with the assistance of armed forces sent by Eumenes II of Pergamum (cf Dan 11:21, 'he will seize the kingdom by dissimulation and intrigue in time of peace,' NEB). There is some evidence from coins and cuneiform documents that in his early years he associated his young nephew Antiochus with himself in the rule of Syria.[2] In the winter of 170–169 Antiochus had to settle some troubles in Cilicia, and during his absence the young Antiochus was murdered by a certain Andronicus, perhaps as a service to the king.

But relations with the Ptolemies of Egypt constituted a much more important political problem. The Ptolemies had never accepted the loss of Coele-Syria, and in the summer of 169 an Egyptian army was mustered to attack Palestine. Antiochus, learning of this, met and defeated the Egyptian force before it traversed the northeast Egyptian desert, and he then proceeded to invade Egypt; after taking Memphis, he captured the young king, Ptolemy VI Philometor, who was in fact his nephew. He then laid siege to Alexandria where a rival king, a younger brother of Ptolemy VI, who was later to be Ptolemy VII, had been installed. It is not clear what precisely Antiochus hoped to accomplish in Egypt. He must have known that Rome would be against annexation. Possibly he had in mind a protectorate. At this point various Hellenistic ambassadors in Alexandria persuaded Antiochus to raise the siege of the city, which he did on condition that Ptolemy VI should be restored to his throne. He then withdrew from Egypt, leaving a garrison in Pelusium. In the following winter, 169–168, the two Egyptian brothers united against their Seleucid uncle, and this brought Antiochus back to Egypt in the spring of 168 BC; again, as in 169, the Egyptian army could offer no effective resistance to him. Then at Eleusis, outside Alexandria, Antiochus met an unexpected obstacle. Egypt had earlier appealed to Rome to intervene, but Rome at the time was involved in a war with Perseus of Macedon, and it was not until the latter's defeat at Pydna in June 168 that a Roman commission, headed by Popillius Laenas, reached Egypt. It was this commission that Antiochus encountered, and he was handed a dispatch from the Roman Senate requiring him to evacuate Egypt. So great was the authority of Rome in the Mediterranean world that Antiochus felt he had no option but to return to Syria. Clearly it was Rome's policy at this time to maintain existing political conditions in the eastern Mediterranean, and in particular to prevent any expansion of the Seleucid kingdom.

Antiochus's actions in Palestine, 169–167 BC, which led to the Maccabean revolt of the Jews, will be dealt with later in this chapter. The Jewish revolt was a relatively minor uprising, and other situations had more pressing claims to the king's attention. His great military review and festival at Daphne in 166 BC was a prelude to his eastern campaign, which he launched in the spring of 165 BC. Our limited knowledge indicates that he first went to Armenia, where his father had campaigned in 212 BC, and where Artaxias was now confirmed as satrap. His real concern, however, was the Parthians, who, under Mithradates I (c 171–138 BC), were turning their forces against western Iran. We next hear of Antiochus in Babylonia, Elymais, and Media. Somewhere in these regions he contracted an illness from which he died at Gabae (Ispahan, Isfahan) early in the summer of 163 BC. His death was a tragedy for the Seleucid dynasty, for it inaugurated a period of political instability which made resistance to Parthia's westward expansion almost impossible.

163–129 BC

Seleucid history during this period is a dismal story. The trouble started with the death of Antiochus IV, who, before leaving Antioch in 165 BC, had appointed Lysias as chancellor and guardian of his son, later Antiochus V Eupator (1 Mac 3:32–4). Two years later, when he was on his deathbed, Antiochus made Philip chancellor and guardian of the boy. So the lad, nine years old in 163 BC, now had two guardians, but this problem was solved when Lysias met Philip in battle, captured him, and put him to death (*Ant* XII, 386).

The subsequent course of events need only be summarized:

Demetrius I, son of Seleucus IV, who had been held in Rome as a hostage, escaped to Syria. He defeated Lysias, and murdered him and his charge Antiochus V.

Alexander (also known as Balas), allegedly the son of Antiochus IV, landed at Ptolemais in 152 BC, and by 150 he had ousted Demetrius who had reigned for twelve years. Alexander's marriage to the Ptolemaic princess Cleopatra at Ptolemais is recorded in 1 Mac 10:51–8.

Demetrius II, son of Demetrius I, began another civil war in 148–147 BC, and by 145 Alexander was defeated and killed.

Demetrius presently had to face Trypho (alias Diodotus), a professional soldier, who sponsored Alexander's son, Antiochus VI. When Demetrius was captured in an expedition against the Parthians, Trypho murdered his young charge and declared himself king.

Antiochus VII, younger brother of Demetrius II, supplanted Trypho 139–138 BC. He was the last Seleucid king of any consequence. Apart from his actions to assert Seleucid rights in Judea (to be discussed later, p 128), his main efforts were directed at containing the Parthians. His campaign against them, begun in 130 BC, was at first successful, and he recovered Babylonia and Media. He wintered at Ecbatana (130–129 BC), where in the spring of 129 BC he had to face the counter-attack of Phraates II (c 138–128 BC), and in this action he was killed. There now began the final disintegration of Seleucid power, which continued until the Romans under Pompey arrived in Syria in 64 BC.

Social and religious policies

The Seleucid kingdom rested upon military conquest and it could be maintained only by military power. For this the Seleucids had to rely principally on Macedonian and Greek soldiers, and the early Seleucid kings, therefore, encouraged immigration from Europe. The new-comers were settled in old or new towns and cities; while a by-product of their presence in Asia was the diffusion of various elements of Greek culture, their primary purpose was to strengthen the power of the Seleucid dynasty. As one example of such military settlements, although it is a non-European one, there is Josephus's record that Antiochus III, probably after 213 BC, ordered the transfer of two thousand Jewish families from Babylonia to various fortresses in Lydia and Phrygia, for he believed that they would be loyal guardians of Seleucid interests there. The terms of their settlement are spelled out and can be described as quite reasonable (*Ant* XII, 147–53). Antiochus IV, who had to deal with a much smaller kingdom than his father had originally ruled, laid considerable stress on the importance of such cities, and no less than fifteen foundations are credited to him. One of the regions to which he gave new life was Babylonia, where such old centres as Babylon and Uruk were restored to something like their earlier vigour. There is some evidence that Antiochus extended citizenship rights in many of these cities to non-Greeks, probably in an effort to develop personnel for posts hitherto given to Europeans.[3]

The religious policy of the Seleucids was, like that of the earlier Persians, one of tolerance towards the variety of religions existing in their realm. This toleration embraced the Jews of Babylonia, as is evident from the passage in Josephus just referred to respecting Babylonian Jews settled in Asia Minor, and also from the extravagant story in 2 Mac 8:19–20. If there is any truth in the latter narrative, it may be that on one occasion the Babylonian Jews helped Antiochus III (or Antiochus I) turn back some Gallic invaders.[4] If there was a change of policy regarding the rights of established religions, it may have been made, at least in one respect, by Antiochus III, who in the difficult times in which he lived seems to have thought that he had the right, as a sovereign king, to plunder temple property. The persecution of the Palestinian Jews by Antiochus IV was a singular exception to the general Seleucid practice of religious toleration, and arose in a particular situation existing only in Judea.[5] This is borne out by the fact that there is no evidence that the Jews of Syria and of Babylonia, both of whom were under Seleucid jurisdiction, were in any way affected by Antiochus's proscription of Jewish practices in Judea.[6] The Babylonian Jews seem to have followed a policy, as did those in Egypt, of cooperating with the secular authority, and to have interfered in any way with what Antiochus IV was doing in Judea would not have served the interest of Babylonian Jewry.

Hellenistic king worship, to which reference was made earlier (p 90), appeared in the Seleucid state, but in a haphazard fashion. By the time of Antiochus II (261–247 BC) the practices of the various cities had been organized and the ruler cult had its temples, professional personnel, and public ceremonies.[7] This cult, with scarcely any religious content, was of interest principally to the Greeks and Macedonians in the kingdom, and participation in it was an acceptable token of loyalty to the crown.

An innovation in this ruler cult was instigated by Antiochus IV, who seems to have claimed divine honours in his lifetime. He was termed Zeus Olympios Epiphanes, and it was probably his hope that Asiatic worshippers of Hadad or Baal would identify him with their god, thus establishing a common religious bond between the various peoples of his kingdom. If this expectation seems unrealistic to us, we must remember that Antiochus was aware of the widespread popularity of the cult of Serapis, founded in Egypt by Ptolemy I as a meeting-point for Egyptians and Greeks, and he may have hoped to duplicate, in some measure, this achievement in the Seleucid state.

JUDEA, 200–143 BC[8]

The early years of Seleucid rule

When Seleucid rule over Judea began, the Jews had been subjected to Hellenistic influences, direct and indirect, for over a hundred years. Some of these influences were very subtle, coming as they did from the dominant culture, while others were less abstract, emanating from the various Greek cities that surrounded Judea – coastal cities such as Ptolemais, Apollonia, Joppa, Ascalon, and Gaza; interior centres such as Samaria, Scythopolis, and Philoteria; and cities east of the Jordan, Philadelphia, Gerasa, and Gedara.[9] The effects on the Jews of such exposure to an essentially alien culture were, as we might surmise, varied. The reaction of some was to withdraw more tightly into their own traditions: these were the Hasideans (*Ḥᵃsîdîm*, 'pious ones').[10] Others seem to have been less rigid, and to have appropriated such features of Hellenism as were consonant with loyalty to Judaism. Others, however, were much more extreme. 'Sinners' and 'scoffers,' long before this, had been known to the author of Ps 1 (see p 8), and this element in the Jewish population, a group which virtually abandoned traditional values, appears to have increased and become more vocal in the Hellenistic Age. The references in 1 Maccabees to 'lawless men' (1:11), those 'who forsook the law' (1:52), 'sinners' and 'lawless men' (2:44), and in Josephus to those 'who adopt the Greek way of life' (*Ant* XII, 240) indicate that Jewish renegades are a part of the whole Jewish picture in this period.

To what extent these Jewish responses to Hellenism were sociologically determined is a nice question, and one to which it is difficult to give a satisfactory answer. We know that Hebrew society had long displayed gaps between the rich and the poor (2 Sam 12:1–2; Amos 2:6–7; 5:11; Isa 3:14–15; Jer 9:23; 17:11; Pro 10:15; 18:23; etc), and we infer from Ben S 13:21–4 that this condition still obtained in Judea in the early second century BC. We may suspect that some wealthy Jewish families, such as that of the tax-collector Joseph the Tobiad, who knew Alexandria at first hand (*Ant* XII, 160–185, 224), may, in the face of the Hellenism all around them, particularly in the large centres, have found traditional Jewish customs too restrictive for the world in which they now found themselves. Such Jews would become basically secular in their outlook, and they would tend to support the policies of their Seleucid overlord.

The commencement of Seleucid rule in Judea probably made little difference to the average Jew. Taxes still had to be paid, and if these now went to Antioch rather than to Alexandria, this did not greatly matter. The various taxes, including a poll-tax, which the Seleucids imposed are referred to in *Ant* XIII, 49–50 (cf 2 Mac 4:8). Antiochus III, if we are to take as historical the substance of the letter which he wrote to Ptolemy, governor of Coele-Syria (*Ant* XII, 138–44), was kindly disposed to the Jews: those parts of the temple complex recently destroyed he would help to restore, and he promised a contribution to the temple sacrifices. Even taxes were to be reduced. A further decree related to foreigners in the Jewish temple, and curtailed the importation of unclean animals into Jerusalem (*Ant* XII, 145–6; cf 2 Mac 3:2–3).[11] It is of interest that in the letter to Ptolemy no specific reference is made to a high priest, although the senate (Gk *gerousia*) is referred to as a governing body in Judea. Possibly the high priest's membership in this body was assumed.

Antiochus III's son and successor, Seleucus IV, ruled from 187 BC, but neither 1 Maccabees nor Josephus has much to say about him. In 2 Mac 3:2–3 it is noted that he supported the temple cultus with gifts, and Josephus records that it was in his reign that Hyrcanus, son of Joseph the tax-collector, was a powerful local ruler of a fortress northwest of Heshbon (*Ant* XII, 228–36). It is 2 Mac 3:4–40 which has the fanciful story (which may have a kernel of truth in it) of the unsuccessful attempt of Heliodorus, Seleucus's chief minister, to confiscate the treasures in the Jerusalem temple.

Antiochus IV (Epiphanes) and the Maccabean revolt, to 163 BC[12]

Two preliminary observations should be made at this point. The first is that Antiochus's primary interest in Judea was its location on the southwest border of his kingdom. It was important to him that there be peace and security in this area. To ensure such peace he looked for the cooperation of the Jewish high priest, who, as the recognized head of the Palestinian Jews, was to all intents and purposes a political figure. Quarrels within high priestly circles might have shocked the religiously sensitive, but to Antiochus they were but evidence that the office of high priest was essentially political.

The second observation is that Antiochus's various actions in Judea were supported by an influential minority of the Jews themselves, those termed 'sinners' and 'lawless men' in 1 Mac 1:11; 2:44. Antiochus seems to have greatly overrated their numbers and standing, but at least he knew that what he was doing had some measure of Jewish support. His greatest error in dealing with the Jews was the result of sheer ignorance. Although he was a well educated man, he was simply not aware of how closely religious, social, and political factors were intermingled in the Jewish tradition, and apparently he had no appreciation of the values for Jews of the ritual in the Jewish temple.

The first move in this high drama occurred shortly after Antiochus's accession to the Seleucid throne in 175 BC. The Jewish high priest, Onias III, was replaced by his brother Jason (Jesus): Josephus claims that Onias III died (*Ant* XII, 237), whereas 2 Mac 4:7–10 suggests that Jason wickedly ousted his brother from office by promising Antiochus more taxes from Judea. It was sometime after this that Antiochus paid a visit to Jerusalem where he was officially welcomed (2 Mac 4:21–2). Jason, who is ignored in 1 Maccabees, is represented in 2 Mac 4:10–17 as very sympathetic to Hellenism: he obtained permission to build a gymnasium in Jerusalem (cf 1 Mac 1:11–15), and to create a *politeuma* (an association of citizens) in the city for the Hellenized Jew (if this is what 2 Mac 4:9 means). He was also responsible for a gift of 300 drachmas being sent from Jerusalem to the quadrennial games at Tyre in honour of Hercules. Such actions as these, especially the setting up in the holy city of a gymnasium, with its pagan associations and its exercises in the nude, were bound to be offensive to the pious and to make many Jews conclude that Jason was unfit for the high priestly office.

At least three years passed, and another change in the high priesthood occurred. In 170 BC Menelaus, brother of one Simon who held a staff position in the temple, was sent to Antioch with the current taxes, and he improved his stay in Syria by offering the king more tribute from Judea, and thus secured for himself the Jerusalem high priesthood (2 Mac 4:23–5). He had, however, no qualifications for this post, and his appointment only outraged the orthodox. Jason subsequently fled to Ammon. Menelaus was soon faced with the problem of raising the taxes he had promised, and 2 Mac 4:27–9 records a visit he was obliged to make to Antiochus in this connection. It was shortly after this that the former high priest, Onias III, who seems to have taken refuge in Syria, was murdered in Daphne (near Antioch), apparently at the instigation of Menelaus (2 Mac 4:30–8). By all accounts Menelaus was a scoundrel, and his brother Lysimachus, who acted as his deputy, no better. Popular resentment, inflamed by the report that the two men had taken some of the temple vessels, expressed itself in a riot in Jerusalem in which Lysimachus was killed (2 Mac 4:39–42). Menelaus got out of this scrape through bribery (2 Mac 4:43–50), but Antiochus must have wondered if all was really well in Judea.

It was in 169 BC that Antiochus invaded Egypt for the first time (1 Mac 1:16–19). On the way back to Antioch he went to Jerusalem and, under the guidance of Menelaus, plundered the temple (1 Mac 1:20–4a; 2 Mac 5:15–20; cf Dan 11:25–8). For an impoverished royal treasury temples were always fair game, and the recent war in Egypt may not have netted the army its customary booty.

Antiochus's second attack on Egypt in 168 BC ended abruptly in the confrontation with the Roman envoy, Popillius Laenas. While the king was thus engaged, an uprising occurred in Judea. The former high priest, Jason, attempted to regain control of Jerusalem, and Menelaus was forced to take refuge in the citadel (2 Mac 5:5–6). It was, however, an unsuccessful coup, and it cost Jason his life (2 Mac 5:7–10). Antiochus was not amused by such insurrectionary activities, and on his return journey from Egypt, doubtless deeply chagrined by his failure there and interpreting events in Judea as a revolt against himself, he went to Jerusalem to discipline its people in an extremely ruthless way (2 Mac 5:11–14; cf Dan 11:29–30). The figures in 2 Mac 5:14 of those killed or sold into slavery seem greatly inflated, but there can be little doubt that Judea was given to understand that anything like insurrection would not be tolerated. It is possible that Antiochus suspected that Jews with Ptolemaic sympathies were behind this trouble. Not long after this, in the spring of 167 BC, an additional force was sent to Jerusalem, probably under Apollonius (cf 1 Mac 3:10), and further disciplinary measures were taken (1 Mac 1:29–32). A hill overlooking the temple was fortified and garrisoned, to become the Acra,[13] which was held by a Seleucid force until 141 BC (1 Mac 1:33–4).

Later in this same year, 167 BC, Antiochus took an epoch-making step in his treatment of the Palestinian Jews: he declared their temple worship and all the other features of traditional Judaism to be illegal (1

Mac 1:41–61; 2 Mac 6:1–11). As has been noted earlier, this was a departure from Seleucid religious policy, and it has to be interpreted in the light of conditions in Judea. As Antiochus presumably had limited knowledge of Jewish religious customs, he must have been advised by some person or persons that the religious peculiarities of the Jews lay behind the recent troubles in Jerusalem, and that, by banning such practices, there was a good chance that tranquility could be established in Judea. If such advice came from Menelaus, then clearly he had no moral right to the high priesthood. It is probable, too, that he argued that the suppression of Jewish religious life would strengthen the hands of the Hellenist Jews, and that this, in turn, would help the Seleucid cause in Judea.

There is no firm evidence that Antiochus issued a decree for his whole kingdom outlawing all local customs, such as is suggested in 1 Mac 1:41–2,51.[14] We know from his city-building activities that he favoured the spread of Hellenism in his realm, but always as something that went hand-in-hand with established traditions. Nor should we confuse Antiochus's actions in Judea with any extension of the long-established older practice of king worship which he had inherited (see above, p 90).

Apart from the prohibition of what were essentially private religious acts, such as the observance of the dietary and sabbath laws, as well as the practice of circumcision and the ownership of sacred books,[15] the most heinous side of Antiochus's decree pertained to the Jerusalem temple. Here the Jewish ritual was prohibited (1 Mac 1:45–6), and the sacred precincts were formally given over, on the fifteenth of Chislev, 167 BC, to the worship of Zeus Olympios (1 Mac 1:54; 2 Mac 6:2), whose Aramaic designation may have been 'Lord of heaven' (b‘l šmyn.). The main structure of the temple seems to have been left intact, as well as the altar of burnt offering, although upon the latter a small pagan altar was erected (1 Mac 1:59; 4:44). It is generally assumed that this pagan object is the 'desolating sacrilege' of 1 Mac 1:54 (cf Dan 11:31).[16] In addition to this altar we might have expected that either a statue of Zeus or some acceptable symbol of Zeus was erected, but this is nowhere specifically mentioned (cf M Taanith 4.6). These temple changes were doubtless intended to make the Jerusalem shrine available to all citizens, and not a place exclusively for Jews. Probably Hellenist Jews like Menelaus would have few qualms about identifying Zeus as the God Israel had always recognized but under another name. It is clear from 1 Mac 1:43,47; 2:15 that Jews in places outside Jerusalem were also obliged to engage in some form of pagan ritual, when called upon to do so, but the ritual is not described nor are the 'idols' involved ever identified.

Not only was Antiochus's decree of 167 BC prohibiting Jewish religious practice a change in traditional Seleucid policy, but it brought to the Jews their first experience of religious persecution. Israel's political independence had been lost since the eighth century BC, but never before had any Gentile overlord interfered with the cult of Yahweh. In 1 Mac 1:43,52 it is indicated that some Jews fully cooperated with the authorities (cf *Ant* XII, 255), and it is clear that the high priest Menelaus was among them, for he was still high priest in 164 BC (2 Mac 11:29,32). It was not until 163–162 BC, after nine/ten years in office, that he was deposed by the Seleucid authorities and killed (2 Mac 13:1–8). There were other Jews, however, who refused to comply with Seleucid orders, and they paid for their defiance by death (1 Mac 1:50,60–4; 2 Mac 6:9–11,18–31; 7:1–42; *Ant* XII, 255–6). Since Antiochus's edict seems to have been directed only against the Jews of Jerusalem and Judea, at first it was only they who suffered. But 2 Mac 6:8–9 records that Ptolemy, the governor of Coele-Syria (cf 2 Mac 8:8), suggested that a similar decree should be issued to 'the neighbouring Greek cities,' which, however, are not identified.

The Samaritans, who seem to have had reliable information about the actions of Antiochus in Judea, are reported by Josephus to have petitioned Antiochus to be exempted from the laws directed against the Jews (*Ant* XII, 257–64). They also asked that their temple be known as that of Zeus Hellenios (in 2 Mac 6:2 the title is Zeus Xenios). Both requests were granted. In the fighting which subsequently developed between the Jews and the Seleucid armed forces, Samaritans were recruited at least once for the Seleucid ranks (1 Mac 3:10).

As we have seen, the initial response of the more devout Jews to Antiochus's decree was passive opposition, and in consequence numbers of them lost their lives (1 Mac 1:62–4). Hundreds who fled to the wilderness perished because when they were overtaken on the Sabbath they would not defend themselves (1 Mac 2:29–39). It soon became clear, however, that such resistance was not an effective tactic. Leadership towards a more positive reaction came from a priestly family recently settled in Modein, headed by Mattathias (of the house of Asamonaios, hence the later term Hasmonean).[17] When the inhabitants of the village were marshalled by a Syrian patrol and ordered to worship at a small altar, Mattathias cut down a local Jew who was about to comply, as well as the king's officer, tore down the altar, and, with the cry 'Whoever is zealous for our country's laws and the worship of God, let him come with me,' he fled with his five sons to the hills (1 Mac 2:1–28; *Ant* XII, 265–71). So began the Maccabean[18] revolt of the Jews, which, to begin with, was both a protest against the Seleucid proscription of Jewish religious practices and an effort to regain the religious freedom which Judea had enjoyed prior to 167 BC. Political independence, at this stage in the struggle, was not an immediate issue.

The resistance movement, spearheaded by Mattathias and his family, was strengthened in its early stages by the accession of some of the Hasideans, who were appalled at the behaviour of the Hellenists (1 Mac 2:42). They were to remain a distinct group within the movement (cf 1 Mac 7:13–4), and at a later date were to become critical of it and separate from it. It is believed that the party of the Pharisees had its origin in this separation.

The first phase of the Jewish struggle was largely within the Jewish community itself. Mattathias and his followers were not involved with the Seleucid authorities, but with renegade Jews. Much of their work was done at night, and on occasion they felt obliged to burn towns and villages (1 Mac 2:44–8; 2 Mac 8:6–7). It was a strenuous kind of activity for an older person, and it is not surprising to learn that Mattathias died in 166 BC (1 Mac 2:49–70). The headship of the movement then devolved upon his son Judas, who proved to be an outstanding leader in this critical time. It was in these early days that the group decided to defend themselves when they were attacked on the Sabbath (1 Mac 2:40–1).

In 166 BC Judas and his followers, now numbering about 6000 men (2 Mac 8:1), had their initial contacts with sizable Seleucid forces. The first of these was led by Apollonius, probably the governor of Samaria and Judea (*Ant* XII, 261), whose men were defeated and who was himself killed in the fighting (the place is not stated), and the second, led by Seron, was also defeated, at Beth-horon (1 Mac 3:10–26). It is remarkable that Judas and his associates had been able, in a relatively short time, to train and equip their followers for encounters of this sort with Seleucid soldiers. It is all the more noteworthy because, except for the relatively few who might have had a period of army service with either the Ptolemies or the Seleucids, the Jews had no previous military experience, and yet they were able to develop very effective tactics, both as guerrillas and in formal battle.

Antiochus was naturally annoyed at these defeats, and before he left for his eastern campaign in 165 BC, he charged his chancellor Lysias with the suppression of the rebellion in Judea. Accordingly Nicanor and Gorgias were dispatched southwards (1 Mac 3:27–41; cf 2 Mac 8:9). The Jewish preparations for the conflict were both military and religious; the latter indicate the genuinely religious temper of Judas and his supporters in these early days of the struggle (1 Mac 3:42–60). The first engagement was fought near Emmaus, and once more the Seleucid force was defeated (1 Mac 4:1–25). Later this same year (probably October-November) Lysias himself led another army southwards, and, while the battle at Beth-zur was not a sweeping victory for Judas, it did send Lysias back to Antioch (1 Mac 4:26–35; cf 2 Mac 11:5–12).

It has been argued, if three of the letters now found in 2 Mac 11: 16–38 (vss 16–21, 27–33, 34–8) are trustworthy, that during the winter 165–164 BC there were peace negotiations between Lysias and Judas, with Menelaus as one of the negotiators (vss 29, 32). Verses 34–7 suggest that Rome, which had a commission on its way to Antioch at this time, was brought into the negotiations. Although J.C. Dancy believes that a peace pact was arranged,[19] it seems to this writer best to assume that the peace efforts were inconclusive.[20]

It is not known what Judas and his men were doing in the spring and summer of 164 BC. Some may have temporarily resumed their agricultural and other duties, or, alternatively, some of the local military actions described in 1 Mac 5 may have taken place at this time. The really important event, the recovery and purification of the Jerusalem temple, occurred near the end of the year.

Seleucid armies had now been defeated three times, and doubtless

Judas knew that most of the state's remaining military resources were involved, like Antiochus himself, in Syria's eastern campaign. It was a propitious time to recover the temple, and Judas acted accordingly (1 Mac 4:36–61; 2 Mac 10:1–8; *Ant* XII, 316–26). Some of his soldiers were detailed to block any effort on the part of the Seleucid garrison in the Acra to interfere with the Jewish plan, which, in fact, seems to have proceeded without let or hindrance. Priests were chosen to cleanse the sanctuary, in which connection Menelaus is nowhere mentioned. The pagan altar was removed, and a completely new altar erected. Necessary repairs to the structures in the temple area were made and new vessels for the service fabricated. On the twenty-fifth of Chislev 164 BC the renovated temple was formally dedicated to the service of Israel's God, three years after it had been taken over by Antiochus in 167 BC. There was an eight-day celebration, and it was decreed that the occasion should be commemorated yearly in a new festival, *Hanukkah* ('dedication'). The finale to these actions took the form of two practical military moves. One was the fortification of the temple hill to guard against any future Gentile attempt to take over the sanctuary, and the second was repairing the walls of Bethsur (Bethzur), northwest of Hebron, to give Judea security on its southern frontier (1 Mac 4:36–61).

Whatever Antiochus may have thought of it, the struggle of the Jews up to this point had been a religious struggle, primarily an effort to recover the religious rights which they had always had. Now, with the recovery of the Jerusalem temple, the Jews had regained what they were deprived of in 167 BC. In this process the military weakness of the Seleucids had been uncovered, and a situation had emerged in which it was not unrealistic to think of political freedom for Israel. The continuation of the rebellion by Judas and his followers after 164 BC therefore takes on increasingly a political character.

In 1 Mac 5 (cf 2 Mac 8:30–3; 10:14–23; 12:10–45) there are details of various incursions made by the forces of Judas against Judea's neighbours or near-neighbours. Some of these conflicts may have occurred before the Jews retook the temple in December 164 BC, but most of them appear to belong to 163 BC. The areas in question, Idumea, Ammon, Gilead, and Galilee, were still under Seleucid control, and their officials must have viewed with dismay the way in which Judea was flouting the authority of Syria. Local Jews in these areas now became the objects of harassment, and it was in response to this situation that Judas and his brothers undertook their raids. These were in fact small-scale wars: the total number of men fighting for Israel is given as at least 13,000 (1 Mac 5:20,60). In two instances (vss 23, 45) the Jews in these Gentile regions were brought back and relocated in Judea. In 2 Mac 12:29–31 it is recorded that the Jews of Scythopolis assured Judas that they were being well treated and asked to be left alone. An ill-planned attack on Jamnia, the administrative centre for Idumea, resulted in the rout of the Jewish forces involved. Likewise, an engagement at Marisa seems to have turned out badly for the Jews. The numbers of Gentile casualties in these wars are unbelievably high (vss 22, 28, etc), and the amount of plunder and damaged property seems incredible (vss 5, 28, etc). In any case lost lives and plundered or ruined property, whatever their true total, must have diminished the goodwill of neighbouring Gentiles towards Judea.

It was in this same year, 163 BC (2 Mac 13:1), or 162 (with 1 Mac 6:20), that Judas determined to remove the Seleucid garrison from the citadel in Jerusalem, and accordingly he began siege operations (1 Mac 6:18–27). Some of the besieged managed to escape and, joined by 'ungodly Israelites,' got word to Lysias in Antioch. Among the Jews who came to Antioch was the high priest Menelaus, and Lysias, who seems to have held him responsible for the deterioration of the situation in Judea, had him put to death (2 Mac 13:3–8). Alcimus, an Aaronite, was appointed his successor (1 Mac 7:5; *Ant* XII, 385; XX, 235).[21] Lysias and the new king, nine-year-old Antiochus V, now came south in the late summer with a large army, including some elephants. They besieged Beth-zur, forcing Judas to abandon his siege of the Acra and attend to this more pressing danger. The Jewish forces met the Syrians in battle at Beth-zechariah and were defeated, and Eleazar, one of Judas's brothers, was killed. Lysias then came to Jerusalem and besieged the temple fortifications. At this point, providentially for the Jews, he learned that his rival Philip had now returned from Media, and, as this necessitated his own presence in Antioch, Lysias entered into peace negotiations with Judas (late in 163 BC). The full terms of the peace are nowhere given, although it may be inferred that the Jews were to have the unrestricted use of their temple

(2 Mac 13:23), and that they could live by their own laws (1 Mac 6:59; cf 2 Mac 11:22–6). The Acra in Jerusalem was to remain in Seleucid hands, and the defensive wall of the temple was to be dismantled (1 Mac 7:61–2 claims that the latter was a breach of the agreement). Taxes would presumably still go to Antioch. In short, what Judas had obtained by force in 164 BC, epitomised by the recapture of the temple, was now accepted as a fact by the Seleucid authorities. The peace of 163 BC marks the end of an epoch in Judea's history.

163 – 143 BC

The power struggle within the Seleucid state during these two decades, and the recurring deaths or murders of the Syrian kings, must have made political decisions for the Jewish leaders very difficult. This political chaos had, however, one positive side for Judea, insofar as no attempt was ever again made by any Seleucid ruler or agent to interfere with the practice of the Jewish religion. The gross errors of Antiochus IV were not to be repeated. Syria, of course, was still interested in Judea as a part of the Seleucid state, and from time to time forces were dispatched from Antioch to maintain or reestablish Seleucid authority there. Thus Bacchides was sent by Demetrius in 161 BC (1 Mac 7:5–25), and Nicanor in 160 BC (1 Mac 7:26–50; 2 Mac 14:12 to 15:36). In the second engagement with Judas and his men at Adasa Nicanor died. Later in 160 BC, to avenge Nicanor's death, Demetrius sent another force under Bacchides, and in the ensuing battle at Berea (possibly Bereth) Judas was killed (1 Mac 9:1–22). The death of Judas, who by all counts was an outstanding military leader, was an irreparable loss for the Jews. He had given the movement begun by his father a drive and direction which none of his brothers could match. Latterly he had been working towards the goal of political independence, but this he did not live to see realized. He was succeeded as leader by his brother Jonathan (1 Mac 9:28–31).

After the battle of Berea the Jewish forces temporarily disintegrated, and Bacchides was able to spend about a year in Judea, fortifying various strategic points and taking hostages (1 Mac 9:50–3). During this year John, Jonathan's brother, was seized and killed by some Nabateans (1 Mac 9:35–6). Bacchides returned to Antioch in 159 BC, but about two years later, when he reappeared in Judea, his men suffered a setback at Bethbasi, and he made peace with Jonathan, although the terms may have secured only an exchange of prisoners (1 Mac 9:58–73; *Ant* XIII, 32–3). This peace gave Jonathan an opportunity to strengthen his forces. He was further assisted by the civil war between Demetrius I and Alexander Balas, which broke out in 152 BC. Demetrius at this critical time offered very favourable peace terms to Jonathan (1 Mac 10:3–6; cf vss 22–46 which may be partly spurious), but Alexander, who needed as much help as he could get and was not to be outdone by Demetrius, determined to make Jonathan his 'friend and ally,' and he appointed him high priest of his nation. Since Jonathan was about to turn down Demetrius's offer, he was in a position to accept Alexander's nomination as high priest (1 Mac 10:46–7). So it was that in October 152 BC Jonathan became high priest of his nation, by the grace of Alexander, claimant for the Syrian throne (1 Mac 10:15–21). The high priestly garments (Ex 28) had evidently been in safe-keeping since 159 BC, when Alcimus the last high priest had died, and they were now placed at Jonathan's disposal (1 Mac 10:20–1). It is noteworthy that Jonathan's acceptance of Alexander's appointment indicates that at this time the Jewish community conceded that the right to make this nomination was a prerogative of the political overlord. Jonathan's status was confirmed in 150 BC, when he was at Ptolemais for Alexander's wedding, on which occasion certain civil and military powers in Judea were vested in him (1 Mac 10:62–5).

Strife within Syria once more cast its shadow on Judea. In the fall of 148–147 BC the young Demetrius II made a bid for the Seleucid throne, and c 146 BC, in the midst of his struggle against Alexander, he sent a general, Apollonius, to Coele-Syria to gain control of that area. Jonathan, in support of Alexander, mustered 10,000 men and defeated the general at Azotus. A by-product of this campaign was that Jonathan was able to occupy Joppa (1 Mac 10:67–89).

Demetrius II succeeded Alexander Balas on the Syrian throne in 145 BC, and he confirmed Jonathan as the Jewish high priest in that year, and promised him certain territorial additions to Judea, as well as tax immunities (1 Mac 11:27,30–7). Jonathan responded to this cordiality by sending Demetrius 3,000 men to help the king maintain his somewhat precarious position in Antioch (1 Mac 11:38–52). But the new king's hold on Syria was tenuous, and he turned Jonathan into an enemy by failing to make good his earlier promises to him (1 Mac 11:59). As a result, when an upstart, Trypho, appeared on the scene, championing the cause of Antiochus VI, Demetrius found himself involved in a civil war that lasted two years. Trypho curried Jonathan's favour by ratifying his high priestly status (1 Mac 11:54–8), and this led Jonathan to take the field against Demetrius and to defeat his forces in Galilee (1 Mac 11:60–74). But Trypho was suspicious of Jonathan and not prepared to tolerate his growing power. Accordingly in 143 BC he marched south to bring him under control. Jonathan met him at Scythopolis, and, while no fighting occurred, Jonathan was inveigled into going to Ptolemais for discussions. Here he was treacherously seized (1 Mac 12:39–48). His brother Simon replaced him as Judea's leader and high priest, and he completed the work on Jerusalem's walls which Jonathan had begun (1 Mac 10:10–11; 13:1–10). Later in 143 BC Trypho again came against Judea, getting as far south as Adida (east of Lydda). He then circled southeastward, via Adora, and ended up in Gilead without joining battle with Simon's men. It was in the course of this fruitless military exercise that Trypho murdered his prisoner Jonathan in 143–142 BC (1 Mac 13:12–30). Jonathan is the least impressive of the sons of Mattathias, and it is perhaps significant that there is no eulogy of him in 1 Maccabees.

The recognition of Jewish religious rights which Judas had secured in 163 BC did not end Judea's internal tensions. Quite apart from the turmoil due to the periodic incursions of Syrian armies, a disturbing factor in the Jewish picture continued to be the existence of dissident Jews who for a variety of reasons opposed the policies of Judas and his brothers. We read that 'After the death of Judas, the lawless emerged in all parts of Israel ... they sought and searched for the friends of Judas and brought them to Bacchides and he took vengeance on them' (1 Mac 9:23,26). The same people encouraged Bacchides to return to Judea in 157 BC (1 Mac 9:58,69). This term 'lawless' occurs again in 10:61; 11:21,25; 14:14; 'ungodly' appears in 9:25. The high priest Alcimus is associated with them in 1 Mac 7:21–5. In 10:14 Beth-zur is described as a place of refuge for those 'who had forsaken the law and the commandments' (cf Ant XIII, 42). Most of those referred to in this way must in fact have been Hellenist Jews, who for one reason or another favoured the Seleucid authorities. In addition to the 'lawless,' there were other groups whose fundamental interests were religious, and who were not always prepared to follow a course of action advocated by Judas. Thus, when Bacchides and the high priest Alcimus came into Judea in 161 BC, Judas refused to see them, but a group of scribes and Hasideans did so, although sixty of them were treacherously murdered (1 Mac 7:8–16).

These years, 163–143 BC, are notable for the fortunes and status of the high priesthood. Just before Lysias and Antiochus v left Antioch for Judea in 163 BC, the high priest Menelaus was put to death (2 Mac 13:3–8), and Alcimus was appointed in his place (1 Mac 7:5; *Ant* XII, 385). Alcimus worked hand-in-glove with the Syrian authorities, and was therefore cast in opposition to Judas (1 Mac 7:9, 21–3; 2 Mac 14:1–10). Judas was able to keep Alcimus out of the temple, of which deprivation the high priest complained in 161 BC to Demetrius (2 Mac 14:3,7,13). After the battle of Berea and the death of Judas in 160 BC Alcimus seems to have gained access to the sanctuary, and it was while he was effecting some structural changes in the sacred area that he died in 159 BC (1 Mac 9:54–7). Demetrius did not name a successor, and in fact the office was vacant for seven years, until, as we have seen, the appointment of Jonathan in 152 BC by Alexander Balas. Jonathan's accession to this office marks an important development in the life of the Palestinian Jews. From 152 BC on, until the coming of the Romans in 63 BC, all authority in Judea, religious, military and political, was to be in the hands of one man, and those who in succession held such great power were all members of one family, the Hasmonean. Whether in the long run it was in the best interest of the Jews to have all spiritual and temporal power vested in one person is highly doubtful.

It was presumably the desire to enhance the Jewish cause that prompted Judas in 161 BC to send two envoys to Rome to establish a friendly alliance with the Roman Republic (1 Mac 8:17–32). We do not know how much Judas knew about the Romans (1 Mac 8:1–16 is a highly idealized picture of them), but he must have been aware of them as a state in the Mediterranean world powerful enough to force Antiochus IV to evacuate Egypt in 168 BC. He may have known, too, of the civil strife in Egypt between Ptolemy VI (181–145 BC) and his brother, and of the Egyptian request that Rome should intervene in this struggle. He may therefore have thought that friendship with such a state would strengthen Judea. Judas's envoys gained what they desired, a formal treaty between the Romans and 'the nation of the Jews' (technically the treaty was probably a *foedus aequum*, which provided for military assistance in defensive wars). This treaty appears to have been renewed c 145–144 BC by Jonathan (1 Mac 12:1–4). Another treaty is said to have been made by Jonathan with Sparta (1 Mac 12:5–23). Jonathan may have had some romantic ideas about Spartan life and organization, but the Sparta of his time was different from what it once had been. The Achaean League had been dissolved by the Roman Senate in 146 BC, and Achaea, including Sparta, then became part of the Roman province of Macedonia. It is not impossible that Jonathan did establish some diplomatic contact with the Spartans, but what good such contact would have done either party is not clear.

VII

JUDEA'S INDEPENDENCE
143/142–63 BC[1]

SIMON, 143–134 BC

In 143 BC Seleucid Syria was involved in one of its chronic civil wars. Demetrius II's title to the crown was being challenged by Trypho, who was sponsor for the young king Antiochus VI. Late in 143 BC Trypho had tricked Jonathan into coming to Ptolemais, where the Jewish high priest was arrested. An assembly of Jerusalem's citizens was then convened, and it agreed that Simon should take Jonathan's place as national leader (1 Mac 13:1–9). Nothing is said in 1 Maccabees or Josephus about Simon also filling the office of high priest, although it must be assumed that he did. After Jonathan's murder by Trypho Simon was the sole survivor of the sons of Mattathias who had first come into prominence in 167 BC.

Trypho's treatment of Jonathan so outraged Simon that he felt he must turn to Demetrius II, although Jonathan's earlier dealings with him offered little hope of a favourable conclusion to such an action (cf 1 Mac 11:52–3). But a Jewish delegation was sent to Demetrius, and it elicited the favourable reply found in 1 Mac 13:36–40. The essence of this letter is that there was to be peace between the two parties, and that the taxes and tribute levied on Judea were ended. Nothing was said about the Acra in Jerusalem, still garrisoned by a Seleucid force. Perhaps Demetrius hoped that the citadel might still be useful to him when circumstances favoured the reassertion of his power in Judea. This letter, probably received in the spring of 142 BC, can be looked upon as the formal abandonment by Syria of its control of Judea, and it marks the beginning of a period of political independence for the Palestinian Jews. This independence, curtailed briefly by Antiochus VII, was to last until Pompey came to Judea in 63 BC.

Early in his new career as leader Simon made two military moves of some consequence. One was a successful siege of Gazara (Gezer, not Gaza as the Greek text reads; cf *Ant* XIII, 215), and the other was a tight encirclement of the Acra that forced its garrison to surrender in May 141 BC and eliminated the last vestige of Seleucid control in Judea (1 Mac 13:43–53).

Apart from his relations with Demetrius II and Antiochus VII, Simon's only ventures into the field of foreign affairs are those described in 1 Mac 14:16–24. He is here said to have renewed the treaties of friendship with both Rome and Sparta which his predecessors had made, although it is improbable that the initiatives in these moves came from either Rome or Sparta.[2]

It was not until September 140 BC that Simon's status in Judea was formally settled by the Jews themselves (1 Mac 14:25–49). A great assembly comprising all the groups in the community met, presumably in Jerusalem, and probably in the temple courts, and decided that Simon 'should be their leader and high priest for ever, until a trustworthy prophet should arise' (vs 41). As verses 42–5 make clear, Simon's power was to be unrestricted in both spiritual and temporal matters, and there could be no appeal against his decisions. The proviso about a future prophet was a tacit recognition that the assembly's decision about Simon was a human one, and might have to be modified if God so declared. Simon, we should observe, was a wealthy man (1 Mac 14:32; 15:32; 16:11–12), and, as an oriental prince, he was probably not too different from other small potentates of the Near East.

Simon's life as high priest and secular leader commenced favourably, but presently he had to cope, as his predecessors had, with a new king in Syria. Antiochus VII, brother of Demetrius II, as part of his preparations for his arrival in Syria, sent from his Mediterranean headquarters a letter 'to Simon, high priest and ethnarch and to the nation of the Jews,' confirming the tax remissions which had been granted by earlier kings (1 Mac 15:1–9). He may have had in mind, particularly, those conceded by his older brother (1 Mac 11:30–7). After Antiochus landed in Syria and was besieging his rival Trypho in Dor, Simon sent two thousand soldiers and much military equipment to assist the new king, but the latter refused this assistance, possibly because he felt that his own position was now secure, and he did not wish to be indebted to the Jewish leader. This was the beginning of a breakdown in the relations between Simon and Antiochus. The latter now queried Simon's right to control Joppa, Gazara, and the Jerusalem citadel, and insisted upon compensatory payment for their continued occupation, as well as for war damages (1 Mac 15:25–31). When Simon was confronted with Athenobius, an envoy of Antiochus, he stoutly defended what the Jews had done, but by way of a compromise did offer to pay one hundred talents for damages in Joppa and Gazara (1 Mac 15:32–6).

After Trypho committed suicide, Antiochus was able to concentrate upon matters pertaining to his kingdom, one of the more pressing being the status of Judea. He delegated Cendebeus to harass Simon, which he did, advancing into Judea and making Jamnia his headquarters. Simon, who had fought in Israel's wars for almost thiry years, now handed over the military leadership to his sons Judas and John. The latter was able to raise twenty thousand warriors (this figure may be inflated) and to fight and defeat Cenebeus in the vicinity of Kedron and Azotus, c 138 BC (1 Mac 16:1–10). It may have been at the conclusion of this encounter that the Jews captured Jamnia (cf *Ant* XIII, 215).

Three or four years now passed with no further attempt by Antiochus to assert his control in Judea. Simon spent this time strengthening the life of the Jewish community and visiting various cities (cf 1 Mac 16:14a). In the course of this activity he came, with his wife and two of his sons, in February 134 BC to Jericho, the centre of a district whose governor was his son-in-law Ptolemy. At Dok, northwest of Jericho, the guests were seized by their host and eventually killed (1 Mac 16:11–7; *Ant* XIII, 228). Ptolemy's attempt to capture and murder a third son, John Hyrcanus, was unsuccessful (1 Mac 16:18–22; *Ant* XIII, 228–35). Ptolemy doubtless hoped to seize the power which Simon had exercised (cf 1 Mac 16:18), but the son who had eluded Ptolemy, John Hyrcanus, succeeded his father as high priest in Jerusalem (*Ant* XIII, 230).

The eulogies on Simon (1 Mac 14:4–15,27–45) indicate that the Jewish tradition held Simon to be one of the most distinguished of the sons of Mattathias. His father had recognized him as being wise in counsel (1 Mac 2:65), and this paternal judgment was borne out by Simon's later career. His military exploits, as we have seen, were not inconsiderable. He was, of course, fortunate in the times in which he lived, for these permitted him to obtain from Demetrius II the abolition of Syria's tax rights in Judea. Most important of all, Simon was chosen high priest and leader of the Jews by the Jews themselves, and not appointed by a foreign power, and he seems to have responded to this appointment by a genuine interest in his responsibilities as head of the religious community of Israel (cf 1 Mac 14:15,42).

JOHN HYRCANUS, 134–104 BC

It was four years after the repulse of Candebeus before Antiochus VII fulfilled his earlier threat to invade Judea (1 Mac 15:31), and thus the new Jewish leader, John Hyrcanus, was confronted by war at the very outset of his rule. Josephus does not record that any resistance was offered to the Syrian army before it surrounded and besieged Jerusalem. The siege lasted for over a year, with one interruption when a seven-day truce allowed the Jews to celebrate the festival of *Sukkoth*. In the end the Jews came to terms with Antiochus. The walls of Jerusalem were to be destroyed, tribute for Joppa and certain other cities was to be paid, and hostages were given for the future good conduct of the Jews (*Ant* XIII, 236–48). Josephus further states that a friendly alliance was made between the Jews and Antiochus (*Ant* XIII, 249).

It was probably this alliance with Antiochus, as well as the latter's recollection that Simon had offered to assist him at the siege of Dor, that explains why John Hyrcanus became involved in 130 BC in Antiochus's expedition against the Parthians. John himself went with an unstated number of Jewish soldiers, but in the defeat which Antiochus suffered in 129 BC, and in which he lost his life, the Jewish high priest managed to survive and get back to Judea (*Ant* XIII, 249–53).

After the death of Antiochus VII John assumed that the Jewish alliance with Syria was ended, as were the limitations imposed in 133 BC on Judea's independence. One indication of this was the alacrity with which he now embarked on a policy of territorial expansion. Behind this was undoubtedly the realization that the time was favourable for Jerusalem to enlarge the territory it governed. Indeed John may have hoped that in the not too far distant future Israel could control all the areas that once comprised the Solomonic kingdom. Josephus's description of John's campaigns is very compressed (*War* I, 62–3; *Ant* XIII, 254–8), but we are told that he employed foreign mercenaries (*Ant* XIII, 249), paying them from plunder obtained by robbing David's tomb. We are bound to ask whether this use of foreign troops points to a lack of popular support for John's plans.

The Jews first moved eastwards into northern Moab, where after a siege of six months they captured the city of Medaba, and later Samoga (Samega). After returning to their home base, they then advanced northwards into the three toparchies of Aphairema, Lydda, and Rathamin, bordering on Samaria (1 Mac 10:30; 11:34), which had been part of Judea since Jonathan's time. Their immediate objectives were the city of Shechem and the Samaritan temple on Mount Gerizim. The destruction of the temple in 128 BC can hardly have improved relations between the Jews and the Samaritans. John also led his forces southwards into Idumea, where he took Adora and Marisa. This was traditionally Judean territory (cf 2 Chr 11:5–10), but in the sixth century BC Edomites had come into it, apparently under pressure from the Nabateans. John's policy was that, if the Edomites wished to stay in this area, they must profess Judaism. So the Edomites submitted to circumcision and agreed to observe the Jewish manner of life. About twenty years after these early military efforts, John again moved northwards. This time his objective was the city of Samaria. The siege of the city was conducted by two of John's sons, Antigonus and Aristobulus, and it was interrupted twice when outside forces came to the assistance of the Samaritans, but in 107 BC, after a siege of a year, Samaria was taken and completely ruined. Later John took Scythopolis and occupied territory as far north as Mount Carmel (*War* I, 64–6; *Ant* XIII, 275–81).

It was probably his success in expanding Judea's borders that induced John to strike his own coins. These bear on one side the inscription, in the Paleo-Hebrew script, 'Yehoḥanan the High Priest and the Council of the Jews,' and on the reverse two cornucopias. The cornucopia was a Greek symbol, but it was widely used on coins, and its heathen association was apparently disregarded by John.[3] The term 'Council' (ḥeber) is ambiguous; it may refer either to the whole Jewish community, or to some advisory group, perhaps the later Sanhedrin.

It is after his treatment of John's wars that Josephus proceeds to give in some detail an account of John's relations with the Pharisees (Ant XIII, 288–98). The times in and the circumstances under which the Pharisees became a recognized group among the Palestinian Jews cannot be precisely determined. The name appears to mean 'separated ones,' but from whom or what they were separated can only be conjectured. The Hasideans, who supported Mattathias early in the Maccabean struggle (1 Mac 2:42; 2 Mac 14:6; cf 1 Mac 14:14), but who, when the temple had been recovered, were anxious to secure peace with Syria (1 Mac 7:12–14), were probably an important group within the larger body of Pharisees. Josephus's first mention of the Pharisees is in his account of Jonathan's life (Ant XIII, 171–3), but what he says about them is quite unrelated to the context. He may merely have wished to record the tradition that they were known at this time as a group within the Jewish community. He is more expansive in Ant XIII, 297–8, where he represents the Pharisees as the custodians of the oral interpretation of the written Torah, and as having considerable support among the people (cf XIII, 288). According to Josephus, John was initially a supporter of the Pharisees and greatly esteemed by them. Later he broke with them and joined the Sadducees. It was at this time that he repealed certain legal innovations which the Pharisees had established (see M Maaser Sheni 5.15; Soṭah 9.10). Josephus claims that these actions deprived John of the general good will which he had hitherto enjoyed.

In the verbal confrontation between John and the Pharisee Eleazar (Ant XIII, 291–2) the latter said to the high priest: 'If you wish to be righteous, give up the high priesthood and be content with governing the people.' It is probable that behind this advice was the conviction that no member of the Hasmonean family was entitled to hold the office of high priest. Possibly Eleazar was also voicing the view of the more devout Jews that there was something inappropriate in Israel's high priest being so involved in political and military undertakings (cf the Chronicler's view that David was debarred from building the temple because he had shed so much blood, 1 Chr 22:8; 28:3).

Two references in Josephus appear to indicate that John had to face and put down civil strife ('the smouldering flames burst out in open war,' *War* I, 67; cf *Ant* XIII, 299). The cause and nature of this trouble are not explicated. In the second reference the allusion to sedition appears after the account of John's break with the Pharisees, and we may perhaps conclude that the turmoil was related to John's poor relations with the Pharisees. His abolishment of certain of their regulations and his punishment of those who continued to observe the cancelled laws (*Ant* XIII, 296) may have stirred up a violent reaction.

In the passage in which Josephus first alludes to the Pharisees (*Ant* XIII, 171–3) he also mentions the Sadducees, and in the material bearing on John he records, as we have seen, that the high priest joined the Sadducees after he left the Pharisees (*Ant* XIII, 293, 295–8). He also tells us that the Sadducees maintained the validity of the written Scriptures and rejected the oral traditions which the Pharisees upheld, and that they had the confidence of the wealthy but not of the common people. From all this it is evident that the Sadducees, like the Pharisees, came into existence in the latter half of the second century BC, that in religious matters they were conservative, and that they were the chief supporters of the social and political structures which the Hasmoneans were creating in Judea (*Ant* XIII, 297–8). The name Sadducee is patently derived from the proper name Zadok. In view of the known history of the Jewish sects, Sadducee, as a sectarian term, must be connected with the Zadokite priesthood, and it may initially have designated a member of the priestly aristocracy, and then by extension anyone who shared in the views and principles of the Zadokite priests.

If we accept the tradition that Judas, Jonathan, and Simon established friendly relations with Rome (1 Mac 8:17–32; 12:1–4; 14:16–24), then it is probable that John followed the same policy. The decrees of the Roman Senate which Josephus records (*Ant* XIII, 259–66; XIV, 145–8) present a number of difficulties which cannot be discussed in detail here, but they appear to indicate that the friendly alliance between the Jewish people and Rome was renewed in John's time. Two other decrees associated with John are one from the Athenians (*Ant* xiv, 148–55), possibly dating c 106–105 BC,[4] and one from Pergamum, in response to envoys sent by John (*Ant* xiv, 247–55).

In both of his accounts (*War*, i, 68–9 and *Ant*, xiii, 299–300) Josephus concludes his treatment of John Hyrcanus with a short eulogy. He credits the high priest with thirty-one years of good government, and he comments upon his gift of prophecy. One instance of the latter (*Ant* xiii, 282) is perhaps better described as an example of clairvoyance, and the other (*War* i, 69; cf *Ant* xiii, 322) might come from a father's knowledge of his own children.

ARISTOBULUS, 104–103 BC

However well John Hyrcanus may have governed Judea, his domestic life must have known few of the blessings of which Ps 127 speaks. If we can trust Josephus's account, one of his sons, Alexander Jannai, was kept out of his sight, and another son, Aristobulus, who succeeded his father, imprisoned and starved his mother to death, murdered one brother Antigonus, and kept his other brothers in chains. It is not a pretty picture, especially of a high priest's family (*War* i, 71–7; *Ant* xiii, 301–10, 320–2).

Josephus says that John Hyrcanus had named his wife heir to his secular power, but that Aristobulus disputed this arrangement and took supreme control of the state. Josephus also claims that Aristobulus transformed the government into that of a monarchy. On his extant coins, however, Aristobulus is not referred to as king, but as high priest.[5] Aristobulus is said to have used the title Philhellene of himself (*Ant* xiii, 318), and if this was so, it can hardly have commended him to the pious. Josephus adds, just after this statement, that Aristobulus conferred many benefits on his country, but it is not clear what such benefits were. His one political achievement was the extension of Jewish control to the Itureans, who lived in the north of Galilee,[6] and who were offered the option of remaining where they were if they became Jews. Thus began the Judaization of northern

Galilee (*Ant* xiii, 318–19). Aristobulus's death, after he had been in office for only one year, is said to have been preceded by remorse for his misdeeds (*Ant* xiii, 314–18).

ALEXANDER JANNAEUS (JANNAI), 103–76 BC

Alexander Jannaeus, the son whom John Hyrcanus did not love, was declared ruler by the widow of Aristobulus, Salina (or Alexandra). Whether Jannai's wife Alexandra is the same person as the widow of Aristobulus is not clear.[7] If the figures given by Josephus (*Ant* xiii, 404, 430) are accurate, Alexandra must have been fifteen years older than her husband. In any case Jannai became not only ruler, but king, for he used the title king on some of his coins.[8] Those in Israel who felt that a legitimate sovereign should be of Davidic lineage would naturally take offence at Jannai's claim.

Jannai exercised his kingly and high priestly powers for twenty-seven years. During this time, as is evident from Josephus, Judea's independence was more than once in jeopardy. For instance, when Jannai attacked Ptolemais, the inhabitants appealed to Ptolemy viii Lathyrus, then ruling Cyprus, for help. Ptolemy's arrival in Syria forced Jannai to raise the siege of Ptolemais. Ptolemy then proceeded inland, took Asochis in Galilee, and defeated Jannai's army at Asophon (Saphon?). He then invaded Judea, but at this point his mother, Cleopatra iii, intervened, apparently alarmed lest her son's success should undermine her own power in Egypt. Ptolemy was forced by this maternal pressure to leave Coele-Syria, and eventually he returned to Cyprus (c 102 BC), but in his place in Judea he now found Cleopatra and an Egyptian army. At Scythopolis Jannai came to terms with her, but the details of the alleged alliance are not given *Ant* xiii, 324–55). This must have occurred before 101 BC, the year of Cleopatra's death.

In the latter part of Jannai's reign another outside power cast its shadow on Judea, namely Armenia under Tigranes i, who came to power in 95 BC. Tigranes formed an alliance with Mithridates vi of Pontus (this is the spelling of Mithradates commonly found in non-Parthian sources), and c 83 BC he was able to annex Cilicia, Phoenicia, and Syria. According to Josephus it was not until after Jannai's death that Tigranes besieged and captured Ptolemais. Queen Alexandra sent envoys to him to seek his favour for Judea, but almost immediately after this Tigranes withdrew from Syria to face an attack by the Roman consul Lucullus (appointed in 74 BC to command the Roman forces in Asia and Cilicia) on his own capital, 69 BC (*Ant* XIII, 419–21). The statement by J. Neusner that Palestine was a dependency of Armenia, c 83–69 BC, appears to be an exaggeration of the few known facts.[9]

It is possible that the expansion of Armenia under Tigranes should be related to an incident recorded in the Jerusalem Talmud (*Berakoth* 7.2). The story concerns a Persian (i.e., Parthian) delegation which visited Jannai in the time of R. Simeon ben Shetah, but the purpose of its coming can only be surmised. Possibly its visit was exploratory, to see if the Jews and Parthians could unite to face Tigranes, and, if so, the meeting probably took place before the death of Mithradates II of Parthia in 87 BC.[10]

Any interest that Jannai had in Transjordan (OT Gilead, Ammon, Moab) was conditioned by the fact that in the early second century BC the Nabatean Arabs had gained control of the trade routes in northwest Arabia, one of which ran between Petra (their capital) and Damascus. Bozrah (61 miles south of Damascus) was one of their important cities. For some undisclosed reason Jannai felt it necessary to attack the Nabatean ruler, Obedas I, c 90 BC, but in the ensuing battle, probably east of the sea of Galilee, he lost his entire army (*War* I 90; *Ant* XIII, 375). Yet a few years later, when a Syrian army under Antiochus XII (87–84 BC) was marching through Judea to attack the Nabateans, Jannai, either to help the latter or to assert his own dignity, tried unsuccessfully to block Antiochus's advance. Antiochus was subsequently defeated soundly by the Arabs (*War* I, 99–102; *Ant* XIII, 387–91). Later Jannai must have irritated Aretas III (c 87–62 BC), for the Nabateans invaded Judea and defeated the Jewish forces near the fortified town of Adida (four miles east of Lydda). The nature of the peace settlement is not given (*Ant* XIII, 392).

It is remarkable that, with all these political complications, Jannai was able to expand the nation's territory. In these military efforts part of his army consisted of mercenary soldiers, described (*Ant* XIII, 374) as Pisidians and Cilicians. At different times Jannai took Transjordan, Gadara (requiring a ten-month siege), Amathus, Gerasa, Dium (Dion), and Pella (which was demolished when it inhabitants refused to embrace Judaism). Josephus (*Ant* XIII, 382) states that the Jewish king had to give back some of the territory conquered in Moab and Gilead for political reasons. Josephus also reports that Jannai's death occurred in Transjordan while he was besieging the fortress of Ragaba, west of Gerasa (*Ant* XIII, 398). East and northeast of the Sea of Galilee he conquered Gaulane (Gaulana), Seleuceia, Gamala, and the 'Ravine of Antiochus' (*War* I, 86, 104–5; *Ant* XIII, 356, 374, 393–4). On or near the Mediterranean coast he took Gaza (requiring a year's siege), Raphia, and Anthedon (*War* I, 87; *Ant* XIII, 334, 357–64). Near the end of his treatment of Jannai's exploits Josephus supplies a list of districts and cities in Syria, Idumea, and Phoenicia which the king controlled (*Ant* XIII, 395–7), some of which had been taken earlier by Simon or John Hyrcanus. In any case it is clear that most of the territory at one time ruled by Solomon was once more under the authority of Jerusalem. Whatever the faults the Jews found in Jannai, they could not but take pride in his expansion of Israel's borders.

That Jannai was able to accomplish what he did is amazing in the light of the considerable opposition to his rule within the Jewish community. In fact his greatest failure was his inability to get along with the majority of his Jewish subjects. Josephus in his *War* nowhere identifies Jannai's opponents. We read of 'the nation which had long hated him' (I, 90), and the people's advice to him was 'Die; even death would hardly reconcile us to one guilty of such enormities' (I, 92). In *Antiquities* Josephus says that 'his own people revolted against him' (XIII, 372). His wife said to him on his deathbed, 'You know how hostile the nation feels toward you' (XIII, 399). Two isolated incidents throw some light on this situation. One occurred at a celebration of *Sukkoth*, when Jannai, as officiating high priest, apparently did something which caused the people to pelt him with citrons and to shout that he was unfit to be high priest. This resulted in a riot in which Jannai's soldiers killed 6,000 Jews (*War* I, 88–9; *Ant* XIII, 372–4). The other incident was the aftermath of Jannai's defeat by the Nabatean king, Obedas I. The loss of the whole Jewish army provoked the Jews into a bloody insurrection which lasted for six years. The Jews finally called in Demetrius III of Syria to help them. After Demetrius had defeated Jannai, many Jews changed sides, and Demetrius then abandoned the Jewish cause and returned to Syria. The rebellion finally ended in a victory for Jannai, who celebrated his triumph by the atrocity of crucifying 800 of his prisoners. The general consternation caused by this display of barbarism led 8,000 of Jannai's opponents to go into exile until after the king's death (*War* I, 90–8; *Ant* XIII, 375–83). It was not until he was on his deathbed that Jannai advised his queen to 'yield a certain amount of power to the Pharisees ... he himself had come into conflict with the nation because these men [the Pharisees] had been badly treated by him' (*Ant* XIII, 400–4). This reference is the only basis, but probably an adequate one, for believing that it was the rigid piety and strict puritanism of the Pharisees that constituted the heart of the Jewish people's opposition to the leadership of Alexander Jannaeus.

QUEEN ALEXANDRA, 76–67 BC

Jannaeus had bequeathed his royal power to his widow Alexandra, and for the second time in Jerusalem's history a woman was sovereign (cf Athaliah in the ninth century, 2 Kgs 11:1–16). The elder son, Hyrcanus II, became high priest, and the younger son, Aristobulus II, was left without any formal responsibility. The nine years of the queen's reign were quiet in terms of Judea's foreign relations. Like John Hyrcanus, Alexandra had mercenary soldiers in the army (*Ant* XIII, 409), but her forces saw no active service except in an abortive mission led by Aristobulus II against Ptolemy of Damascus. Her contact with Tigranes of Armenia (c 70–69 BC) has been commented on earlier in this chapter.

Alexandra's real problems concerned the internal life of Judea, particularly the role of the Pharisees. Following her husband's final words of advice, she established cordial relations with the Pharisees; for instance, when she reinstated their regulations which her father-in-law, Hyrcanus, had abrogated (*Ant* XIII, 296). Josephus says that the Pharisees were permitted 'to do as they liked,' and that the queen commanded the people to obey them. This may mean that the

Pharisees now had a generous share of those civil appointments made at the pleasure of the queen. It may also mean that in the national council (*gerousia*, the later Sanhedrin) members of the Pharisaic party were now well represented.[11] The remainder of the council would still be Sadducean. One immediate result of all this was that exiles who had fled the country in the time of Jannai were now free to return to Judea, and those imprisoned by the late king were released.

Unhappily the Pharisees were not content with righting the wrongs of the past. Their new power made them, or some of them, arrogant and vengeful, and they began to exact retribution for the 800 prisoners whom Jannai had crucified. As far as one can judge from the data given by Josephus, numerous people were put to death without due process of law, and the leading citizens of Jerusalem, headed by Aristobulus II, made vigorous representations about such lawlessness to the queen. The queen was in a quandry, for she wished to retain the support of both parties in the dispute. Her solution of the matter was to permit those Sadducees who wished to do so to live in some of the country's fortresses, where they would be out of reach of the Pharisees in Jerusalem.

Aristobulus II was, however, not satisfied either with this arrangement or with the general way in which his mother was conducting the nation's affairs. While the queen was sick with what proved to be a fatal illness, Aristobulus II took the first steps to seize power. Within fifteen days he had control of twenty-two fortresses and had gathered a small army. When the high priest, Hyrcanus II, who appears throughout as a singularly weak character, and the council drew the queen's attention to these developments, the poor woman, who was seventy-three years old, had no strength to cope with them, and she could only suggest that they should do what was expedient. Not long after this she died, after a reign of nine years.

ARISTOBULUS II, 67–63 BC

Hyrcanus II, who had been high priest since 76 BC, assumed the kingship on his mother's death. But his brother, Aristobulus II, was determined to seize power. A battle was fought near Jericho, but most of Hyrcanus's troops went over to Aristobulus. Negotiations were begun in Jerusalem, and it was agreed that Aristobulus should be king and, as is clear from Josephus (*Ant* xiv, 97; xv, 31; xx, 243), also high priest. Hyrcanus was to be left undisturbed as a private citizen. This arrangement, however, although publicly confirmed with oaths, was not destined to remain long unchallenged. The partisans of Hyrcanus felt that he had been ill-treated, and out of this smouldering discontent there presently flared up full-scale civil strife.

This was an unfortunate time for the Palestinian Jews to engage in fratricidal war, for Rome's interest in this part of the world had been increasing rapidly. Since 133 BC, when Rome had acquired the kingdom of Pergamum, to become the province of Asia, it had had a territorial stake in the Near East, which grew when, c 102 BC, the province of Cilicia was organized, primarily to deal with Mediterranean piracy. The bequest of Cyrenaica to Rome in 96 BC led to the establishment of that province in 74 BC. In the latter year Nicomedes of Bithynia left his kingdom to Rome. In 67 BC Pompey was given almost unlimited powers against the Mediterranean pirates, and in 66 BC he was put in charge of Rome's interests in the Near East, with special responsibility for the war against Mithridates vi of Pontus. This led in 64 BC to an enlargement of the province of Cilicia, the annexation of Crete, and the creation of the province of Syria. In short, Rome was no longer a republic whose territory was confined to Italy. It was now directly involved in the life of the Near East, and it was not likely to tolerate political chaos on the borders of its domains. If in the preceding century Judas, Jonathan, Simon, and John Hyrcanus had thought is prudent to establish friendly relations with Rome, this was all the more desirable in the first century, with Rome a next-door neighbour. The situation demanded that Judea be a peaceful, unified state, but Aristobulus and Hyrcanus were either too politically naive, or too ill-informed, or too self-centred to be concerned about such matters. Josephus's diatribe against the two brothers has therefore considerable justification. Of the events leading up to 63 BC he wrote: 'For this misfortune which befell Jerusalem, Hyrcanus and Aristobulus were responsible, because of their dissension. For we lost our freedom and became subject to the Romans' (*Ant* xiv, 77).

The most important of the friends of Hyrcanus ii was a wealthy

Idumean named Antipater, presumably Jewish in his religious practices. His father, Antipas, had been appointed governor of Idumea by Jannai, and it is probable that the son held the same office under Queen Alexandra; if so, he may have been apprehensive regarding his future if Judea was to be ruled by Aristobulus II. In any case Antipater appears to have been the prime mover in persuading Hyrcanus to assert his claim to the high priesthood. The first step was to seek help from the Nabatean ruler, Aretas III (85–60 BC), who was prevailed upon to give Hyrcanus military assistance. A Nabatean force was accordingly dispatched against Aristobulus. The latter was defeated and retreated to Jerusalem, where he was besieged in the temple by Aretas (c 65 BC).

At this point in the course of events the Romans entered the scene. After wintering in 65–64 BC in Armenia Minor, Pompey, who had sent Gabinius and Scaurus on ahead, came down into Syria which was in a state of anarchy.[12] When Scaurus reached Damascus, he heard of the civil strife in Judea, and, advancing southwards, he was met by envoys from both Aristobulus and Hyrcanus, each asking for aid, and each offering the usual bribes. Scaurus decided to support Aristobulus, and he ordered Aretas to lift the siege of the Jerusalem temple or risk being declared an enemy of Rome. Aretas raised the siege and started back for Nabatea, and Scaurus returned to Damascus. Aristobulus, taking heart at this development, then pursued the Nabateans and defeated them at Papyron (thought to be near Jericho).

In 64 BC, while Pompey was in Syria, he received envoys from both Hyrcanus and Aristobulus, but took no action on their allegations. By the spring of 63 BC he had reached Damascus, and once more the problems of Judea came before him: Hyrcanus and Aristobulus were on hand, and a third delegation, claiming to represent the Jewish people, argued against any form of monarchical government. Pompey avoided making any immediate decision; his immediate objective was the Nabateans, probably because of the trade which they controlled.

Aristobulus's subsequent actions aroused Pompey's suspicions, and he decided to postpone the Nabatean expedition. Coming to Coreae (southeast of Shechem), he summoned Aristobulus to appear before him, and required him to surrender all his strongholds. After some delay Aristobulus promised Pompey both money and admission to Jerusalem, but, when Gabinius was sent to take over the city, Aristobulus's soldiers refused to let him in. Pompey therefore arrested Aristobulus and made preparations to besiege the Jewish capital. Hyrcanus's supporters let the Romans inside the city walls, but the forces of Aristobulus occupied the temple precincts and prepared to withstand a siege. The Romans, who had brought the necessary siege machines from Tyre, now began the siege, which was terminated three months later, in July 63 BC. It is said that 12,000 Jews were killed in the operation, in addition to those taken prisoner. Pompey and some officers went inside the sanctuary itself, but apparently no plundering of the temple treasures took place. Pompey is credited with encouraging the priesthood to resume the temple cultus as soon as possible.

THE CONSEQUENCES OF POMPEY'S INTERVENTION

The consequences of Pompey's intervention in Judea's affairs were tragic for the Palestinian Jews.

1 / Judea lost the political independence it had enjoyed since 143 BC and became tributary to Rome. Josephus claims that within a short time the Romans exacted 10,000 talents (a very high figure) from Judea, but he does not elaborate this. In 64 BC what was left of Seleucid Syria had become the Roman province of Syria, and Judea was now made part of this province, whose legate (governor) was Scaurus.

2 / The borders of Judea were considerably reduced, principally by restoring to their various inhabitants most of the districts and cities that John Hyrcanus and Jannaeus had added to the original Jewish state, although Galilee, Peraea, and Idumea remained under the jurisdiction of Jerusalem. One of the regions to be freed of Jewish control was Samaria, which meant that the Samaritans were again able to maintain their own version of Yahwism.

3 / The high priesthood was restored to Hyrcanus II; whether he had any other legal title is uncertain. In a decree of Julius Caesar (quoted in *Ant* XIV, 191) Hyrcanus is referred to as high priest and ethnarch, and in popular parlance he was called 'king' (*Ant* XIV, 157, 172).

4 / No special role was assigned to Antipater, who may have continued as governor of Idumea. In any case he was to prove to be a figure of importance in the coming years.

5 / Aristobulus and his family were put under arrest, and eventually they accompanied Pompey back to Italy. It was not until December 62 BC that Pompey and his forces landed at Brundisium, and when, in September 61 BC, the conqueror had his triumph in Rome, among the prisoners then displayed was Aristobulus II of Judea.

VIII

JUDEA UNDER THE ROMANS
63–4 BC[1]

FROM 63 BC TO THE COMING OF THE PARTHIANS[2]

It was an unhappy circumstance that Judea came under Roman control when it did, for the Roman Republic was in its death throes. This was the period of the dictatorships, and there was considerable chaos and malpractice in the administration of the overseas provinces. These conditions were to be greatly improved once the principate was established in 27 BC, but in the meantime all parts of the Roman world, including Judea, were to suffer from the weakness of the central government and the ineptitude and cupidity of provincial administrators.

Administrative arrangements

Hyrcanus II remained as high priest throughout these years, being confirmed in this position by Gabinius, governor of Syria (57–54 BC), and by Julius Caesar in 47 BC. If the high priest also had the office of ethnarch, there is no evidence in Josephus of his acting in such a capacity. The status of Antipater in the early part of this period is not clear. In 62 BC he was under orders from Hyrcanus, but he seems to have been impatient with the high priest, and gradually to have usurped some of the latter's secular power. This was the charge made against him before Antony by some Jews at a later date.

It was Julius Caesar who in 47 BC legitimized Antipater's status by making him procurator of Judea, and giving him the rights of Roman citizenship, as well as certain tax exemptions. Subsequently Antipater gave governorships to two of his sons, that of Jerusalem and vicinity to Phasael, and that of Galilee to Herod (who was about twenty-five years of age, not fifteen, as in *Ant* xiv, 158). After Caesar's murder in 44 BC there were echoes of the civil strife in the Roman world in Syria, and in the midst of this turmoil Antipater was assassinated in 43 BC. Cassius and Murcus, in search of support in their struggle with Antony and Octavian, made Herod governor of Coele-Syria (not of Syria, as in *War* I, 225), and, when Antony and Octavian emerged victorious from Philippi in 42 BC, and the Near East became Antony's bailiwick, the latter confirmed the positions of Antipater's sons. Phasael and Herod now became tetrarchs, presumably of southern Judea and Galilee respectively. It is probable that Antony still considered Hyrcanus II to be the titular head of Judea.

Josephus records that Gabinius, legate of Syria, after putting down an insurrection in Judea c 57 BC, divided the area into five districts, with centres in the cities of Jerusalem, Gazara (rather than Gadara), Amathus, Jericho, and Sepphoris. As Josephus speaks of the setting up of five councils (*sunedria*) and five districts, it has been thought that this was an effort to decentralize the administration and perhaps to weaken the civil power of Hyrcanus. How permanent this measure was we do not know.

Judea and Roman politics

Since Judea was now a part of the Roman world, it was inevitable that the Jewish leaders should become involved in the kaleidoscope of Roman politics. For instance, in 62 BC Scaurus led a force against the Nabatean king, Aretas III, but, when the Romans got into difficulties, Hyrcanus and Antipater used their influence with Aretas to persuade him to buy Scaurus's withdrawal for 300 talents.

Some years later, when Crassus had become proconsul of Syria, he needed money for his proposed Parthian campaign, and in the winter of 54–53 BC he came down to Judea and plundered the Jerusalem temple, taking about 10,000 talents of booty. Six years later, in 48 BC, Hyrcanus and Antipater, who had been supporters of Pompey, had to switch their allegiance quickly to Julius Caesar after Pompey's defeat at Pharsalus. As a token of their new loyalty they responded to the call of Mithridates of Pergamum, who was raising a force to help Caesar in Alexandria, and sent 3,000 Jewish soldiers, led by Antipater himself, to Egypt. This assistance to Caesar was not without its benefits to Judea, for, when Caesar came to Syria in 47 BC, he confirmed Hyrcanus as high priest, and gave Antipater the rights and privileges noted previously. The territory of Judea was slightly extended; for example, the port of Joppa was restored to Jewish control. These benefactions, we may suppose, were granted to ensure that Judea would be a stable element in Rome's eastern domains.

Four years after this, in 43 BC, Cassius, one of Caesar's murderers, came to Syria and demanded extremely heavy tribute from that province. Judea was ordered to pay 700 talents, and to Antipater fell the task of collecting this money. Herod quickly gathered the 100 talents demanded from Galilee, but the four Judean towns that were dilatory Cassius reduced to slavery. By 42 BC Antony was in charge of the Roman Near East, and it was before him, both in Bithynia and at Daphne (near Antioch), that Phasael and Herod had to appear to justify themselves against the allegations of Jewish deputations that they were usurping Hyrcanus's power. From such incidents as these we infer that successful relations with the Roman leaders demanded considerable political know-how, and that at times bribery was indispensable.

Periodic disturbances

These two decades are notable for the recurring tumults in the life of Judea. Frequently these were reactions to Roman rule. The Maccabean revolt and its aftermath had revived Jewish nationalism, and thus the loss of independence in 63 BC was very hard to accept. Another important factor in these disturbances was the persistence of sentiment in favour of Aristobulus II and his sons. Still another factor, although it can hardly have amounted to much in 63 BC, was the influence exercised by Antipater and his family. That this group of Idumeans consistently showed themselves to be friendly to the Romans did not enhance their standing in the eyes of many Jews. In addition there was the problem of lawlessness: while society was being convulsed by numerous other causes, banditry found a perfect setting for its activities. It was various combinations of the factors just noted that led to the unruliness in Judea in the period being considered.

For six years after Pompey's conquest the land appeared to be tranquil. Then in 57 BC Alexander, the son of Aristobulus II, who had escaped from Pompey's custody, launched a rebellion. Neither Hyrcanus nor Antipater could cope with this uprising, and it required the intervention of Gabinius of Syria to defeat the considerable force (according to Josephus, 11,500 men) which Alexander had collected. In the next year, 56 BC, another outbreak occurred, led by Aristobulus himself and his other son Antigonus, both of whom had escaped from Rome. Once again Gabinius had to intervene, the insurrection was suppressed, and Aristobulus and his son were sent back to Rome. In a rather strange move, for which Josephus's explanation is not entirely convincing, the Roman authorities allowed the children of Aristobulus to return to Judea. In 55 BC, when Gabinius came back to Syria after restoring Ptolemy XI to his throne in Egypt, he found Judea once more in a tumult instigated by Alexander. The latter was defeated near Mount Tabor with a loss, Josephus claims, of 10,000 men. That the Romans had to face three serious uprisings 57–55 BC can only mean that there was a strong anti-Roman and anti-Hyrcanus sentiment in the Jewish community.

In 52 BC more trouble developed. Pitholaus, a partisan of Aristobulus II, rallied another force in Galilee in the town of Tarichaeae. Cassius, proquaestor of Syria, came south to nip this incipient insurrection in the bud. He quickly took Tarichaeae and enslaved 30,000 of its men. Pitholaus himself was captured and put to death.

It was only the caprice of fortune that prevented further fighting in 49 BC. In this year Caesar, in the course of his struggle with Pompey, freed Aristobulus II from detention in Rome, and sent him to win over to his side Judea, whose leaders, Hyrcanus II and Antipater, were presumed to favour Pompey. This plan was never to be fulfilled, for Aristobulus was poisoned by some Pompeians. His son Alexander, active in the troubles of 57 and 55 BC, was, at Pompey's order, tried in Antioch for his offences against the Romans and put to death.

After Antipater had seen Caesar depart from Syria in the spring of 47 BC, he had to suppress various disorders in Judea (not detailed by Josephus), and at the same time, in traversing the countryside, he argued for the support of Hyrcanus and the acceptance of the Romans. His efforts to establish public order were not entirely successful, as his son Herod discovered when he took over the governorship of Galilee. Here Herod had to act energetically against a large body of brigands under one Ezekias, but Herod was then called before the Sanhedrin for putting persons to death without due legal process. Josephus's accounts of the trial are confused, although it seems likely either that the case was dismissed, or that, under pressure from Sextus Caesar, Herod was acquitted. It is possible that some of the brigands were in fact Herod's political enemies.

Another expression of the support which the family of Aristobulus II continued to have in Judea is seen in the delegations of Jews who went from time to time to Roman leaders to complain about what was going on in Judea. In 47 BC, for instance, Antigonus, son of Aristobulus II, appeared before Caesar, probably in Ptolemais, and condemned the unjust actions of both Hyrcanus and Antipater in Judea, and the outrage they had done to his own family. Five years later a group of Jewish leaders came to Antony in Bithynia and complained that Phasael and Herod were robbing Hyrcanus of his civil powers. This same accusation was made later in the year before Antony at Daphne. A few months later a deputation of 1,000 Jews came to Antony at Tyre and repeated the charges. When their protests got out of hand, Antony in exasperation turned his troops on the Jews, and many of them were killed or wounded.

The evidence of Josephus makes it clear that the population of Judea was virtually polarized into two camps, those who supported Hyrcanus, Phaesael, and Herod, and those who did not. It was a situation that only the superior force at the disposal of the two tetrachs, mostly because of the proximity of the Roman legions in Syria, kept under control. As we shall see in the next section, once Roman authority was undermined, civil strife in Judea was almost inevitable.

THE PARTHIAN INTERLUDE AND THE EMERGENCE OF HEROD AS KING[3]

The Parthians in Judea

Ever since the acquisition of Syria in 64 BC Rome had Parthia on its eastern borders, and it was perhaps to be expected that, when Roman leaders were in an expansionist mood, they should consider the feasibility of conquering Parthia. It fell to Crassus, who became legate of Syria in 54 BC, to attempt this task. His expedition ended in his defeat at Carrhae, 53 BC, one of the worst military disasters Rome ever suffered. Two years later a Parthian force entered Syria but was turned back by the legate Cassius. In the subsequent civil commotion in the Roman world Cassius and Brutus, who were ultimately to face Antony and Octavian at Philippi, did not hesitate to seek Parthian help, and with this in mind even sent Labienus to the Parthian court. After the battle of Philippi, 42 BC, this envoy was still in Parthia, and he eventually persuaded Orodes II that the time was ripe for an attack on Rome. There were no troops of any account in Asia Minor, and it was known that the two legions in Syria were disaffected. Therefore in 40 BC Barzapharnes and the king's son Pacorus invaded Syria, while Labienus led another force westwards, penetrating as far as Lycia and Caria.

It was not until early in 39 BC that Ventidius, sent by Antony, landed in Asia and began a campaign to drive the Parthians back across the Euphrates. Labienus was killed in this fighting, and the Parthians who had advanced into Syria and Judea were obliged to evacuate these regions. In 38 BC Pacorus led a strengthened Parthian army towards Syria, but Ventidius stopped his advance at Gindarus and Pacorus himself was killed. This ended the danger of a further Parthian attack.

At this point we shall go back a few years to pick up the story of Antigonus, son of Aristobulus II, who had been released from custody in Rome in 56 BC. It was not until 42 BC that Antigonus, with assistance from Marion of Tyre and Ptolemy of Chalcis, felt able to attack Galilee.

Although he was defeated by Herod and banished, he remained a potentially dangerous leader. The coming of the Parthians into Syria in 40 BC must have seemed providential to Antigonus, for they were likely to further his own ambitions. Negotiations with the invaders were opened, and for a bribe of 1,000 talents and 500 women the Parthians agreed to depose the Jewish high priest, Hyrcanus, and to replace him by Antigonus.

The Parthians then proceeded into Judea, Pacorus along the seacoast and Barzapharnes through the interior. As far as can be determined from Josephus's somewhat confused account of the Parthian advance, Herod in Galilee had insufficient forces to stop the invaders and he therefore moved south into the Jerusalem area. Pacorus sent a reconnoitring troop of cavalry from Phoenicia into Judea, and this encouraged Antigonus's supporters to congregate in Jerusalem. Armed clashes between them and the high priest's party became a daily feature of the city's life, but it appears that neither party had enough military power to defeat the other decisively. Antigonus, with the consent of Phasael, invited Pacorus (not the royal prince) into the city to mediate the dispute, and Phasael and Hyrcanus were subsequently persuaded, against the advice of Herod, to go to Barzapharnes in Galilee to arrange for a cessation of hostilities. This only resulted in their seizure by the Parthians, and a scheme to trap Herod was set afoot. Herod, however, learned of what had happened to his brother and Hyrcanus, and, since he had no troops to resist Antigonus and the Parthians, he fled to Idumea in the fall of 40 BC.

In the meantime the Parthians controlled Jerusalem, where they carried out some pillaging, and they proceeded to install Antigonus as ruler of Judea.[4] Phasael and Hyrcanus were handed over to Antigonus, who at once mutilated his uncle's ears so that he could never again function as high priest (Lev 21:17–23). Phasael, to avoid a worse fate, committed suicide. When the Parthians, under Roman pressure, later retired from Jerusalem, they took the ex-high priest with them as a prisoner.

Herod's flight to Rome

Herod's initial purpose in going to Idumea was to place his family and treasures in the safety of Masada, and then to proceed to Malchus I (47–30 BC), the Nabatean king, from whom he hoped to obtain funds to buy off the Parthians. But Malchus refused Herod entry into his kingdom, and thus the fugitive headed for Egypt. What happened at his reception by Cleopatra is obscure, but in any case Herod was determined to push on to Rome. His motive for doing so can only be conjectured. Josephus suggests that he hoped to obtain the kingship of Judea for Aristobulus III (whose sister, Mariamme, was to marry Herod in 37 BC), but that he himself might be declared king cannot have been absent from his thoughts. Cassius had earlier promised that, when the civil war of 43 BC was ended, he would make Herod king of Judea (*War* I, 225).

Herod, journeying via Pamphylia, Rhodes, and Brundisium, reached Rome in December 40 BC, and gave Antony a first-hand account of what had happened in Judea. Antony realized that the situation demanded strong local leadership, and, as he had a very favourable impression of Herod (cf *War* I, 244), he determined to recommend Herod as king of the Jews. Although in *War* Josephus makes no allusion to a bribe, in *Ant* XIV, 382 he speaks freely of the money promised to Antony if Herod were to become king. As the pact of Brundisium between Octavian and Antony had been in force since October, Octavian was now brought into the discussion, and he proved amenable to Antony's wishes, for he had some knowledge of Antipater's services to his foster-father Caesar in Egypt in 48 BC. The proposal was duly presented to the Senate, and in December 40 BC Herod was declared to be king of Judea. On this occasion the new king did not hesitate to join in the sacrifices to Juppiter Capitolinus, which act sheds some light on his religious convictions as a Jew.

Herod's struggle to possess his kingdom

When Herod landed at Ptolemais early in 39 BC, he must have expected that the Palestinian Jews would not welcome his coming. This proved to be the case, and it required a sustained struggle of two and a half years before he was actually in control of Judea. Most of Galilee early came over to his side, but Joppa yielded only after a siege. He moved on successfully to relieve his beleaguered family and treasures in Masada, despite the opposition of Antigonus's forces. He then went back to Jerusalem, where he temporarily besieged Antigonus, but a Roman force under Silo, which was supposed to be helping him, proved of doubtful value. It is evident that Herod did not yet have the resources to subdue Antigonus. After his Roman allies took to winter quarters, 39–38 BC, Herod sent his brother Joseph to occupy Idumea, while he himself went back to Galilee where two campaigns were needed to take and hold the strongholds that had not surrendered to him earlier. He also had to deal with the brigands of the district.

It was not until the Parthians under Pacorus had been finally defeated in 38 BC that Ventidius, who had previously recalled Silo, sent a sizable force of two legions and 1,000 cavalry under Machaeras to assist the Jewish king. But Machaeras's conduct was so equivocal that Herod felt obliged to complain to Antony in person, who, as he had learned, was now at Samosata in northern Syria, besieging Antiochus I, an ally of the Parthians. Josephus records that Herod gave Antony some much appreciated help, although, while Herod was thus engaged, his brother Joseph suffered an ignominious defeat by Antigonus near Jericho, and was killed in the action. This led to revolts against Herod in both Galilee and Idumea. When the king returned to Judea, he came with additional military support from the Romans, and in the winter of 38–37 BC he was able to defeat Antigonus's forces at Jericho and later near Isana. It was not until the spring of 37 BC that he renewed the siege of Jerusalem. It was during this operation that Herod took time off to go to Samaria to marry Mariamme,[5] the granddaughter of the high priest Hyrcanus II. Sosius, who had been appointed governor of Syria and Cilicia by Antony in 38 BC, now arrived with reinforcements, and the siege of the capital was energetically pressed forward. The city was finally taken in July 37 BC.[6] Antigonus surrendered to Sosius, but his supporters were massacred. Herod, by promising large rewards to the Romans, was able to safeguard the temple and to check the pillage of the city. Antigonus was taken to Antony, now in Antioch, and at the request of Herod was put to death. The son of Antipater was at last king of Judea.

HEROD, KING OF THE JEWS, 37–4 BC[7]

Herod as king

Herod was about thirty-seven years of age when he became master of his kingdom. He brought to his office a considerable fund of military and political experience, not the least of which was his acquaintance with Roman leaders and Roman ways. In addition, he was free of personal financial worries, for he seems to have inherited the wealth of his father (*War* I, 123). This inheritance was considerably increased during his reign by careful management, and it was augmented by numerous confiscations of property, as well as by revenue from copper mines in Cyprus (a gift from Augustus). The result was that at his death Herod was able to leave generous bequests to his sister Salome and other relatives, as well as even larger gifts to Augustus and the empress Julia.

It is tempting to speculate on what Herod's plans for Judea were in 37 BC. From the way things worked out, he must have hoped to persuade his subjects to accept Rome's domination of the Near East, including Judea. If he was at all successful in this, then Judea could become a stable and prosperous unit within the Roman world. There is no evidence that Herod wished to alter radically the way of life favoured by most Jews. He himself, while nominally a Jew, was in fact cosmopolitan in his tastes and values, and in those parts of Palestine that were traditionally non-Jewish, such as the cities of Samaria and Caesarea, he supported the more external features of Graeco-Roman culture, although his own appreciation of Greek thought and literature must have been minimal. He was essentially a Near Eastern prince (endemic in this area), gifted in many respects, and determined to exercise his absolute power in such a way as would justify the confidence placed in him by Antony and Octavian. That Herod ever hoped, as J. Neusner suggests,[8] to establish 'an empire in the Near East, particularly in Palestine, Syria, ... and Babylonia' seems to this writer quite improbable, and certainly after Octavian's formal accession to a new kind of power in the Roman world in 27 BC the idea would be fantastic.

Herod and Rome

Since Herod owed his position to the Roman Senate, his first political obligation was the maintenance of good relations with Rome. As Antony's jurisdiction was the Roman East, it was Antony whom Herod had to recognize as his immediate superior. Antony's marriage to Cleopatra of Egypt in the autumn of 37 BC introduced a new complication into Herod's situation. Cleopatra was a powerful as well as ambitious woman, and she coveted the territories in Asia which her third-century predecessors had once controlled. Antony refused to give her Judea, but she did obtain some balsam-producing land at Jericho, for which Herod gave her annual rent of 200 talents. Antony also gave his queen some tracts of land east of the Sea of Galilee which were nominally Nabatean, and King Malchus I (47–30 BC) agreed to pay a tax of 200 talents annually on this gift, for the collection of which Herod assumed the responsibility, and because of which Herod became involved in 32 BC in a military action against the Arabs when the payment was not forthcoming. It was this episode which saved Herod from being implicated directly in the battle of Actium, 31 BC.

After Actium, when Octavian was at Rhodes,[9] Herod was summoned to meet the new master of the Roman world. He frankly admitted his allegiance to Antony, but he promised Octavian the same loyalty that he had given Antony, and Octavian very sensibly accepted this and confirmed Herod's kingship in Judea. This was the beginning of a friendship between the two men from which both Herod and Judea derived considerable gain. For instance, the territory which Cleopatra had received now came back to Judea, and the regions of Trachonitis, Batanaea, and Auranitis, east of the Sea of Galilee, were put under Herod's jurisdiction, as in c 20 BC was the domain of Zenodorus, north of Lake Semechonitis. In 12 BC Augustus gave Herod part of the copper mines of Cyprus as a gift. It was at about this time that he also gave him a role in the administration of the province of Syria, but the precise nature of the appointment is not clear. The acquisition of Trachonitis was a mixed blessing, for it presently involved Herod in a small war against Arab brigands. When this was reported to Octavian (Augustus after 27 BC), he resented what appeared to be Herod's high-handed actions, and it was only the effective pleading of Herod's envoy, Nicolaus of Damascus, that convinced Octavian that Herod's conduct had been above reproach.

In various ways Herod showed his fidelity to Rome. In 25 BC he sent 500 soldiers to assist Aelius Gallus in his ill-fated expedition against the Arabs of Arabia Felix, and in 14 BC he went in person with a small fleet to the Black Sea to give such help as he could to Marcus Agrippa, the life-long friend of Augustus, who was engaged in settling affairs in the Bosporan kingdom. In Judea itself some of Herod's extensive building was an expression of homage to Rome and Augustus, as at Caesarea, Sebaste, and Paneion, where temples were erected to honour Rome and Augustus. These temples are of interest, for the imperial cult was still in its formative stages. Even within the Jewish temple a daily sacrifice on behalf of Caesar and the Roman people was offered. This practice was instituted by Augustus, probably at the suggestion of Herod. Further recognition of Caesar is seen in the institution at Caesarea in 10–9 BC of athletic contests every fourth (or fifth) year in honour of Augustus. An oath of loyalty which Herod required of his subjects, and which plunged the king into a tussle with the Pharisees and the Essenes, seems to have been expanded to include Caesar's name. Herod's acknowledgment of Rome's suzerainty is seen also in his visits to the empire's capital. In 17 BC he went to Italy to meet Augustus and to bring home Mariamme's sons, Alexander and Aristobulus, whose studies in Rome were now complete. About five years later Herod went to Rome again, taking with him the same two sons, and accusing them before Augustus of plots against himself. Augustus effected a reconciliation between the father and his sons, and the whole occasion became a kind of gala state visit.

Herod's administration

Herod commenced his rule in a manner typical of the era in which he lived: he exterminated the supporters of Antigonus, including forty-five of Judea's leading citizens, and he was responsible for Antigonus being put to death by Antony. The fortress of Hyrcania, held by the sister of Antigonus, was the last centre of resistance to be taken. In the years that followed there was never any open rebellion against Herod, largely because of the king's firm measures. No public assembly was permitted, except when one was called by Herod, and a strict surveillance of the populace was exercised, principally through the employment of spies. The use of torture to obtain information or confession was routine. A formal but unavailing complaint about Herod's tyrannical power was made by the people of Gadara to Augustus when he was in Syria in 20 BC.

Almost nothing is known about the administrative structure of Herod's kingdom. There may have been a council which the king consulted when necessary, but the evidence for this is scanty. An assembly of the people of Jerusalem and its suburbs was held from time to time, but such an occasion was used by Herod solely to make a public speech, and the gathering had no executive or legislative power. The king's chief official and minister of finance (*dioiketes*) was one Ptolemy, who survived Herod and read his last will to the army. Taxes were basically of two kinds. The first was the tribute due to Rome; in the time of Julius Caesar this was one-fourth of the sown crops and was payable at Sidon. The other type of tax was whatever was levied regularly by Herod, including a sales tax, and in addition such special imposts as the king established from time to time. The only revenue figures we have relate to the situation at Herod's death. We are told that the annual taxes collectable by Archelaus, Herod Antipas, Philip, and Salome from their respective lands amounted to 1020 talents (*Ant* XVII, 317–21).[10] Taxes were reduced temporarily under conditions of drought or pestilence or as a political gesture (*Ant* XV, 365; cf 299–316; XVI, 64). Whether the sum total of Judea's taxes was greater than what might be called the normal tax-load of other Mediterranean states we do not know, although Herod's extensive building program must have strained the country's finances. After the king's death Archelaus conceded that his father had injured the people, and the people in turn demanded a reduction in taxes and elimination of the sales tax (*Ant* XVII, 201, 204–5).

Herod's army and the maintenance of public order

Behind all the royal edicts was the power of the army, but the details of Herod's military structure elude us. Detachments of soldiers were assigned to garrison duty in the various fortresses strategically located throughout the kingdom. The cavalry was one of the units of the army, and men on being discharged from this service were settled in the town of Gaba near Mount Carmel. The king had a personal body-guard of 400 Gauls, who came to him as gift from Octavian after Cleopatra's death in 30 BC. Herod also employed mercenaries, as we learn from the description of his funeral procession: first came his bodyguard, and then the Thracians, Germans, and Gauls, and after them the whole army. In the turmoil after his death 3,000 of his best men adhered to the Roman cause: these are described as Sebastenians (from Sebaste), and probably they were not Jews. That many of Herod's soldiers were Jews is implied both in his address to the disconsolate survivors of the Arab war, c 31 BC (*War* I, 373–9), as well as in the statement in *Ant* XVII, 265–6 that most of Herod's army sided with the Jewish malcontents in the troubles in Jerusalem after the king's death. The relation of Herod's forces to the Roman soldiers in Judea is not clear. In Antony's time a Roman legion, one of the thirteen (or fifteen) assigned to Syria, was stationed in Jerusalem. Its duties were essentially those of a garrison. This legion appears to have been withdrawn in 30 BC by Octavian.[11]

Apart from serving as a deterrent to insurrection, Herod's armed forces appear to have been used mostly against groups in Transjordan variously known as Arabs, rebels, robbers, and brigands. The relation of these troublesome people to the Nabatean Arabs is not easy to determine. After one of these small-scale wars, c 31 BC, in which the Arabs were twice defeated near Philadelphia, the Arabs proclaimed Herod their ruler (*prostates*), although the precise meaning of the term in this context is obscure. It was not until 12–8 BC that Herod was once more obliged to deal with the Arabs, this time in Trachonitis which he had recently acquired. His first efforts to rid the area of bandits were unavailing, and eventually with the consent of Saturninus, legate of Syria, he led a larger force to a place called Rhaëpta (location un-known) which was demolished. Afterwards Herod tried to stabilize the situation by settling 3,000 Idumeans in the region (*Ant* XVI, 285). The area, however, continued to be a trouble spot, and somewhat later Herod persuaded one Zamaris, a Babylonian Jew, with a small army of 500 men, to settle in Batanaea to help maintain peace and order (*Ant* XVII, 23–7).

Herod's building activities

It was a convention in the ancient Near East, which was perpetuated in the Hellenistic Age, that kings should erect public buildings. When Herod was given the kingship of Judea, he was therefore under some obligation, if he wished to prove his kingly qualities, to carry on this tradition. Besides, as Josephus notes, he loved honours and fame, and there can be little doubt that many of his buildings were intended to enhance his reputation as a beneficent ruler. Others, such as those which were built at Caesarea and Sebaste, had a more obvious political motivation.

Apart from the Jewish temple in Jerusalem, which will be treated later, Herod's chief structures were these: in Jerusalem a magnificent palace for himself and a greatly improved fortress protecting the temple, renamed Antonia after Antony;[12] in Samaria, renamed Sebaste, new walls and a great temple in honour of Augustus; at Strato's Tower on the coast a new city, Caesarea, with theatre, amphitheatre, hippodrome, a serviceable harbour, and a temple dedicated to Rome and Augustus;[13] at Paneion, near the sources of the Jordan, a temple for Augustus; at Jericho a fortress, Cypros, in honour of Herod's mother; north of Jericho a city, Phasaelis, named after his brother; east of the Dead Sea the castle of Machaerus; southeast of Bethlehem an elaborate fortress called Herodium; in the plain of Esdraelon a new city, Gaba; in Perea a rebuilt Esebonitis.

What must have infuriated many of Herod's subjects were his benefactions to foreign cities. It was obvious to all that these gifts diverted funds which could well have been put to good use in Judea itself. This was one of the criticisms of Herod made by a Jewish deputation before Augustus after the king's death (*War* II, 85). Furthermore to the pietistic groups in Judea Herod's erection of pagan temples and various secular structures, usually dedicated to the locally acknowledged deity, was a flagrant violation of a basic Jewish dogma that pagan worship must not be aided or abetted in any way. While, therefore, Herod may have gained a widespread reputation in the Gentile world as a benefactor,[14] in Judea these gifts must have been looked upon by many as but another indication that Herod's Jewish faith sat lightly upon him.

Herod and Judaism

HEROD AS A JEW

As four years of his boyhood were spent at the court of Aretas III of Nabatea, it was probably not until he was back in Judea that Herod began to acquire, in bits and pieces, some knowledge of the externals of the Jewish religion, but how far he ever proceeded beyond these is a matter of speculation. He was, on occasion, ignorant of or indifferent to accepted Jewish practice, as in his laws about theft (*Ant* xvi, 1–5), which were more severe than those in the Torah (cf Ex 22:1–2), and he was prepared, when circumstances demanded it, to participate in a non-Jewish religious ceremony, as in Rome in 40 BC. It is instructive, however, that he insisted that Syllaeus the Arab be initiated into the customs of the Jews before marrying his sister Salome, and that he was willing to support the appeal of the Jews of Ionia to Agrippa (c 14 BC) that they be allowed to practise their own customs, and in particular to send their temple tax without molestation to Jerusalem. The speeches which Josephus puts into the mouth of Herod are difficult to assess, but if they in some measure reflect the king's thoughts, then they suggest that Herod had a formal belief in the Jewish God (e.g., *Ant* xv, 127–46). It is harder, however, to accept that Herod ever publicly said that God 'exhorts us to hate arrogance and injustice' (*Ant* xv, 135). On the other hand the challenge to the view that misfortunes come as a sign of God's wrath (*Ant* xv, 144) may in fact have come from Herod.

THE HIGH PRIEST

As the Hasmonean days when the religious leader of the community was also the king were gone, Herod took upon himself the duty of both appointing and dismissing high priests, although he may not have known that there was some biblical support for his so doing.[15] Since Hyrcanus II had been multilated by Antigonus in 40 BC, Herod had to appoint a high priest at the very beginning of his reign. He selected a Babylonian Jew of correct lineage, Ananel,[16], whose tenure of office was temporarily interrupted by the appointment of Aristobulus III (Jonathan), the last of the Hasmonean line. The latter served for one year before his strangulation, at which time Ananel resumed his office.[17] Josephus notes that Herod kept the high priest's robe under his control in the citadel (Antonia), and released it only when required. The reference is probably to the special raiment worn by the high priest on the Day of Atonement (Lev 16:4, 23; M *Yoma* 7.5).

Apart from the murder of Aristobulus III, Herod's worst treatment of a high priest was given to Hyrcanus II. This man, after being disfigured and taken to Parthia in 40 BC, was later allowed by the Parthians to return to Judea, possibly through the influence of the Babylonian Jews. About 30 BC he became involved in a plan to take refuge with the Nabatean king, Malchus I, and, as Herod was apprehensive that as a Hasmonean Hyrcanus was planning to usurp the throne, he put the case before the Sanhedrin (probably on a charge of treason), and Hyrcanus was put to death by strangling. Josephus felt obliged to comment that 'What he [Hyrcanus] experienced ... was neither just nor an act of piety' (*Ant* xv, 179–82).

THE SANHEDRIN

The Sanhedrin comes into Josephus's account of Herod, but the references do not permit us to speak with much confidence about its role in Jewish life at this time. It is usually assumed that the court of priests and laymen of 2 Chr 19:8, the elders of 1 Mac 7:33; 11:23; 12:35; etc, and the senate (*gerousia*) of 1 Mac 12:6; 2 Mac 1:10; 4:44; 11:27 point to a kind of supreme court or national council in the post-exilic and Maccabean ages, and that the later Sanhedrin was the descendant of this body. The Mishnah's data on the Sanhedrin, while reflecting the practices of the first century AD, probably contain much pre-Christian material. The head of the Sanhedrin was the high priest, but how its members were selected we do not know.

Herod's first brush with the Sanhedrin (over his treatment of the brigands of Galilee) has been commented on earlier in this chapter. Probably his view of the Sanhedrin after this incident was rather cool. After he was established as king in 37 BC, he liquidated all the supporters of Antigonus that he could seize. In *Ant* xiv, 175 he is said to have killed all the members of the Sanhedrin except Samaias. We may assume, however, that under the presidency of the new high priest

Ananel, the Sanhedrin was reconstituted with a membership more to Herod's liking. When, some years later, Herod's suspicions were aroused against the former high priest, Hyrcanus II, he turned the matter over to the Sanhedrin, and the man was put to death. On the evidence we have, it is hard to see how Hyrcanus could have been found guilty of any crime, and we can only conclude that the Sanhedrin was virtually forced to abandon equity and agree with the king's wishes (*Ant* xv, 165–73).

THE JEWISH SECTS

According to Josephus the sects played a relatively minor role in Jewish life in Herod's time. The Sadducees are not mentioned at all, we presume because their numbers had been drastically reduced both in the civil war of 67–63 BC, and in the rebellions of 57, 56, 55, 52 BC, as well as by the slaughter of Antigonus's followers in 37 BC. As for the Pharisees, Herod seems to have had a favourable attitude to them, partly because two of their leaders, Pollion and Samaias, had urged the citizens of Jerusalem to admit him when he was besieging the city in 37 BC, and partly because their scholarly activities appeared to be harmless to him politically. His only major confrontation with the Pharisees, said to number over 6,000, was over the oath to Caesar and the king's government. An earlier oath to Herod himself they had been excused from, but this expanded oath they refused to take. Herod punished them with a fine, which was paid for them by the king's sister-in-law. The aftermath of this incident was that some of the Pharisees, who had ventured to predict to some members of his household that Herod, by God's decree, would be removed from the kingship, were put to death. A more serious event, probably involving Pharisees (although they are not named in the narrative), occurred shortly before Herod's death. In his rebuilding of the temple Herod had placed a huge golden eagle over the main entrance, and he had been reproached for this flagrant disregard of the Jewish law against images. Thinking that the king's illness was a propitious time to act, two scholars, Judas and Matthias, now ordered their disciples to pull down the eagle, which they did. The authorities at once arrested the persons involved, and Herod had them brought to Jericho, where in the presence of 'the Jewish officials' the two scholars and forty young men were condemned to death.

The only other sect which appears in Josephus' chronicle of Herod is the Essenes. Herod is said to have honored the Essenes because one of them, Manaemus (Menahem), had told Herod as a boy that he would some day become king of the Jews. Whatever the reason, Herod treated the Essenes tolerantly, and exempted them, in accordance with their principles, from the oath of loyalty.

THE REBUILDING OF THE TEMPLE

Herod's public announcement that he proposed to rebuild the Jerusalem temple seems to have caught most people unawares, although it is probable that he had had prior discussions with the high priest and his associates. While he avowedly looked upon the erection of a new temple as an act of piety in honour of God, there can be little doubt that his main motive was political. He hoped thereby to win popular praise and to establish more firmly his claim to be a legitimate king. The existing temple was almost five hundred years old, and, apart from its increasing maintenance costs, its sixth-century architecture may have seemed very old-fashioned to a ruler whose tastes were formed by the Hellenistic Age.

Herod was astute enough not to offend Jewish religious sensibilities needlessly, and he must have taken counsel with Jewish leaders regarding building plans and procedures. After elaborate preparations, including the training of 1,000 priests as artisans, the work began in 20–19 BC.[18] We do not know what parts or materials from the old temple were utilized in the new one. The sanctuary itself, built solely by priests, was completed in one and a half years. This stage of the rebuilding was celebrated with appropriate sacrifices. The rest of the construction (retaining walls, courts, porticoes, gates, etc) was carried out by 10,000 skilled workmen, and required eight years to finish. John 2:20 refers to a building span for the temple of forty-six years, and Josephus (*Ant* xx, 219) suggests that the work was completed only in 64 AD, and that its completion made 18,000 men idle. These references to the prolongation of the construction must refer to supplementary or decorative activites, and not to the main structures of the temple area. Josephus claims that Herod's resources paid the entire cost of the new temple, but this may mean only that no special taxes were levied, and it does not preclude a considerable contribution from Herod's personal fortune.

No attempt will be made here to describe Herod's temple,[19] but the sources of our information about it can be noted. The archaeological data, while important, are meagre,[20] and we have to rely almost exclusively on literary sources. In addition to a few details in Philo and the NT, these are the writings of Josephus (*War* I, 401; V, 184–247; *Ant* XV, 391–425) and the Mishnah (*Middoth* – literally 'measurements' of the temple as it was before 70 AD). Other tractates of the Mishnah supply various traditions about temple usages, e.g., *Shekalim* (the temple dues), *Tamid* (the twice-daily burnt offering), etc. When the literary data are assembled, certain differences between the accounts in Josephus and the Mishnah become apparent, and the resolution of these is not easy. Josephus, who had served as a priest in Herod's temple, eulogized it succinctly: 'The expenditure devoted to this work was incalculable, its magnificence never surpassed' (*War* I, 401).

Herod's family life

Herod, as Josephus observed (*War* I, 431), enjoyed prosperity in the public domain, but the very reverse in his own home. His family troubles were the result partly of his marriages, of which he had ten,[21] and partly of his ambition, as a kind of parvenu, to become accepted in influential Jewish circles. The marriages meant that the king was involved in the affairs of numerous families, and the tensions at the court resulting from the making and breaking of the royal alliances can easily be imagined. Josephus refers to the cabal (*suntagma*) of women at court who created tumults (*War* I, 568). One of these was Alexandra, daughter of the high priest Hyrcanus II and mother of Mariamme I whom Herod married; and another was Herod's sister, Salome (who survived her brother, dying c 9–12 AD). It was ambition that led Herod to marry into the Hasmonean family in 37 BC. This was, of course, an arranged marriage, and, while the king seems to have had a genuine affection for Mariamme, she, as a member of a well-established line, never seems to have really loved her upstart husband.

While it will serve no useful purpose to reproduce here the details, which Josephus supplies, of Herod's domestic adversities, we shall note briefly what happened to various individuals in the course of Herod's life.

Aristobulus III, brother of Mariamme, who had been appointed high priest 37–36 BC, alarmed Herod by the favourable reception he received, and the king contrived to have him drowned at Jericho.

Joseph, the husband of Herod's sister Salome, was accused of irregular relations with Mariamme and killed without a trial.

Hyrcanus II, the former high priest, was, as earlier noted, put to death c 30 BC on a trumped-up charge of planning to usurp the throne.

Mariamme was accused of unfaithfulness to the king, and, when the matter was presented to a council of Herod's friends, she was condemned to death c 29 BC (Josephus offers two accounts of this: *War* I, 438–44; *Ant* XV, 202–39).

In 28 BC, when Herod was ill, Alexandra, Mariamme's mother, tried to seize power and was put to death.

Fifteen years or so now passed in relative quiet, and then the next round of troubles began, centring on three of Herod's sons: Antipater, a son by Doris of Jerusalem, Herod's first wife; and Alexander and Aristobulus, sons by Mariamme I. Between Antipater and his half-brothers there was little love lost.

Alexander and Aristobulus were the next victims, being calumniated by both Antipater and Salome. It was suggested that these young men planned to oust Herod from the throne, and, despite a trip to Rome, c 12 BC, which resulted in a temporary reconciliation of father and sons, the mischief had been done, and Alexander was subsequently accused of planning to kill Herod. The trial at Berytus was something of a farce, but the death sentence imposed on both sons was carried out at Sebaste in 7–6 BC. When it was learned that many army leaders were sympathetic to Mariamme's sons, 300 of them were also put to death.

Antipater, at one time high in Herod's esteem and actually designated his successor in one of his wills, was the next victim. He was accused of plotting to poison the king, and after a somewhat protracted trial, during which the case actually came before Augustus, he was executed in 4 BC and buried in Hyrcania.

Five days later Herod himself died (March 4 BC), apparently from cancer.[22]

Herod in retrospect

Josephus refers to Herod as a tyrant (e.g., *War* II, 84), meaning, we may presume, an absolute ruler unlimited by law. If Herod had been a benevolent tyrant, Josephus might have viewed him differently, but in fact Herod was largely a law unto himself. Like many rulers through the centuries, he loved public recognition, the pleasures of pomp, and the exercise of power, and these point to his human weaknesses, but the charges that he was irreligious, unjust, cruel, given to excessive punishment, and murderous are a damning indictment of his character and performance (*Ant* XVI, 402; XVII, 191, 201, 304–10). The paranoia from which he suffered in his later years did nothing to improve these moral deficiences (*Ant* XVI, 259–60).

If Herod reflected on his life as the years closed in on him, he must have been a disappointed man. True, he had maintained public order, and he could view with some pride both the buildings he had erected and the employment he had created for countless artisans. His family, however, with the exception of his sister Salome, can only have been a constant source of concern and frustration to him. The fact that in his last will his kingdom was distributed among three of his sons indicates that only by this act of political madness could some semblance of family peace be maintained. His greatest failures lay in the refusal of most of his subjects to treat him as a legitimate king, and in his inability to persuade the majority of the Jews to accept political subordination to Rome.

We can hardly leave Herod without reference to a singularly important event which occurred near the end of his life. According to the New Testament the birth of Jesus took place in the time of Augustus, during the reign of Herod, in Judea (Matt 2:1; Lk 1:5; 2:1–7). While this is partisan evidence, in the absence of other data it is commonly accepted as a statement of fact. This birth must have passed unnoticed except among the family and friends, but from it were to flow consequences which no one at the time could possibly have anticipated.

EPILOGUE[23]

After Herod's death Salome and her husband Alexas summoned the soldiers and the people of Jericho to an assembly in the amphitheatre, where Ptolemy, the king's minister of finance, read the latest version of the royal will.[24] Archelaus, as the chief beneficiary, was charged with taking the will to Augustus in Rome for ratification. Then followed preparations for the funeral, a very impressive occasion, which ended in Herodium where the burial took place. Subsequently there was serious trouble with malcontents in Judea, and, before order was restored, 3,000 Jews perished in the fighting. Archelaus and a large party of supporters then felt free to go to Rome.

When Augustus had received all the necessary papers and information about Judea, he proceeded to call a council to deal with Palestine's future. Two sessions of the council were held, at which various speakers and delegations were heard. A few days after the second meeting the emperor announced his decision. Essentially it followed the wishes of Herod, as expressed in his last will, except that Archelaus was to be ethnarch, not king. Roughly half of Herod's territory (Judea, Idumea, Samaria) now came under Archelaus; his brother Antipas, who had been designated chief heir in Herod's third will, and who had opposed Archelaus's claims in Rome, was made tetrarch of Galilee and Perea; while Philip, whose mother was Cleopatra of Jerusalem, was made tetrarch of Batanea and the surrounding regions. Herod's kingdom, and indeed the state which the Hasmoneans had earlier created, was now shattered beyond repair. An irony in this situation was that most of the Jewish population of Palestine was now to be governed by two men whose father, Herod, was an Idumean, and whose mother came from Samaria.

While Augustus in Rome was dealing with the disposition of Herod's kingdom, the political situation in Palestine was going from bad to worse. After Archelaus had sailed from italy, there was a breakdown in public order, and Varus, legate of Syria, who had come to Judea in answer to Archelaus's earlier appeal, took some punitive action and then returned to Syria. But the situation continued to deteriorate, and Varus had to come south again, bringing with him two legions with their auxiliaries. This time it required considerable military effort to pacify the country once more. When the legate went back to Syria, he left a legion behind him in Jerusalem to maintain peace.

The situation in Judea at the end of the first century BC did not augur well for the future. General dislike of the Romans, the ruthlessness and insensitivity too commonly found in the local representatives of Roman power, stubborn resistance to many of the features of Graeco-Roman culture, unrealistic nationalistic aspirations, fanatical allegiance to traditional religious values and customs – all these were present in varying degrees in Judea in 4 BC. They constituted the tinder for the political and religious brush-fires which were to break out from time to time. The ministry of Jesus and the growth of the early Christian Church do not seem to have appreciably affected either this situation or the general direction in which the Palestinian Jews were moving. Two major confrontations between the Jews and the Romans – the rebellions of 66–70 and 132–5 AD – were many years away, but when they occurred, much of what was most precious in the life of Israel perished.

PART THREE

LITERATURE, 200–4 BC

IX

THE SCHOLARLY AND
PIETISTIC LITERARY TRADITIONS
AND EARLY
SCRIPTURAL EXPOSITION

THE SCHOLARLY TRADITION

Ben Sira

Ben Sira (Jesus the son of Sirach; Ecclesiasticus) is the longest literary product of Israel's wisdom movement (see pp 61–2). Its prologue, written in 132 BC by the author's grandson, who relates why, when, and where he translated his grandfather's book from Hebrew to Greek, supplies the principal evidence for dating Ben Sira and his work c 180 BC. This date is favoured because the work cannot be earlier than Nehemiah's time (49:13), nor later than the Maccabean struggle, to which there is no clear reference in these 51 chapters. The book in some respects is similar to Proverbs in that it presents a good deal of prudential advice on how to cope with the problems of life, but it deals with a wider range of topics than does Proverbs, stretching from bringing up children (30:1–13) to propriety in mourning for the dead (38:16–23). On the whole the treatment of the themes is sensible and moderate. The admirable little essay on forgiving one's neighbour (27:30 to 28:7) anticipates Jesus' words in Matt 6:14–15. While Ben Sira must have been indebted to current Jewish traditions, and perhaps also to aphoristic writers in the Greek world, his book is essentially his own work and it bears the stamp of a single personality. It is difficult to detect any orderly scheme in the arrangement of the material, and this tempts one to conclude that these proverbs, essays, etc were brought together haphazardly. Some think that chapters 1–23 may have been collected first, and chapters 24–50, 51, added at a later date.[1]

Anything we say about Ben Sira as a person has to be inferred from his book. A Palestinian layman, probably from Jerusalem, he was a devout man, as his prayers, meditations, and hymns testify (18:1–14; 23:1,4–6; 36:1–17; 39:12–35; etc), and he was a sincere participant in the temple cultus and firm supporter of the priesthood (7:29–31; 34:18–20; 38:9–11; etc). But he was also a scholar (or scribe, *sopher*), and as such he would have been familiar with the laws and traditions of Israel. The use of 'my son' in some of his discourses (2:1; 3:17; etc) and the one reference to 'my school' (*beth midrash*, 51:23) support the conclusion that he was a teacher. The well-known passage (38:24 to 39:11) in which he exalts the work of a scribe over that of craftsmen (the latter, he concedes, 'keep stable the fabric of the world') reflects Ben Sira's view of the importance of his own vocation, and at the same time serves as his epitaph.

The following aspects of Ben Sira's teaching call for a brief comment. 1 / If our date for Ben Sira is correct, it is probable that there is an apologetic interest behind much that he has to say. At the beginning of the second century Hellenistic culture had surrounded Judea for over one hundred years, and Jewish values and the Jewish way of life were being challenged as never before. Ben Sira was undoubtedly aware of this, and he tried to present Israel's traditional religion and ethic in such a way as to show that only in loyalty to her received culture could Israel find peace and strength. The 'ungodly men who have forsaken the law of the Most High' (41:8) must be a reference to Jews whose faith had buckled under the secular pressure of the age (cf 2:12–14; 30:19; 42:1–2).

2 / In contrast to both Proverbs and Qoheleth, Ben Sira is more nationalistic in the sense that his basic concern is the well-being of Israel. He recognizes the gifts of God to all men, and he allows that these include knowledge and the law of life (if this is the point of 17:1–14; cf 10:19). Similarly we read in 18:13 that 'the compassion of the Lord is for all living beings.' It is also undeniable that most of Ben

Sira's ethical advice, while directed primarily to Jews, relates to the common situations of all men. Nevertheless it is Ben Sira's view that the divine Wisdom eventually made her dwelling-place in Zion (24:8–12; 36:13). Israel is the Lord's own portion (17:17), and it is the famous men of Israel who are celebrated in 44:1 to 50:24. Moreover, when the Gentile world is specifically alluded to, the references tend to be negative (36:7–9; 48:18–21; 49:5–6; 50:25–6). Our author's main concern is 'that peace may be in our days in Israel' (50:23).

3 / Ben Sira's use of the term 'wisdom' is equivocal, and in a given case it is often difficult to determine which particular meaning he wishes us to attach to it. In many instances wisdom is the expertness for dealing intelligently with day-to-day human situations, and the young can learn it by listening to their elders (6:18,32–6). Ben Sira himself claims to have poured out such wisdom (50:27).

Another facet of Ben Sira's concept of wisdom belongs to the tradition of Pro 8:22–31, where wisdom, as the first of the Lord's creations, is almost personified. Thus Ben Sira holds that 'Wisdom was created before all things' (1:4). Thereafter she appears to have had a semi-independent existence, although she was eventually ordered to 'make your dwelling in Jacob' (24:8). 'In the holy tabernacle I ministered before him, and so I was established in Zion' (24:10).

This almost metaphysical view of wisdom is given a less abstract form by Ben Sira when he associates wisdom with the Law. The Law has now become a tutor in the wisdom of God. 'If you desire wisdom, keep the commandments' (1:26). 'Reflect on the statutes of the Lord ... and your desire for wisdom will be granted' (6:37). 'He who holds to the Law will obtain wisdom' (15:1); 'the Law which Moses commanded us ... fills men with wisdom' (24:23–4; cf 21:11; 39:1–8).

4 / It is of interest that in an age which was beginning to have some ideas about the resurrection of the dead (as in Dan 12:1–3), Ben Sira's views on death remain largely traditional. The praise of the Lord ceases when one goes to Sheol or Hades (17:27–8). Death is the inevitable end of life (14:17–19; 38:21–3; 41:1–4); and when man dies he can expect to inherit only the worms of the grave (10:11).

5 / After Ben Sira's rather sombre view of the meaning of death for the individual, it is refreshing to find that he can offer a prayer in 36:1–17 which is essentially an expression of hope for the future blessedness of

Israel. In these verses it is the Lord who is to act against the nations, and one result of the divine intervention will be the return of all the exiles of Jacob to their inheritance in Palestine. Although it is to be an earth-centred restoration, there is something almost unearthly about it, for the temple will be filled with the glory of the Lord (cf Ezek 42: 4–5).

The growth of the oral law

While oral tradition can scarcely be termed literature, in the present instance 'the traditions of the elders' (Matt 15:2; Mk 7:3), while originally oral, became the foundation of a later but very important body of Jewish literature (Mishnah, Tosephta, Talmuds), and it seems appropriate to treat its early stages very briefly here.

As we have seen in chapter 4 (p 53), the acceptance of the Torah as an authoritative law for Israel carried with it the necessity of studying its text in order to understand its full meaning and implications. Obviously there must have been oral traditions in Israel relevant to both ethics and cultic practices long before 400 BC, but, once the Torah was accepted, tradition tended to focus on the interpretation of its laws. Ben Sira is an important witness to this growth of scribal tradition. There were in his time schools for instructing the disciples of scholars (51:23). Scholars are given an impressive encomium in 39:1–11 (cf 8:8–9), and their role in the community is cited in 21:16b–17 and implied in 38:33. Ben Sira's book is probably a good example of one kind of teaching that went on in the scribal schools. When later in this century the Pharisees emerge as a party in Palestine, Josephus reports of them: 'The Pharisees passed on to the people certain regulations handed down by the fathers and not recorded in the laws of Moses' (Ant XIII, 297).

The rabbis of a later age, whose work was enshrined in the Mishnah, recorded in the tractate Aboth 1.1–18 some of their beliefs regarding the early stages of this oral tradition.[2] In Aboth 1.1 the men of the Great Synagogue are described as the successors of the prophets. Nothing is really known about such a Synagogue, but it is a reasonable supposition that Ezra and his contemporaries constituted in fact a kind of school for the study and teaching of the Torah. The reference to Simeon the Just as a survivor of the Great Synagogue is probably to Simeon II, to whom Ben Sira refers (50:1–21), and the saying attributed to him in *Aboth* 1.2 could be authentic. That the Jewish tradition had nothing to report about the century between Ezra and Simeon II is rather surprising. The next scholar mentioned in *Aboth* is Antigonus of Soko, a pupil of Simeon (1.3), and after him are the five pairs (*zugoth*) of scholars who exercised joint leadership in the principal rabbinical court or school (*Aboth* 1.4–12), from Jose, son of Joezer and Jose, son of Johanan (c 160 BC), to Hillel and Shammai (c 30 BC to 10 AD). Of these ten scholars, Nittai the Arbelite (*Aboth* 1.6) was a contemporary of John Hyrcanus; Simeon, son of Shetah (*Aboth* 1.8), lived in the time of Alexander Jannaeus; and Shemaiah and Abtalon (*Aboth* 1.10) are probably the Pharisees Pollion and Samaias (Sameas), contemporary with Herod (*Ant* XV, 3, 370).³ Hillel and Shammai (*Aboth* 1.12–15) founded somewhat distinctive schools of thought, and there was considerable scholastic controversy between the two groups.

A few examples will illustrate the nature of the Shammai-Hillel disputations. Take, for instance, the Shema (Deut 6:4–9): in what physical posture should it be recited? Against the school of Shammai, the school of Hillel held that each man should say it in his own way (M *Berakoth* 1.3). Regarding the benediction on the Sabbath: should it be pronounced first over the day and then over the wine? or vice versa? The school of Hillel favoured the latter (M *Berakoth* 8.1). Or take Deut 22:9, which prohibits the sowing of a vineyard with two kinds of seed. The question arises: What is a vineyard? The school of Shammai claimed that, if a man plants a row of five vines, this counts as a vineyard, but the school of Hillel said that it is not a vineyard unless there are two rows (M *Kelaim* 4.5). Apropos of Sabbath observance, the school of Shammai claimed, against the school of Hillel, that the dyeing of certain specified items must not be begun on Friday unless it can be finished by sunset (M *Shabbath* 1.5). Regarding the abstention from lighting a fire on the Sabbath, with the concomitant prohibition of sabbath cooking, if a stove has been heated before the onset of the Sabbath, what can one place upon it? The school of Hillel argued, against the school of Shammai, for both water and cooked food (M *Shabbath* 3.1).

Since the Torah contains 613 laws, all of them subject to the kind of careful scrutiny illustrated above, it is clear that Jewish scholars had abundant material to work on, and that by the end of the first century BC they had reached a considerable level of sophistication in dealing with the biblical text. It came to be believed, we do not know how early, that reputable scholars had the authority to introduce ordinances that were essentially extensions of laws found in the Torah. Occasionally some of the scholarly enactments were at variance with the Law, as when Hillel devised the legal fiction called *Prosbul* (M *Shebiith* 10.3–9), which effectively negated the law for the release of debtors found in Deut 15:1–3.

THE PIETISTIC TRADITION

The synagogue

The Jewish piety, which expressed itself in various literary forms which we shall examine presently, is also seen in the creation and development of the synagogue. If, therefore, we are concerned with the pietistic tradition in Judaism, some reference here to the synagogue appears to be desirable.

In the Graeco-Roman world the Jewish synagogue was a unique religious and social institution. Curiously, it is the NT that offers some of the earliest literary references to its existence. We learn from Lk 4:16,31–8 that there were synagogues in Nazareth and Capernaum in Jesus' day, and we know that Paul's activities led him to speak in synagogues in various eastern Roman provinces (Damascus, Acts 9:19–20; Salamis on Cyprus, 13:5; Antioch of Pisidia, 13:14; etc). We also learn from the NT that on the sabbath day there was a gathering of Jews in the synagogue, that portions of the Law and the Prophets were read,[4] and that the Scripture readings were followed by a discourse by someone thought to be suitable (Lk 4:16–22,31–8; Acts 13:14–16; cf 14:1; 17:1–3; 18:4; 19:8).

The origins and early history of the synagogue are not known, and anything said about them is conjectural. From the NT references we infer that the synagogue was a well established institution in the first century AD, as Philo[5] and Josephus (*Life* 277) also testify, and thus we assume that it must have come into existence in an earlier age. Greek inscriptions from Egypt point to synagogues there in the third century BC, and Josephus alludes to a synagogue in Antioch (Syria) in the early second century BC (*War* VII, 44). Since the synagogues referred to above in Acts served the religious needs of Diaspora Jews, very few of whom could ever get to the temple in Jerusalem, and since after the loss of the temple in 70 AD the synagogue remained the only focal point (apart from the home) for Jewish religious ceremonies, it is reasonable to conclude that the earliest synagogues arose among Jews of the dispersion. Such Jews would find in a local sabbath gathering both fellowship and an incentive to remain loyal to traditional Jewish customs. Probably they prayed to the Lord, even though they were in a foreign land (as Jeremiah had earlier said they should, 29:12–13), and if they had access to sacred writings, these were probably read and even studied. Such assemblies were essentially private groups, and the precise activities doubtless varied from community to community. Eventually Jews living in the homeland, especially those some distance from Jerusalem, adopted this sabbath custom, and we may surmise that from the second century BC on the Pharisees had a share in developing in Judea a kind of standard sabbath procedure for the synagogue, so that it slowly became a community institution. The Babylonian Talmud records the tradition that some of the synagogue's blessings and prayers go back to the men of the Great Synagogue, i.e., to about the time of Ezra (*Berakoth* 33b). As matters turned out, the synagogue – and it was often associated with a school[6] – was one of Judaism's most effective devices for maintaining its religious values in a world that seemed to be increasingly hostile to it. It is little wonder that Josephus thought that its beginnings went back to Moses (*Apion* II, 175; cf Acts 15:21).

Baruch (1 Baruch)

Baruch, the amanuensis of the prophet Jeremiah (Jer 36:1–32), became a figure of some importance in later Jewish thought as the supposed author of various books. 1 Baruch of the Apocrypha, which we are now considering, is one of these; 2 Baruch, the Syriac Apocalypse of Baruch, and 3 Baruch, the Greek Apocalypse of Baruch, are two others.

1 Baruch, extant in Greek, consists of three parts. As these sections appear to be independent of one another, they will be dealt with separately.

1 / The first section is in prose, 1:1 to 3:8. The introduction, 1:1–14, describes a document written by Baruch in Babylon in the fifth year (possibly after 587 BC). After the scroll was read to those in exile in Babylon, it was sent with a gift of money to Jehoiakim, the high priest in Jerusalem. The text of the scroll, 1:15–3:8, contains a confession of the sins that Israel and Judah have committed over the generations, followed by two prayers for forgiveness. The introduction is really an attempt to give verisimilitude to the description of Baruch's presence in Babylonia, but a number of details, which need not be cited here, make us suspicious of the historicity of the narrative. The date of this section can be established only on very general grounds. The reference to Belshazzar in 1:11–12 suggests familiarity with Dan 5, while the phraseology of 1:15 to 2:17 shows striking resemblances to Dan 9:4–19. These considerations suggest a date after 165 BC for this part of Baruch. The supposition of some scholars that the 'Chaldeans' of 1:2 is a veiled reference to the Romans, and that the book relates to the Jewish war of 66–70 AD, seems to this writer far-fetched.

2 / The second section, 3:9 to 4:4, a didactic poem in praise of true wisdom, is reminiscent of similar material in Pro 8, Job 28, and Ben S 24. This wisdom is in the Law, 'the book of the commandments of God,' and 'all who hold her fast will live' (4:1). There is almost nothing in the poem that can be used to establish its date. The reference to Israel being 'in the land of your enemies' (3:10) is probably a general allusion to the Jewish Diaspora, which in the Hellenistic period became quite extensive. The author may have taken the identification of wisdom and the Law from Ben Sira (cf Ben S 24:23–5). If so, we can date him somewhat later than Ben Sira.

3 / The third section, 4:5 to 5:9, is a group of poems comprising both laments over Jerusalem and songs of comfort. Jerusalem has had great sorrow, but her desolator will be brought to ruin, and the exiles will return from the east and the west, rejoicing in the glory of God. The language of this section is in places very close to that of Deutero-Isaiah, but it offers no real clue about the historical situation out of which the poems arose. It is often claimed that 4:36 to 5:9 is indebted

to Pss Sol 11:1–7, but this writer is not impressed with these resemblances and cannot accept the inferences drawn from them. The absence of references to the building of the temple or to the repairing of Jerusalem's walls may indicate an age later than Nehemiah and Ezra.

It is commonly held that all three parts of Baruch were written in Hebrew, and, as there is no clear indication of another locale, that their provenance was Judea. The book was translated into Greek probably before the Christian era began.

Esther

Esther, a beautiful Jewess, becomes the queen of the Achaemenid king Xerxes (*Khshayarsha*, Heb *'hashwerosh*, Eng *Ahasuerus*, 486–465 BC). About five years later, when the king's vizier, Haman, launches a scheme to destroy all the Jews in Persia (theoretically this would include those in Palestine), Esther is able to act on her people's behalf, and, when the day appointed for the extinction of the Jews comes, they are authorized to defend themselves. This they do so effectively that over 75,000 Persians perish in the fighting (the Jewish casualties are not recorded). Esther and her uncle Mordecai, who had earlier replaced Haman as vizier, send a letter to all Jewry within Persia to enjoin them to celebrate this deliverance in an annual festival, to be called Purim, on the fourteenth day of Adar (in some centres on the fifteenth as well).

The Book of Esther is a good example of the Hebrew short story, such as we find elsewhere in the books of Ruth, Jonah, Tobit, Judith, and Susanna. The tale is well told, and the author manifests a sense for dramatic effect as well as irony. One of the weaknesses is that the motivation for some of the actions is not very convincing. The readiness of Xerxes, for instance, to condone civil strife by promulgating Haman's anti-Jewish measures is not readily intelligible from what the book of Esther tells us.

Esther is primarily concerned with commending the observance of the feast of Purim by the Jews, and it is important for its account of the origin of this festival. The question at once arises of how reliable the story is as a record of historical events. The general view of critical scholars is that the book is an historical romance. There are so many items in the story that tax the historical sense (e.g., we know from Herodotus VII, 61, 114 that Xerxes' queen was Amestris) that no other conclusion is possible. This view does not preclude the belief that there may be a genuinely historical kernel behind the book. For instance it has been theorized that some Jews in Susa or elsewhere in Persia may have been saved from disaster by the influence of a highly placed Jewess, and that the Jewish community celebrated its deliverance by a feast, possibly adapting a local Persian festival for their purposes. As the actual incident receded into the past, the basic tale became embellished with various imaginative additions, and eventually the book of Esther as we have it emerged.

If Purim originated among the eastern Jews, it must have taken time for the festival and the book to become known in Palestine. There is no reference to any person prominent in the Esther story in Ben Sira's list of famous men in 44–50, which must indicate that the book was unknown in the circles in which Ben Sira moved. The first literary reference to the Esther story is in 2 Mac 15:36, which alludes to 'the day of Mordecai.' As 2 Maccabees is thought to date from the first century BC, Esther may have become known in Palestine only in the latter half of the second century BC. The proposition that Esther should be included in the third division of Israel's Scriptures (the Writings) appears to have met with some opposition, the chief objection being that the feast of Purim is not found in the Law of Moses, which, by definition, was complete.[7] When this difficulty was overcome, Esther's place in the canon was assured, and in the Jewish community it became one of the most cherished books of the scriptures. One indication of importance is the fact that it is the only biblical book to be given special treatment in the Mishnah, where the tractate *Megillah* deals with the time and manner of its public reading.

The Book of Esther shares with the Song of Solomon the distinction of being an essentially secular work. It nowhere mentions the name of God,[8] a defect which was remedied by the Greek translators who proceeded to add some material not found in the Hebrew text in an effort to supply a specific religious interest wanting in the canonical Esther.[9] What has made Esther such a favourite in the Jewish community is that, despite its lack of a formal religious orientation, it has served to keep alive the hope that Israel cannot under any circumstances be annihilated by the Gentile world. It was only in the Hellenistic and Roman periods that Jews first became aware of tensions between themselves and their environment,[10] tensions due partly to the unassimilable character of most Jews. The Jews tended to be isolated culturally as well as religiously from their neighbours, and in this situation the Book of Esther seemed to speak directly to them. The story could be taken as a kind of allegory: no matter how dreadful the situation in which the Jews found themselves, they knew that in the end the Haman confronting them would meet his downfall. As for the lack of specific religious details in Esther, it need only be said that in Israel there has always been a close connection between the nationalistic spirit and the religious spirit. The perpetuation of the Jewish community was a basic condition for the survival of the worship of the Lord.

The Additions to the Book of Esther

The popularity of the Book of Esther led to some additions being made to the story at a fairly early date, principally to give it a religious dimension which, as we have seen, the original Hebrew narrative lacks. If some or all of these passages were intended for the Hebrew text, they did not prove acceptable, but they were added to the Greek translation. No less than five sizeable blocks of text (a total of 107 or 108 verses) were added to the Greek story at points thought to be suitable. The Greek text of Esther which Josephus used seems to have had most of these additions in it (*Ant* XI, 184–296). When Jerome made his Latin translation of the scriptures (to become known as the Vulgate), he could not find these Septuagint additions to Esther in the Hebrew, and he therefore took them out of their Septuagint contexts and placed them in a group at the end of Esther. In the RSV these selections are presented in the order in which they appear in the Greek Bible, but the numbering is that of the Vulgate and the KJV.

The purpose of some of the additions is, as suggested above, to give the story of Esther a religious orientation. All of the additions except 13:1–7 mention God ('God' or 'Lord' appears nine times in 10:4–13), and two of them, 13:8–17 and 14:3–19, are prayers to God uttered, respectively, by Mordecai and Esther. On the other hand, two of the additions, 13:1–7 and 16:1–24, purport to be the texts of royal decrees, presumably to give an air of authenticity to the narrative.

There are a number of discrepancies between the additions and the Hebrew text, and these appear to nullify the arguments of those scholars who claim that the additions are part of the original Hebrew story. For instance, in Est 2:16–23 Mordecai discovers the plot against the king in or after the seventh year of his reign, whereas in Additions 11:2; 12:1–6 it is implied that the plot occurs in the second year. In Est 6:1–11 Mordecai is rewarded for his discovery of the plot some time afterwards, but in Additions 12:1–5 the reward comes immediately. In Est 3:1 Haman is an Agagite, but in Additions 16:10 a Macedonian. In Est 3:1–6 Haman's animosity towards Mordecai is the result of the latter's refusal to bow down to him, but in Additions 12:1–6 it is because of the incident involving the two eunuchs. And so on. Such differences would have been obvious to any alert Jewish scholar, and their existence must have been a factor in the Jewish decision not to recognize the Septuagint additions as part of the authentic text of Esther.

The Book of Esther displays a rather negative attitude to the Gentile world, and the additions do not substantially change this (10:8–12). The tension between the Jews and their Gentile environment is reflected in 13:3–5.

The colophon of the additions (11:1) indicates that the Greek translation of Esther, done by one Lysimachus, was brought to Egypt in the fourth year of Ptolemy (Ptolemy XII?) and Cleopatra, which indicates a date c 76 BC.

Judith

The books of Judith and Esther have in common the fact that both record how Israel was saved from disaster, and in each case through the intervention of a Jewish woman. Their chief difference is that Judith, in contrast to the secularism of Esther, is a patently religious narrative.

Judith falls into two sections, 1–7 and 8–16. The first part supplies the alleged historical background. Nebuchadnezzar, king of Assyria, planned a war to conquer all of western Asia and selected his chief general, Holofernes, to carry out the campaign. Eventually Holofernes came into Palestine and encamped in the plain of Esdraelon, near Dothan. In the meantime the Israelites determined to resist Holofernes, and the town of Bethulia (unidentified, but the geography points to Dothan or Shechem) was chosen as the king-pin of the Hebrew defence. When Holofernes learned that Israel was prepared to oppose him, he was angry, and was little mollified when Achior, leader of the Ammonite contingent in his army, gave him a lecture on Israel's history, ending with the astonishing claim that Israel's God would look after his people, provided they fell into no sin. Achior was lucky that all that happened to him was to be handed over to Bethulia, where it was presumed that presently he would suffer the same fate that was soon to befall the town. Holofernes then went ahead with his plans and besieged Bethulia, whose inhabitants now began to suffer all the discomforts and misery of siege warfare.

Chapter 8 introduces us to Judith, a beautiful, wealthy, and pious widow of Bethulia, who was astounded that the rulers of the town, in reaponse to complaints from the citizens, had vowed that, unless the Lord God relieved them within five days, they would surrender to the enemy. Judith rebuked their lack of faith, but went on to assure them, without revealing any details, that the Lord would indeed deliver the city through her hand.

Judith and her maid, after careful preparations, then left Bethulia and, on coming to the Assyrian lines, were taken to the headquarters of Holofernes. The Jewish woman echoed what Achior had earlier said, that it was Israel's sins that would betray them, and promised that, when they sinned, as hunger and thirst would force them to, she would tell Holofernes and he would then have the victory he longed for. For three days Judith was Holofernes' guest, during which time she made a practice of leaving the camp temporarily each night to say her prayers. The fourth day was crowned by a private dinner for Holofernes and Judith. The general, however, who had drunk too much wine, dozed off, and his guest siezed the opportunity she had apparently been looking for and decapitated the sleeping man. The head was put in the food bag, and Judith and her maid then left the camp, ostensibly for the usual prayers, but in fact to go straight back to Bethulia. Their arrival there marked the turning-point in the siege. In the morning the Assyrians' discovery of Judith's trick so demoralized them that the whole army withdrew in a panic, hotly pursued by Israel's forces. The Jews celebrated their deliverance with dance, song, and feasting, both in Bethulia and in Jerusalem, and in the capital there were special sacrifices in the temple. A finely constructed psalm of thanksgiving uttered by Judith is found in 16:2–17. After the excitement died down, Judith resumed her life in Bethulia, where, still a widow, she died at the age of 105.

The first part of the book is prolix and tedious, but, once the figure of Judith is introduced in chapter 8, the pace quickens, and we find ourselves caught up in a neat little plot, with the characters well drawn. Whether the author himself concocted the story, or whether he drew upon earlier material, it is impossible to say. As some glaring historical errors in the tale can be set right from the Hebrew Scriptures, it is quite possible that the author never intended his work to be a record of sober fact. In any case it cannot be accepted as history; it is a moral tale designed to teach religious truth. That there is a substratum of fact behind it, some tradition of a valorous deed performed by an Israelite woman (cf Jael in Judg 5:24–7) cannot be ruled out. But the real heart of the narrative is the character and performance of Judith. Her piety, reflected in her supererogatory fasting and mourning, her prayers, her strict observance of dietary laws (even in the Assyrian camp), as well as her readiness to act in a way appropriate to the situations in which she found herself, delineate the type of person whom the Lord favours and through whom his good purposes for Israel are advanced. The interest of the story centres quite naturally upon Israel, although it is noteworthy that it is a Gentile, Achior the Ammonite, who first warns Holofernes of the nature of the opposition he is confronting (5:5–21), and his point is presently confirmed by Judith herself (11:9–19). This same Achior later becomes a Jewish proselyte.

Judith appears to have been written at a time when a high priest headed the Jewish state, when the territory of Judea did not extend as far north as Galilee nor as far west as Jamnia, Azotus, and Ascalon, and when existing political conditions threatened Judea's security.

The unsettled age when Jonathan was high priest (c 150 BC) would appear to meet all these conditions.

Susanna and Bel and the Dragon

Reference was made in chapter 5 (pp 95–6) to a cycle of stories centring on Daniel, some of which now appear in Dan 1–6. Three other tales, Susanna, Bel, and the Dragon, found only in the later versions of the biblical Daniel, seem to come from the same source. In the Latin Vulgate these stand at the end of the canonical Daniel, as chapters 13 and 14. In the Greek manuscripts the position of Susanna varies: the Theodotion version uses it as a preface to the biblical material.

SUSANNA

Susanna is a compact and well told tale. Its background is the Jewish community in Babylonia, and its central figure is Susanna, the attractive wife of one Joakim, a much honoured citizen. Two elders, recently appointed as judges, conceived a passion for Joakim's wife, and, when she refused to yield to their desires, charged her before the court with immoral conduct with a young man. As both elders testified against Susanna, she, despite her protests of innocence, was condemned to death and was led off to execution. At this point Daniel enters the story. He heard Susanna's cry and was stirred by God to demand that the case be reopened. When it was, Daniel insisted upon examining the two elders separately, and, when he did so, he found their testimony to be in conflict. Thus Susanna was freed, and the two elders were put to death (cf Deut 19:15–9).

Apart from its merits as a story, Susanna seems to have some didactic overtones. It obviously illustrates the efficacy of prayer and God's care for the innocent. It is probable, too, that it is meant as a rebuke to a judicial system that had become too casual about the evidence of witnesses. This is a weakness to which judicial systems in most societies are prone, and it is of interest that Simeon, son of Shetah (c 80 BC), felt it necessary to urge: 'Examine the witnesses diligently and be cautious in your words, lest from them they learn to swear falsely' (M Aboth 1.9).

BEL AND THE DRAGON

This is an amalgam of two tales with few merits of any sort. The probable sources will not here concern us.

The story of Bel is simply a demonstration by Daniel that an idol, Bel, revered by the Babylonians in the time of Cyrus, was a lifeless man-made image, incapable of consuming food, and that the offerings made to it daily were in fact eaten by the priests and their families. Cyrus, when he was shown that this was the case, had the priests put to death and authorized Daniel to destroy the image.

The dragon episode is in part the tale of how Daniel put a large dragon, worshipped by the Babylonians, to death by feeding it a concoction of pitch, fat, and hair. The rest of the narrative is an inferior variant of Dan 6. The Babylonians, humiliated by these affronts to their religion, demanded that Daniel be handed over to them, and Cyrus felt obliged to accede to their demands. Daniel was then thrown into a den with seven lions. For six days nothing happened, but on the seventh day the prophet Habakkuk and a bowl of food were brought to Daniel from Judea by an angel. Later in the day when the king found that Daniel was still alive, he formally acknowledged Daniel's God, pulled Daniel out of the den, and put in his place the men who had tried to destroy him.

The purpose of Bel and the Dragon is obscure. It is doubtful that a Jew who was seriously thinking of adopting some form of paganism would have been put off by these fairy-tales, and devout pagans might well have taken offence at this travesty of their religion.

The Psalms of Solomon

The Psalms of Solomon are eighteen poems, probably written originally in Hebrew, but extant now only in a Greek translation thought to have been made before 70 AD. The Syriac version is believed to have been made from the Greek. As there is nothing in these psalms that has any relation to Solomon, the title may be an attempt to distinguish them from those ascribed to David, and to profit from the tradition that Solomon composed 1005 songs (1 Kgs 4:32). The heading of Ps 8 ('of the chief musician') and the presence of 'Selah' in 17:31 and 18:10 may indicate that some of them were put to cultic use.

If these psalms are not from one author, they are from a small group sharing a common religious tradition. The language and concepts are basically biblical, although as poems they are on the whole inferior to those in the canonical Psalter. Most of the types of poems which scholars have identified in the biblical Psalms are to be found here, but usually there is a mixture of types, the commonest being a combination of lament and hymn. There may be some literary relation between Ps 11 and Bar 4:36 to 5:9, but this is too detailed a matter to be discussed here.

The date of the Psalms of Solomon has to be determined from the internal evidence. There appear to be clear references to Pompey's attack on and capture of Jerusalem in 63 BC (2:1–3,20–3; 8:16–24; 17:8–10,13–15) and to the death of Pompey in Egypt in 48 BC (2:30–3). The tensions within the Jewish community between the pious and the sinners, involving pollution of the temple and altar (1:8; 2:3; 8:12–13,26), moral sins (4:1–15; 8:9–11,14; 12:4), and the establishment of a non-Davidic monarchy (17:5–8), seem to indicate the situation in Judea during and after the time of Alexander Jannaeus (103–76 BC). The imprecation on the wicked in 4:16–25, which suggests that their punishment is yet to come, could be an allusion to Jannaeus or his son Aristobulus II, as could Ps 12, whereas Ps 13 celebrates some improvement in the lot of the pious. A fair conclusion from these data is that the Psalms of Solomon belong to the first century BC, some as early as the time of Jannaeus, but, since there is no manifest allusion to Herod's accession, none as late as 37 BC.

Apart from the testimony they bear to a deep and sincere piety, a faith in a God to whom Israel (or the godly) can turn in times of distress (1:1; 2:24; etc), and whose praise is appropriate in the mouth of the righteous (3:1f; 5:1f; etc), these psalms are chiefly important for the light they shed on first-century BC Jewish eschatology.

1 / There is to be a return of the Diaspora (8:34; 9:1–2; 11:1–9; 17:28,50), which implies the hope of a better life for Israel here on this earth.

2 / A resurrection is considered desirable but not elaborated (3: 16; 14:7). In 3:13; 14:6 sinners do not share in this rising.

3 / As men have freedom of choice (9:7), they will find themselves eventually under the judgment of God (2:37–8; 15:13–14). The righteous will have life eternal (3:16; 13:9; 14:7; 15:5), but sinners can look forward only to Sheol, darkness and destruction (13:10; 14:6; 15:11–15).

4 / Ps 17:23–49 is a vivid description of a Davidic king whom God will raise up, and who will reign, apparently on earth, as the anointed one (vs 36; cf 18:6,8) in the days to come. This personage, made mighty by God's Holy Spirit, will purge Jerusalem, destroy the sinful Gentiles, judge the nations, and shepherd the flock of the Lord. The psalmist makes it clear that this anointed king is subordinate to the Lord himself (vs 38).

5 / The non-Hebrew world occupies a rather negative position in these psalms. The Gentiles are usually cast as real or potential oppressors of Israel (2:20; 7:6; 8:27; 17:27) or as servants of the Davidic king (17:32,34,38); in the new Israel there will be no aliens (17:31). The general view is that Israel is the object of the Lord's love (9:16): as verse 14:3 puts it: 'The portion and the inheritance of God is Israel.'

The Prayer of Manasseh

Manasseh, king of Judah (c 687–642 BC), is reported in both 2 Kgs 21:1–18 and 2 Chr 33:1–9 to have been a very wicked ruler, principally because of his support of non-Yahwistic religion. This, presumably, is why later rabbinical opinion, as recorded in the Mishnah, claimed that Manasseh would have no share in the world to come (*Sanhedrin* 10.2). It is 2 Chr 33:10–13, however, that supplies the additional information that Manasseh was taken by his Assyrian overlord to Babylon, where in his distress he repented of the evil he had done and prayed to God; God accepted his repentance and returned him to Jerusalem. The Chronicler later states that further details regarding Manasseh, including his prayer, are to be found in the 'Chronicles of the Seers' (2 Chr 33:18–20). It was doubtless this repentance of the king that led R. Judah to argue, against the majority, that Manasseh would have a share in the world to come (M *Sanhedrin* 10.2).

If the prayer to which the Chronicler alludes ever existed, it was lost along with the 'Chronicles of the Seers,' and to fill this gap a later

Jewish writer composed the Prayer of Manasseh now found in the Apocrypha. As a penitential psalm, it is a sincere expression of contrition, well constructed and consisely written, although not quite of the same calibre as the OT Ps 51. Verses 1–8 are the invocation, verses 9–10 the confession, verses 11–13 the entreaty, and verses 14–15 the ascription. Manasseh is not referred to in the text of the psalm, and the closest allusion to any specific sin is in verse 10 (RSV):

> I ... have done what is evil ...
> setting up abominations and
>   multiplying offenses.

It is thought that the author was a Palestinian Jew living after the time of the Chronicler (350–300 BC), probably in the second or first centuries BC. The evidence regarding the original language of the prayer is inconclusive, although we might expect a Jewish writer to use Hebrew. The earliest evidence for the prayer's existence is in the Syriac Didascalia (a Syrian church manual) of the third century AD. Later it found its way into some MSS of the Septuagint, where it was included among the hymns and odes appended to the Psalter.[11]

EARLY SCRIPTURAL EXPOSITION
(EXCLUDING THE DEAD SEA SCROLLS)

Jubilees

Jubilees, after an introductory chapter, offers an exposition of parts of the Torah from Gen 1 to Ex 14; the last chapter, 50, is based on Lev 25:8–17 and Ex 20:8–11. The author's method displays both targumic and midrashic traits,[12] and it may be assumed that the lore upon which he drew was current coin in those Jewish circles, probably Pharisaic, in which he moved. His work belongs, in a general way, to the same literary genre as the Testaments of the Twelve Patriarchs, the Genesis Apocryphon (from Qumran), and Enoch. The book takes its title from the author's method of presentation. Events are described as happening in a series of 'jubilees,' each of which comprises forty-nine years (seven units of seven years each). The period from the creation to the events on Mount Sinai is equated, in 50:4, with forty-nine jubilees, one week and two years. This is an arbitrary use of the term 'jubilee,' for in the tradition represented in Lev 25:8–17 the jubilee year is every fiftieth year. While the book says nothing about its author or compiler, it is generally held, mostly on the basis of the treatment of Levi (31–2; 45:16), that he was a levitical priest.

The more important features of Jubilees are noted below.

1 / Jubilees claims to be, in some sense, a revelation of God to Moses, although there is some ambiguity regarding the mode of the revelation. In the prologue and in 1:7,26 (cf 50:1) the Lord speaks directly to Moses and enjoins him to write down what he hears. But in 1:27 the Lord instructs the angel of the presence to write down the revelation for Moses (cf 50:6, 13); in 1:29 the angel of the presence takes the tables of the divisions of the years; and in 2:1 he speaks to Moses and tells him to 'write the complete history of the creation.' In any case it is of interest that some members of the Jewish community would tolerate a written supplement to the existing Law, and would ascribe to this supplement a divine origin.

2 / As we should expect, Jubilees presents us with traditional Jewish ideas and practices: the Law received by Moses from the Lord (Prologue 1:1), and seemingly related to the preexisting heavenly tablets (3:31; 6:17); the assignment of Levi to the priesthood (30:18; 32:1–3); the absolute necessity of observing both the Sabbath and circumcision (2:17–32; 50:6–13; 15:11–34; 16:14); the law against eating blood (6:12–14; 7:31); the separation of Israel from the Gentile world by neither eating with nor marrying them (20:4; 22:16, 20; 25:1–10; 30:7). A somewhat curious feature of Jubilees is that the patriarchs are represented as observing the Law. Noah and his sons kept the feast of Weeks, and then after a lapse of time Abraham revived the practice (6:17–19). And Abraham also began the celebration of *Sukkoth* (16:29–31).

In numerous cases the author expands the biblical material from some non-biblical source or sources: the twenty-two distinct acts of creation (1:1–16); the explanation of the law of purification after childbirth (3:8–14; cf Lev 12:2–5); the building of Babel (10:18–27); the war of Jacob and his sons against the Amorites (34:1–9; cf Gen 48:22); Esau's battle with Jacob (37:1 to 38:14; cf T Jud 9:1–8); the wreaths to be borne upon the head and the procession around the altar at *Sukkoth* (16:30–1; cf Lev 23:39–43); burning with fire for a woman who fornicates (20:4; cf Lev 21:9); the twelve kinds of wood which may be used for the altar fire (21:12–14; cf M *Tamid* 2.3, where any wood is acceptable save the vine and the olive); wine at Passover (49:6); abstinence from sexual intercourse on the Sabbath (50:8; cf M *Nedarim* 8:6); etc.

3 / The nature of Jubilees was such that it gave its author limited scope to express any eschatology he may have favoured. Apart from a reference in 1:29 to a future renewal of all creation, his views are found in chapter 23. Israel will experience many woes (vss 18–25), but a new era will be inaugurated by a renewal of Torah study (vss 26–31). There will be a gradual transformation of Hebrew society until human life extends to 1,000 years of peace and joy, and Israel's enemies will meet their judgment (vss 11,30). Verse 31 is obscure, but it may point to some post-mortem bliss apart from the body. The reference in 31:18 is probably to a descendant of Judah ruling over Israel, and need not refer, as R.H. Charles thinks, to a Messiah.

4 / Jubilees gives us another glimpse of the angelology and demonology of pre-Christian Judaism. Unlike the Book of Noah, there are no named angels: the description of angels is purely by function; there are angels of the presence, angels of sanctification, angels of the phenomena of nature, and guardian angels. The first two of these classes were created circumcised (15:27), and they were expected to observe the Sabbath (2:18). Over against this angelic world are the demons ('wicked spirits' in 10:3), whose aim is to seduce men (7:27; 10:1; 11:5; etc). Their chief is variously named: Beliar (1:20; 15:33), Mastema (10:8; 11:5, 11), and Satan (10:11; 23:29).

5 / To a pious man like the writer of Jubilees the calendar was important, for it was necessary to observe the religious festivals at their proper times, a point made in 49:14–15 with reference to Passover. The author's concern over the calendar was shared by all Jewish groups, including the author(s) of Enoch, chapters 72–82, as well as the Qumran community. His solution of the calendar problem was to advocate, as does Enoch 74:10–17, the adoption of a solar year of 364 days, or 52 weeks of 7 days each (6:29–38). If the months are to have 30 days each (cf 5:27), he does not indicate when the four additional days

are to be added to the year. Nor does he recognize, as does the Book of the Secrets of Enoch (14:1), that a solar year ought to have 365¼ days.

Date, language, and provenance / The outside dates for Jubilees are, on the one hand, 400–350 BC, when the Torah was accepted by the Jewish community, and on the other, whatever date we give to the fragments of Jubilees found in cave IV of Qumran. A more precise date within these limits has to be derived from the internal evidence of the book itself. The allusion to Israel's conquests (of Edom, 38:1–14; of Philistia, 24:28–32; of Shechem, 30:4–6) are thought to refer to the Maccabean wars under Simon and John Hyrcanus. The phrase used to describe Levi, 'priest of the Most High God' (32:1), can also designate the Hasmonean leaders (*Ant* XVI, 163; Assump M 6:1; T Levi 8:14). That no antagonism towards the Hasmoneans is in evidence may suggest, if we can assume that the author of Jubilees was a Pharisee, that he lived before John Hyrcanus broke with the Pharisees. The reference to the need to cover the pudenda (3:31) may be an attempt to discourage Jews from exercising naked in the Jerusalem gymnasium (1 Mac 1:14–15; 2 Mac 4:12–15; *Ant* XII, 241), and the allusion to some Jews who will not circumcise their sons (15:33) may also point to the Maccabean age. In short, the limited evidence favours a second-century BC date for Jubilees, probably in the latter half of the century.[13]

The finding of Hebrew fragments of Jubilees at Qumran would seem to indicate that the original language of the book was Hebrew. This Semitic text was the parent of a Greek version which, except for some fragments, is lost. A Latin version was made from the Greek, possibly in the fifth century AD, but only about one-quarter of it is extant. The Ethiopic version, which may belong to the sixth century, was also made from the Greek, and, as it survives in its entirety in mediaeval manuscripts, it is our primary source for the text of Jubilees.

The fragments of Jubilees found at Qumran and the affinities between Jubilees, the Zadokite documents, and the Genesis Apocryphon have led some scholars to conclude that Jubilees originated in the Qumran community (so Eissfeldt, pp 607–8). This theory, however, is too detailed to be discussed here. For the same reason we cannot examine the relation of Jubilees to the Jewish oral tradition, although it should be noted that J. Neusner in *The Rabbinic Traditions about the Pharisees before 70* virtually ignores Jubilees (III, 73, 77).

The Testaments of the Twelve Patriarchs

This work consists of twelve sections, each of which purports to be the deathbed speech of one of the sons of Jacob. These discourses all display essentially the same structure. The father (Reuben, Simeon, etc), knowing he is about to die (the age, when given, ranges from 114 to 137 years), calls his sons together and speaks to them. He relates something of his life: this is basically biblical, but it is usually expanded with Haggadic[14] additions. To this are added various admonishments and exhortations, and frequently a forecast of history and even some eschatology. The father then dies and his children dutifully bury him in Hebron.

The common pattern which the Testaments display favours the view that one person was responsible for the basic material of the present work. Further, the general contents identify the author as a pious Jew. The importance attached to the Law, the confession of sin, repentance, and a high moral standard confirm this inference. The author may be thought of as a Pharisee, but the sort of Pharisee who found Ben Sira a congenial spirit. Since 1948 it has been asked if he and his associates could have been members of the Qumran community. The parallels between the Qumran literature (especially the Zadokite documents) and the Testaments are quite striking, and have led some scholars to conclude that the whole of the Testaments originated at Qumran.[15] This opinion seems, in the present state of our knowledge, to be premature.

The Testaments became part of Judaism's life and literature, but it is evident that as time passed they were interpolated by various interested parties. Initially these must have been Jews, but the first century BC, in which it is assumed these interpolators lived, was a troubled age, and, as our knowledge of it is imperfect, the identification of these additions is often hazardous. When Christianity arose and the Testaments became known in Christian circles, Christian writers left their mark on the text. Some of these Christian additions can be readily identified, as in T Sim 6:7; 7:2; T Levi 10:2;

14:2; 18:7; T Dan 6:9; etc, but there may be others that are not so easily detected.

The date of the primary text of the Testaments can be established only on the basis of the internal evidence, although the finding at Qumran of fragments of T Levi and of T Naphtali (or of works closely related to them) indicates that a pre-Christian date is now certain.[16] The reference in T Naph 5:8 to Syrians (in a list of nations that enslaved Israel) must point to c 200 BC as the earliest date. The allusions in T Reub 6:7a,10–12 to Levi as chosen both to bless Israel and to be king over the nation, and in T Sim 5:5 to Levi as waging the war of the Lord (cf T Reub 6:12), have been thought to indicate the early Maccabean period (cf 1 Mac 14:41, where Simon is accepted as leader and high priest). In T Levi 8:1–19 (especially vss 14–15) the reference must be to John Hyrcanus, who is credited in *War* I, 68–9, with the gift of prophecy. Several passages mention Enoch (T Sim 5:4; T Levi 10:5; T Jud 18:1; etc), and these may indicate a date in the late second century BC, although Charles is doubtful of their value for dating purposes.[17]

If the principal text of the Testaments comes from the second century BC, before John Hyrcanus broke with the Pharisees, there are some other passages which are highly critical of the Levitical priesthood and which demand a first-century BC date. The struggle between Alexander Jannaeus and the Pharisees and the unhappy spectacle of the civil war between Hyrcanus II and Aristobulus II must have convinced many that the Lord's purpose for Israel was going to be fulfilled outside the Hasmonean family. This, it is theorized, led to the revival of the earlier ideal that political leadership would come from Judah. For references to Levi's failure to live up to God's hopes, see T Levi 10:1–5; T Dan 5:6–7. T Levi 14:1–8 seems to be a clear allusion to Alexander Jannaeus (cf *Ant* XIII, 380), and T Zeb 9:1–6 to the civil strife of 67–63 BC. It is possible that other passages of a somewhat similar tenor belong to this same era (T Jud 17:2 to 18:1; 22:1 to 23:4; T Naph 4:1–5; T Gad 8:2; T Ash 7:4–6).

As an indication of the ambiguity of some of the evidence for dating the Testaments, the work of M. de Jonge can be cited. This scholar argued that the older view is correct – that the Testaments are a Christian work – and he fixed the date between 190 and 225 AD. Later, under the impact of the material found at Qumran, he modified his opinion to the extent of conceding a Jewish nucleus behind the present work.[18]

The Testaments were written in Hebrew, but, except for fragments found at Qumran, none of the original text is extant. The book is preserved in Greek manuscripts, although the date of the first translation into Greek is speculative. R.H. Charles believes that it was done before 50 AD.[19] The text is found also in numerous Armenian manuscripts as well as in a Slavonic version.

Certain noteworthy features of the Testaments are listed below.

1 / Since the law was basic to Judaism, references to it are found in all the Testaments except Simeon (T Reub 3:8; 6:8; T Levi 13:1–4; etc). It is curious, however, that the minutiae of the Law, as well as of the great festivals, are ignored, as are such important practices as circumcision and sabbath observance.

2 / The Testaments, like Jubilees, illustrate how Haggadah, related to the Law, developed in the Jewish community. Thus in T Reub 3:13–15 we have a popular expansion of Gen 35:22 (cf Jub 33:2–8). Simeon's jealousy of Joseph, referred to in T Sim 2:6–8, is based upon the general statement in Gen 37:4. T Levi 6:3–11 is a Haggadic rationalization of Levi's share in the murder of the Shechemites (Gen 34:25–6). T Jud 2:1–7, which describes Judah's exploits as a hunter, appears to be related to Gen 49:9. And so on. The longest of these Haggadic embellishments is in T Jos 2–9 (cf Gen 39:7–23) and 11–16 (cf Gen 37:25–36); chronologically these two sections should be reversed. It was the continuous development of such Haggadah that led at a later date to Judaism's Midrashim (plural of Midrash).

3 / The primacy of Levi and Judah is a fundamental article of faith in the Testaments. As T Sim 7:1–2 puts it: 'And now my children, obey Levi and Judah ... for the Lord shall raise up from Levi as it were a high priest, and from Judah as it were a king' (cf T Reub 6:5–12; T Levi 2:11; T Jud 21:1–5; T Iss 5:7; T Naph 8:2; T Gad 8:1; T Jos 19:11). Such references as T Levi 10:1–5 and T Dan 5:6–7 appear to reflect a more realistic view of the Levitical priesthood as examplified in the Hasmoneans.

4 / Each of the twelve patriarchs includes in his disquisition a substantial amount of ethical teaching, such as we find in Ben Sira (T Reub 3:9–10; 4:6–7; 5:1 to 6:4; T Sim 3:1–6; 4:7–8; 5:3; 6:2; etc). The various

virtues – patience, truthfulness, love, generosity and sexual purity –
are commended and their opposing vices condemned. In T Ash 1:3–9
the moral framework is supplied by the doctrine of the two inclina-
tions (singular *yeṣer*) given by God to men, the good inclination and
the bad (cf Ben S 15:14–17). Here is what is said on forgiveness and
love: 'Love ye one another from the heart, and if a man sin against
thee, speak peaceably to him, and in thy soul hold not guile; and if he
repent and confess, forgive him' (T Gad 6:3).[20] For the same sentiment, see T Gad 4:1–7; 5:2; 6:1; T Dan 5:3; T Iss 5:2; 7:6; T Zeb 5:1; etc.

5 / Angels and demons appear in the Testaments, although there are
no named angels. 'The holy ones' are mentioned in T Levi 3:3. In some
of the Greek MSS there is a reference in T Levi 3:5 to archangels. In T
Levi 5:6 and T Dan 6:2 an angel who identifies himself as the one who
'intercedes for the nation of Israel' is presumably Michael. 'The angel
of peace' (T Dan 6:5; T Ash 6:6; T Ben 6:1) may be a member of the
angelic hierarchy. T Ash 6:5 suggests that angels meet the soul at
death.

The demons ('spirits of deceit' or 'of wickedness,' T Sim 4:9; 6:6; T
Dan 5:6), also called 'angels of Satan' (T Ash 6:4), may have their own
internal divisions, for 'seven spirits of deceit' appear in T Reub 2:1.
The demons are headed by Beliar (T Levi 3:3; etc), the Devil (T Naph
8:4), the Prince of Deceit (T Sim 2:7), and Satan (T Dan 6:1' T Gad 4:7).
Beliar is said to rule over those who yield to their evil inclination
(T Ash 1:8). In T Dan 5:6 Satan is described as Dan's prince, and this
tradition, plus Dan's association with idolatry in Judg 18:29–31, may
account for the omission of Dan from the NT list of Israel's tribes in Rev
7:5–8.

6 / The Testaments are of interest because they record various eschatological ideas current in some Jewish circles in the second and first
centuries BC. These notions are in fact a *pot-pourri*, for the authors or
editors were quite unable to impose upon this material anything like
consistency and logical arrangement. The chief items in this mixture
are noted below.

Some disaster to Israel will precede the end of the age (T Levi
15:1–3; T Ash 7:1–2).

God himself will come and save Israel (T Ash 7:3; T Judd 22:2; cf 'save men' in T Sim (6:5), and thereafter he will be in Israel's midst (T Dan 5:13).

R.H. Charles identifies a good many references to a Messiah in the Testaments,[21] but this writer finds some of these identifications very doubtful. Actually the term 'Messiah' does not occur in the Testaments, and all that we can be sure of is that a personage is referred to who, under God, is going to assist in the salvation of Israel (cf 'a man working righteousness' in T Naph 4:5; 'a prophet' in T Ben 9:2). In T Jud 24:5–6 he is to arise from Judah (24:1–3 need not refer to a leader from Levi, as Charles suggests). In other Testaments he is to come from Levi (T Levi 18:1–14; T Dan 5:10–13, assuming that 'Judah' is an intrusion in vs 10). This person will establish peace on earth, open the gates of paradise, and bind Beliar (T Levi 18:4,10,12).

There will be a resurrection to life on this present earth (T Ben 10:6–8, 'some unto glory and some unto shame'; cf T Jud 25:1; T Zeb 10:2); there will be a judgment, first of Israel, and then of all the Gentiles (T Ben 10:8–9). Beliar and the ungodly will be cast into eternal fire (T Jud 25:3; T Zeb 10:3). Thereafter, we must assume, the saints will rest in Eden, also called the New Jerusalem (T Dan 5:12).

While the Testaments, by their basic premises, are concerned with the children of Israel, it is noteworthy that their hopes frequently embrace the Gentile world. An angel (Michael?) is said in T Levi 5:7 to intercede for all the righteous. At the end of time the Lord shall appear and himself save men (T Sim 6:5). T Naph 8:3 makes this more explicit: 'God shall ... gather the righteous from among the Gentiles' (cf T Ash 7:3; T Dan 6:7; T Ben 9:2; 10:5); and T Levi 4:4 speaks of the time when 'the Lord shall visit all the Gentiles in his tender mercies.'

X

APOCALYPTIC AND
HISTORICAL WRITINGS

APOCALYPTIC WRITINGS*

Daniel

The book of Daniel appears to have originated in Judea about 166 BC.[1] In an earlier age its author would have been a prophet known by his own name, but in the second century BC it was accepted that prophecy had ceased, and our author, convinced that God had spoken to him and that he had a message for his contemporaries, was obliged to use a pseudonym. He selected Daniel as his pen-name, probably because his basic sources were a number of Daniel stories now found in chapters 1–6 of his book (see pp 95–6). He adapted these stories for his immediate purpose, and to them he affixed, in chapters 7–12, accounts of visions which he himself had had. These visions, as they now stand, have all the marks of literary creation, but some of them may be elaborations of genuine psychological experiences. The ultimate sources, literary and mythological, which lie behind all this material constitute an area of critical inquiry which cannot be dealt with here. Another facet of the book, which will also be merely noted, is its language division: 1 to 2:4a and 8–12 are in Hebrew, whereas 2:4b to 7:28 is in Aramaic. This means that the division of the text on linguistic lines does not correspond to a division based on content.

*For an introduction to apocalyptic writing see chapter 5 (pp 100–2).

The structure of Daniel is basically simple. The narratives about Daniel and his friends, chapters 1–6, serve as an introduction to the visions of chapters 7–12, in which the friends nowhere appear. Chapter 7, Daniel's vision of the beasts and the man (lit. 'son of man'), portrays, like chapter 2, a series of earthly kingdoms. The real interest, however, is in the fourth kingdom (the fourth beast, the Hellenistic Age), and in one of its kings (the little horn of vss 8, 20, 24), who makes war on the saints. This is clearly an allusion to Antiochus IV and his treatment of the Jews. 'A time, two times, and half a time' (vs 25) is a cryptic forecast of the length of Antiochus's oppression. The chapter is noteworthy for its picture of the final judgment (vss 9–10, 26); for its introduction of the figure 'one like a son of man' (vs 13), who, in the sequel, turns out to be 'the saints of the Most High' (i.e., the godly ones of Israel, vss 22, 27); for its forecast of the destruction of the little horn (vss 11, 24–6); and for its affirmation, as in chapter 2, that in the end an eternal kingdom for the saints will be established (vss 14, 27). It is difficult to determine precisely what is meant when it is said that in this kingdom all peoples and nations shall serve Israel (vss 14, 27).

Chapter 8, Daniel's vision of the ram and the he-goat, is an expansion of certain parts of chapter 7. Daniel, who does not understand what he has seen is instructed by Gabriel about the meaning of the vision (vss 16–26). The ram, it turns out, symbolizes the Achaemenid Persian Empire, and the he-goat which attacks it is Alexander the Great. The he-goat's four horns, standing for the divisions of Alexander's empire, presently produce a little horn, which as in chapter 7, designates Antiochus IV. Verses 10–12 and 23–5 refer to the king's attack on the Jewish religion, and verses 13–14 (part of a celestial conversation) to the duration of the oppression (1150 days). Verse 25 brings the assurance that at the end of this period the evil king will be broken.

Chapter 9 is somewhat different from the two preceding chapters insofar as there are no symbolic animal figures and the only object that Daniel sees is the angel Gabriel. Daniel has been concerned about the meaning of Jeremiah's seventy years, the period which must pass before Jerusalem's troubles end (Jer 25:11–12; 29:10), and Gabriel comes to elucidate the matter. It seems that by 'seventy' Jeremiah meant seventy weeks of years, i.e., 490 years. Sixty-nine of these weeks (483 years) have passed, and Judea is now in the midst of its last week (of seven years). It is a troubled time: an anointed one (probably the high priest Onias III) will be killed, and sacrifice in the Jerusalem temple will cease (vss 26–7). The conclusion, verse 27, forecasts the destruction of the oppressor.

The last vision, chapters 10–12, consists of three parts. The prologue, 10:1–21, is of interest for the light it throws upon the author's conception of the angelic world. At least four different angels are referred to, although only one of them is named (Michael, 'your prince'), and two are designated as 'the prince of Persia' and 'the prince of Greece' (vs 20; cf vs 13). Chapter 11 is the explanation by an angel, possibly Gabriel, of the vision referred to in 10:1,7. It is, in fact, not a vision in the usual sense, but rather a revelation of the course of history from the Persian period (in which Daniel supposedly stands) down to the Greek age. Curiously, no proper names are mentioned, but a schoolboy with some knowledge of history would have no difficulty in identifying the persons and events alluded to. The last king mentioned is given more space than any other (vss 21–45) and clearly he is Antiochus IV. His treatment of the Jews and his profanation of their temple are referred to in verses 30–6. Antiochus's death is mentioned in verse 45 as something yet to occur. If this verse means that the king will die in Palestine, its forecast was wrong, for in fact he died at Gabae in 163 BC in a war against the Parthians.

Chapter 12 offers a sketch of the dénouement of history which is to begin with the death of Antiochus. There will be a time of trouble in the world but the saints ('everyone whose name shall be found written in the book') will be delivered. There will be a resurrection, although the details are not spelled out: 'Many of those who sleep ... shall awake, some to everlasting life, and some to shame and everlasting contempt.' Verse 4, 'shut up the words and seal the book,' reads like the end of the original revelation. Whether the remainder of the chapter, verses 5–13, comes from the same author or from another hand or hands is debatable. In verse 5 Daniel asks an angel: 'How long shall it be to the end of these wonders?' and the verses which follow give three answers to this question. The starting-point is evidently the desecration of the temple in December 167 BC by Antiochus: in verse 7 the end will come when 'a time, two times, and half a time' (cf 7:25;

8:14; 9:27) have passed, usually thought to indicate three and a half years; in verse 11 it is 1290 days; and in verse 12, 1335 days.

Apart from its literary merits – and parts of Daniel are vividly and imaginatively written, as, for instance, chapters 2, 3, 6, and 7 – Daniel stands out as a unique declaration of Israel's religious faith. In these chapters what belief in the living God really means is presented to us. He is the God of history who removes and sets up kings, and who, amid the sequence of earthly empires, holds before his people the prospect of the subjugation of their enemies and the establishment of a kingdom that can never be destroyed. This God encourages his servants to resist evil in all its forms, and if in doing so they die, there is for them the sure and certain hope of an awakening at the end of time to everlasting life. Such beliefs must have given power and courage to those involved in the Maccabean struggle, and at the same time offered grounds for believing that their struggle was not in vain.

The book of Daniel was to become the prototype for later apocalyptic writers, and as such it was to have a considerable influence on Jewish as well as Christian literature. Its anonymity was to become standard apocalyptic practice, and its deterministic view of history, its angelology, and its eschatology were to be appropriated by later apocalyptic writers in varying degrees. In view of what we find elsewhere, it is interesting that there is no real dualism in Daniel, nor is there any reference to a future leader such as the Davidic king or the Messiah as found in other writings. In this earliest of the apocalypses the chief actor is God himself.

The Prayer of Azariah and the Song of the Three Young Men

This prayer and the song are not apocalyptic in any sense, but their association with the book of Daniel makes this an appropriate point to comment on them.

In the ancient Greek and Latin versions of the Bible the Prayer of Azariah and the Song of the Three Young Men, which form no part of the Hebrew text of Daniel, appear as part of Daniel 3, being introduced between verses 22 and 23. It cannot be determined when, where, or by whom these additions were made. Some scholars aver that they had become part of the Hebrew text before it was translated into Greek, others that the Greek translator, thinking them suitable, added them to his Greek rendition of the Hebrew. It may be that some Greek MSS of Daniel displayed these additions, while others did not. Josephus seems to have used a text of Daniel without these additions (*Ant* x, 213–15).

The Prayer of Azariah, verses 3–22 (vss 1–2 are introductory), is a well constructed prayer, although it has no relevance to its context in Daniel 3. It is best described as a lament for the community, with an invocation (vss 3–4), a confession of sin (vss 5–8), a description of the nation's situation (vss 9–10), and a plea for God's intervention and acceptance (vss 11–22). The references to lawless enemies and an unjust king (vs 9), and to the absence of prince, prophet, leader, and sacrificial system (vs 15), can only point to the Maccabean age, soon after 167 BC, and the prayer must have been written about this time. That it should have become attached eventually to the book of Daniel is not surprising.

The Song of the Three Young Men, verses 29–68 (the introductory verses, 23–8, are a midrashic expansion of Dan 3:22–5), is a lyrical and beautifully phrased hymn of praise. It calls upon all the works of the Lord, in heaven and on earth, to praise and bless their Maker, and in a sense it is an elaboration of Ps 148, its conclusion (vss 67–8) being a slight variation of Ps 136:1–3. There is nothing in this song to indicate its date of composition. It may well have been known in the Jewish community in Palestine long before the second century BC. When an editor or translator added it to Dan 3, he inserted verse 66 to make it appear more acceptable in its new milieu.

In some Greek MSS the prayer and the song appear twice, once in the text of Dan 3, and again, like the Prayer of Manasseh, in a group of hymns and odes appended to the Psalter.[2]

Enoch

The book of Enoch was written originally in Aramaic; fragments of the original Semitic text have been found in cave IV at Qumran.[3] The work was translated into Greek, and it was apparently this Greek version that was known to the author of the NT Jude (vss 14–15) of the early second century AD. Only part of this Greek version has survived. For the complete text of Enoch we are dependent upon the Ethiopic translation which was made from the Greek, and which is extant only in relatively late MSS. The problems caused by this history of the text are too numerous and too technical to be discussed here.

Initially the book of Enoch represents a Midrashic expansion of Gen 5:24: 'Enoch walked with God; and he was not, for God took him.' Thus in Enoch 14: 8f (cf 39:3) we have a description of Enoch's vision wherein he was translated into heaven, and was addressed by the Lord and given a message for the Watchers (the fallen angels). Whether the same author gave us chapters 37–71, a series of three parables revealed to Enoch by God (37: 1–5), is problematic,[4] but he may be responsible for including the fragments of the book of Noah in our present text (see chapter 5, pp 101–2). This basic material was subsequently added to by other writers, in much the same way that anonymous prophetic oracles were attached to the words of the eighth-century Isaiah, and the end result was our present book of Enoch.

We presume that it was the editor or latest author who arranged Enoch as it now stands in its five sections.

1 / Chapters 1–36: an introduction (1–5) is followed by material from the book of Noah (6–11), an account of a vision (12–16), and accounts of Enoch's various journeys (17–36).

2 / Chapters 37–71, the Parables (37:5, 'Now three parables were imparted to me').

3 / Chapters 72–82: data re the heavenly bodies, etc, shown to Enoch by the angel Uriel.

4 / Chapters 83–90: Enoch's account to his son Methuselah of various visions.

5 / Chapters 91–105: a hortatory section, addressed to Methuselah and his brothers, in which woes which befall sinners figure prominently. The two verses of chapter 105 may be an independent fragment.

This listing may seem to be a tidy analysis of the book, but in fact it conceals numerous literary problems which we shall have to bypass here.

The material for dating Enoch, admittedly scanty and ambiguous, can be summed up as follows:

1 / In the description of Sheol in chapter 22 the fact that there is no

specific reference to martyrs is thought to point to the pre-Maccabean period.

2 / The references to the kings and mighty ones, often implied as being in opposition to the just and holy (38:5; 46:4; 48:8; 53:5; 63:1–12), and to the shedding of the blood of the righteous (47:1), may allude to the age of Alexander Jannaeus. For the same reason 103: 9–15 may belong to the same period.

3 / While the use of 'Son of Man' in 46:2; etc, as a title for the coming deliverer cannot be examined here, it is probable that it is to be related in some way to the same phrase in Dan 7:13 (where it designates Israel). This may mean that this part of Enoch postdates the book of Daniel.

4 / The section in Enoch dealing with physical phenomena (72–82) seems to be referred to in Jub 4:17,21. The date of Jubilees is taken to be 150–100 BC.

5 / In the dream-visions of chapters 83–90, which survey history from Adam onwards, 90:6–12 appears to refer to the Seleucid rule in Judea; the great horn of verse 9 is then Judas Maccabeus. As, however, there is no allusion to Judas's death in 160 BC (90:13–19 can be taken as a forecast of future developments), the dream-visions of 83–90 can probably be dated before 160 BC.

6 / In the Apocalypse of Weeks (93; 91:12–17) the seventh week (93:9) indicates the post-exilic period as an age of apostasy, but there is no allusion to the Maccabean struggle.

The conclusions about the date of Enoch to be drawn from these considerations must be tentative. All that we can say is that there is material in Enoch ranging from the early second century to the early first century BC. As there is nothing in the book that can be confidently identified as reflecting conditions in the Roman era, 63 BC would appear to be the latest date.[5]

In summarizing the principal religious views of Enoch we shall ignore the internal divisions of the book and treat it, including its interpolations, as a unity, and its contents as a medley of the varied ideas held in some Jewish circles between 200 and 63 BC.

1 / God, whose throne in heaven is described in 14:8–23, is most commonly referred to as the Lord of Spirits (37:2; etc); cf the Head of Days in 46:1–2; 47:3; etc. He is served by angels, the more important

of whom are the Seraphim, Cherubim, and Ophannim (71:7); the four archangels are Michael, Raphael, Gabriel, and Phanuel (40:1–10; 71:8), although Uriel (9:1; 21:5) and Raguel (23:4) appear to have equally high status. Saraqael and Remiel appear in another list of seven archangels (20:1–8). That God's will is absolute, and that human history is predetermined, is implied in the visions of chapters 83–90 and the Apocalypse of Weeks (93; 91: 12–17).

2 / The incipient dualism of the fragments of the book of Noah is not developed in Enoch. The demons, the offspring of the primaeval giants, are to have a free hand in the world until the day of judgment (15:11; 16:1), and Satans are referred to (40:7) as having a role in heaven similar to that exercised by Satan in the book of Job.

3 / Unlike the Testaments of the Twelve Patriarchs, Enoch offers little in the way of moral instruction. What there is is found in 94:6–9; 95:4–6; 96:5–8.

4 / Chapters 72–82, while showing that the created universe reflects the power and wisdom of God, are of particular interest because they bring together all that the Jews of this age knew and theorized about the world of nature, especially with regard to the heavenly bodies. In 72:32 and 74:10–12 the solar year of 364 days is taken to be normative (cf Jub 6:29–38).

5 / While Enoch's echatology largely follows well known paths, in some important respects it is innovative.

Sheol / although the traditional Hebrew belief in an underworld to which all the dead go persists in Enoch (51:1; 56:8; 63:10; etc), there is found in chapter 22 the novel notion that the land of the dead is in the west and that it exhibits three (or four) internal divisions appropriate to the chief varieties of the spirits who enter its precincts.

Woes preceding the end of the age / The final troubles of the world, a familiar theme in apocalyptic (e.g., Dan 7:25; 12:1), are referred to in 56:5–8; 90:13–19.

The advent of God / When the 'Holy Great One' comes, even the high mountains shall be shaken (1:3–6).

The resurrection / Enoch accepts the idea of a resurrection of the dead (51:1; 62:15; 91:10; etc), but does not develop it.

The return of the Diaspora / Just as the book of Daniel ignores Israel's Diaspora, so Enoch says virtually nothing about the return of the dispersed Jews to the homeland. In 57:1–3 wagons (presumed to carry Jewish exiles) come from the east and the west, and their rumbling is remarked on even in heaven. In 90:33 the 'dispersed' are to share in the future kingdom.

The future leader / A common view of Israel's future associated it with the appearance of a leader (e.g., Jer 23:5–6; Mal 3:1; Zech 9:9–10), although, as previously noted, no such personage appears in the book of Daniel. Enoch's eschatology not only has a place for such a leader, but it designates him by no less than five titles: the Righteous One (38:2; 53:6); the Elect One (39:6; 40:5; 45:3–4; 51:5a,3); the Anointed One (Messiah, 48:10; 52:4), the earliest literary reference to the use of this title for the future leader; The Son of Man (46:2,4; 48:2; 62:9, 14; 63:11; etc); and My Son (105:2; cf the same term in 2 Esd 7:28–9; 13:32; etc). It should be noted that the first four titles appear only in the Parables (37–71).

Of these titles, the Anointed One or Messiah (Gk *Christos*) was to become in the Jewish community the standard word for the future deliverer, while in the early Christian Church Christ, Son of Man, and Son were to become accepted titles for Jesus.

It is curious that in the Parables the Son of Man is represented as having some kind of preexistence before coming to earth (48:2–3,6; cf 46:1–2; 49:2; 62:7; 2 Esd 12:32). This may reflect the same kind of thought that is found in the personification and preexistence of Wisdom in Pro 8:1–36.

It may be noted that in the visions of chapters 83–90, which offer a sketch of Israel's history, a white bull appears in 90:37. Apparently this is the Messiah, who has arisen out of the community, but, as the judgment has already taken place (90:31–6), his function is not clear.

Judgment / The notion of a future judgment, primarily of Israel, goes back at least as far as Amos's conception of 'the day of Yahweh' (Amos

5:18–20). This limited judgment seems to appear in Mal 3:5. The idea was often expanded to denote a judgment of all mankind (e.g., Zeph 1; Jer 25:30–1; Joel 3:1–3). Daniel takes up this conception and presents it as the great assize (7:9–27), and Enoch repeatedly uses it (1:3–9; 16:1; 22:4; 38:1–6; 48:8–10; 90:20–7; etc). The novelty in Enoch's presentation is that the Elect One (the Anointed One in 69:27) is to be the future judge (51:1,5a,2; 55:3–4; 61:8; 62:1–3). The wicked do not fare very well on this occasion: the fallen angels, and even some sinful men, end up in a great abyss of fire (21:7–10; 90:24–7); elsewhere sinners shall be cursed for ever and have no peace (102:3; 103:5–8).

The future blessedness / Enoch's statements about the post-judgment era for the righteous are on the whole rather restrained and couched in traditional language. In 93:16 he states that a new heaven will appear, but elsewhere that there is to be an transformed earth, cleansed from all sin (5:7–9; 45:5–6), a kind of New Jerusalem (90:28–38), where God and the Son of Man will dwell with the righteous for ever. The latter will be given the fruit of the tree of life, and their joy will be that of the angels in heaven (25:4–6; 58:1–6; 62:13–16; 104:4; 105:1–2). What share the non–Hebrew world will have in all this is none too clear. In 90:30 the animal symbolism suggests that the nations will be subservient to Israel, but in 48:4 the Son of Man is to be the light of the Gentiles (cf 91:14). The editor of Enoch may have endorsed the view of the book of Noah that in the end all men will become righteous and worship the Lord (Enoch 10:21), whereas 50:2–5 (which is not from the book of Noah) appears to indicate that only repentant Gentiles will be saved.

2 Esdras

The chronological limits of this volume should exclude 2 Esdras which comes from the latter part of the first century AD or later, but because of its inclusion in the Apocrypha, as well as its apocalyptic character, it warrants a brief mention here, although a summary treatment can hardly do justice to this extremely interesting book.

Chapters 1–2 and 15–16 are additions, mostly Christian, to the primary text of 2 Esdras, and they will receive no further notice.

Chapters 3–14, the heart of the book, comprise seven visions seen by Ezra. In 3:1, where Ezra is identified with Salathiel, an editorial touch may be noted. This is a highly creative work by a sensitive and pious Jew who has discerned the nature of God's love for his creation (8:47). Actually the first three visions (3:1 to 9:25) are more accurately described as dialogues, with God, Ezra, and various angels participating in what is often a sprightly exchange of views. In the third of these visions (6:35 to 9:25) a long theological discussion is initiated by Ezra's question: 'If the world has indeed been created for us, why do we not possess our world as an inheritance?' (6:59).

In 9:26 to 10:59 there is a vision of a sorrowing woman whose son has died, which is interpreted by an angel in 10:38f as representing the destruction which had befallen Jerusalem. The vision ends with Ezra being invited to view the splendour of the new Jerusalem (10:55–7).

The fifth vision (11:1 to 12:39), which must be from a different source from those in chapters 3–10, is an allegorical dream, centring on a three-headed, multi-winged eagle. This creature clearly represents the Roman world of the first century AD. The lion-like creature who emerges from a forest in 11:37 is identified in 12:31–4 as the Davidic Messiah whose role is principally that of a judge, although (in a way not specified) he will also deliver the remnant of God's people.

The sixth vision (13:1–58), described as a dream, centres on a winged man who comes from the sea, and a great multitude assembles to make war against him. The man sends a stream of fire from his mouth and burns up his adversaries. God, not an angel, then explains that the man is his Son. The reunion of all the tribes of Israel is the theme of verses 39–50.

The most important feature of the seventh vision (14:1–48, which is really a theophany), is that Ezra suggests to the Lord that, since the Law has been destroyed, he should send his Holy Spirit into him (Ezra), and thereby enable him to reproduce the Law. The Lord acts on this proposal, and Ezra and five assistants are enabled in forty days to write 94 books, 24 of which are to be made public (the Scriptures?), but the remaining 70 kept for 'the wise among your people' (vs 46; cf vss 4–6). Probably these 70 books represent the oral tradition, with its assortment of Halakic, Haggadic, and Midrashic elements.

2 Esdras is a typical apocalyptic work in its accounts of the signs which herald the end (5:1–13; 14:17), in its view that the consumma-

tion of history is near (4:26; 5:55; 14:10–12), and in its concern with resurrection and judgment (7:32–8; 14:35). Only a few, it seems, will in the end be saved (7:60; 8:3; 9:20–2). The final victory of goodness is the theme of 6:25–8. The Messiah is described as God's Son 7:28; 13:32; 14:9), as preexistent (13:25–32), and (most curious of all) as reigning 400 years and then dying (7:28–9), although 7:30–1 may imply that his death is a temporary sleep.

2 Esdras was undoubtedly written originally in Hebrew or Aramaic, but no part of that text has survived. A Greek translation has also perished (except for a few verses on a papyrus), but not before various translations were made from it, of which the most important is the Latin. In the Vulgate it appears as 4 Esdras.

HISTORICAL WRITINGS

1 Maccabees

1 Maccabees is an account of events, chiefly political and military, in Judea from 167 to 134 BC. The plan of the book is quite transparent.

1 / Introduction, 1:1–64: from Alexander the Great to the accession of Antiochus IV of Syria, 175 BC (vss 1–10); Antiochus IV and the Jews (vss 11–64; vss 54–9 describe the desecration of the temple)

2 / The beginning of the revolt against Antiochus: Mattathias and his five sons, 2:1–70

3 / The leadership of Judas, called Maccabeus, 3:1 to 9:22 (the rededication of the temple, 4:36–61)

4 / The leadership of Jonathan, 9:23 to 12:53 (Jonathan's death 13:23)

5 / The leadership of Simon, 13:1 to 16:17

6 / The accession of John Hyrcanus, 16:18–24

If, as seems reasonable, we assume a single author for 1 Maccabees, he must have lived after the accession of John Hyrcanus to power in 134 BC. It is probable, too, in view of the account of the treaty between Judas and Rome, recorded in chapter 8, that he lived before Pompey's conquest of Palestine in 63 BC. A more precise date depends upon the interpretation of the last two verses (16:23–4). If these verses are thought to imply that John Hyrcanus was dead, the author wrote sometime after 104 BC. If, however, verse 23 does not refer to John's death, but to his early career and to his rebuilding of Jerusalem's walls, razed by Antiochus VII of Syria (*Ant* XIII, 247), then the author could have lived in the early years of John's leadership, before the latter's break with the Pharisees, perhaps c 125 BC.

What sources the author used is a matter of speculation. If he wrote c 125 BC, he himself could have lived through many of the events he describes, and to that extent he wrote out of personal knowledge. Doubtless he would have gathered first-hand oral and written reports from various witnesses. Verse 9:22, which refers to 'the rest of the acts of Judas' as not having been recorded, is ambiguous. It may mean that there was a document, which our author used, chronicling some of the deeds of Judas. If he had access to the temple treasury, he may have consulted such records as were there (14:48–9); the latter must have included the chronicles of the high priests (16:24). The bits of poetry scattered throughout the chapters (1:24b–8,36–40; 2:7–13; 3:3–9; etc) must come either from the author himself or from some collection of contemporary psalms.

Another type of material which 1 Maccabees exhibits is the official document or letter, of which there are twelve (8:23–32; 10:18–20,25–45; 11:30–7; etc). While most of these writings conform to the norms of Hellenistic epistolography, the possibility of forgery beclouds them, and the authenticity of each has to be determined on the general grounds of probability. The difficulties of these documents are not reduced by the translation process: the author translated, perhaps rather freely, from Greek to Hebrew, and then at a later date the Hebrew was translated back into Greek to give us our present text. Finally, all the material which our author had assembled was presented within a framework of Seleucid history, and for this he was probably indebted to some Seleucid source. This created a chronological problem, for the official Seleucid era began in October, whereas the Jewish calendar had been influenced by the Babylonians, who began their year in the spring, as is illustrated by 1 Mac 4:52, which makes Chislev (December) the ninth month. The ramifications for 1 Maccabees of this double calendar cannot be pursued here.

While the main emphasis of 1 Maccabees is secular, specifically religious matters are dealt with in appropriate places: the laws against

Judaism promulgated by Antiochus IV (1:41–61); the recovery of the temple in 164 BC and its rededication to Israel's God (4:36–61); Jonathan's appointment as high priest by Alexander Balas in 152 BC (10:15–21); the people's decision to make Simon their high priest and leader (13:7–9; 14:25–49). As we would expect, allusions to the Torah are fairly common (1:52,56–7; 2:21,26,48; etc). Sacrifices in the temple are taken for granted (4:53,56; 5:54; etc), as is the practice of prayer (3:44,50–3; 4:10,30–3; 7:36–8; etc). But it is curious that the terms God and Lord are avoided by the author. The Deity is referred to in the third person in 2:61; 3:60, and as 'Saviour of Israel' in 4:30, but normally the surrogate 'Heaven' is used (3:18,19,50,56; 4:10,24; etc).

It is generally agreed that the author-editor of 1 Maccabees was a serious historian, who has given us what is, on the whole, an honest and sober narrative. His sympathies were with the Hasmoneans and with the revival of Jewish nationalism which their leadership brought about. If he belonged to the Pharisees, he wrote before the troubles between them and the Hasmoneans had come to the surface. While his work is extant only in the Greek of the Septuagint, it is believed that it was composed in Hebrew. This assumption is supported by later Christian traditions,[6] as well as by the existing Greek text, which has many phrases implying translation from a Hebrew original.[7]

2 Maccabees

SOURCES AND PLAN

2 Maccabees records events in Judea from the time of Seleucus IV (187–175 BC) to the defeat of the Seleucid general Nicanor by Judas Maccabeus at Adasa (so 1 Mac 7:40) in 160 BC. It therefore covers some of the same ground as 1 Maccabees 1:10 to 7:50. The main part of the book (2 Mac 3:1 to 15:36) has a prologue (2:19–32) in which the author explains that his work represents a summary of the five books of Jason of Cyrene, which outlined the history of Judas Maccabeus and his brothers. A short epilogue (15:38–9) concludes the work of the epitomist-author. To all of this there has become attached the material in 1:1 to 2:18, which consists of two letters from the Jews of Judea to the Jews of Egypt, 1:1–10a and 1:10b–2:18. As the whole of 2 Maccabees is

extant in Greek, and as the text from 2:19 onward shows no evidence of translation from a Semitic original, it is commonly assumed that both Jason and his epitomist wrote in Greek. While it is probable that the prefaced letters, 1:1 to 2:18, were also composed in Greek, a Hebrew or Aramaic original cannot be entirely ruled out.

Although the two letters in 1:1 to 2:18 are of little importance as historical documents, they have received considerable attention from scholars because of the numerous problems they present. The first one, 1:1–10a, is dated 124 BC, and it urges the Egyptian Jews to celebrate *Hanukkah* (called, oddly, the feast of Booths, vs 9; cf 1 Mac 10:6, where the festival starting on the twenty-fifth of Chislev is said to be like the feast of Booths). Reference is made in verses 7–8 to an earlier letter written on the same subject in 143 BC, possibly by Simon who had lived through what led to the institution of the *Hanukkah* festival. There is little ground for questioning the genuineness of this letter. The second letter, 1:10b–2:18, which is not dated, is generally thought to be a forgery, although some short epistle aimed at getting the Egyptian Jews to observe *Hanukkah* may lie behind it. In 1:11–17 there is a legend about the death of Antiochus (either IV of VII), which seems to relate in some way to the death of Antiochus III in Elymais in 187 BC. The letter is further embellished by midrashic accounts about Nehemiah (1:18b–36; 2:13), Jeremiah (2:1–8), Solomon (2:9–12), and Judas (2:14–15).

Nothing is known about Jason of Cyrene whose work is the basis of 3:1 to 15:36. We know from Josephus that there was a Jewish settlement in Cyrene (*Ant* XIV, 114–16; *Apion* II, 44), and we may suppose that there were various contacts between the Cyrenaic Jews and those in Alexandria and Judea. The knowledge of the Maccabean struggle which Jason acquired through these channels, both written and oral, must have prompted him to produce his five-volume record of the Maccabean age. It is probable that some of his details of Seleucid history come from a Seleucid source (4:21,27; 5:22–6; 6:2; 8:8; 9:29; etc). The epitomists's description in 2:19–22 of Jason's five volumes is too vague to permit us to infer how much ground the work actually covered, or how thorough the coverage was. In view of the known literary achievements of the Hellenistic Age we may suspect that Jason produced a somewhat romanticized combination of fact and fancy.

All we know about the epitomist himself has to be inferred from his prologue (2:19–32), and from what he chose to present as a summary of Jason. He clearly had some literary gifts, and he directed these to producing a book which, by eliminating many of Jason's details, would be a reliable history of the Maccabean age, and which at the same time would please its readers (2:25). As we know so little about either Jason or his epitomist, no effort will be made in what follows to identify their separate contributions to the history now found in 3:1 to 15:36.

The plan of 2 Maccabees, like that of 1 Maccabees, is quite simple. After the prologue (2:19–32), the first part of the narrative, 3:1 to 7:42, deals with Judea under Seleucus IV and Antiochus IV. The latter's oppression of the Jews is the theme from 4:7 on. The second half of the book, 8:1 to 15:37, is an account of the Maccabean rebellion down to 160 BC. Here Judas is the chief actor: Mattathias's share in initiating the revolt is ignored, and the role of the brothers is minimized. The one reverse suffered by Jewish forces occurred when they were led by Simon (14:17). Judas's death in May 160 BC is not recorded.

2 MACCABEES AS HISTORY

There are many instances where 2 Maccabees repeats or corroborates the data found in 1 Maccabees: 2 Mac 4:9–17 and 1 Mac 1:11–5, re the gymnasium in Jerusalem; 2 Mac 5:11–21 and 1 Mac 1:20–4, re Antiochus IV's plundering of Jerusalem; 2 Mac 6:1–6 and 1 Mac 1:44–59, re the desecration of the temple; etc. There are other instances where 2 Maccabees records traditions not found in 1 Maccabees, and where general probability suggests that the essential data thus given may be reliable. For example, the highly coloured tale about Heliodorus in 3:1–40 may preserve the simple fact that an unsuccessful attempt was made to rob the treasury of the Jerusalem temple. Again, the traditions about the high priests Onias III, Jason, and Menelaus, and about the share of the last two in furthering Hellenism in Judea, may be substantially sound (3:1,9–12; 4:1–20,22–38), as may be the story of the death of Menelaus (13:3–8). It is more difficult to appraise three of the documents now found in 11:16–21,27–33,34–8. As 1 Mac 6:55–62 indicates that Lysias made peace with the Jews late in 163 BC, it is not inconceivable that the advantages of a peaceful solution to Judea's problems may have occurred to him at an earlier date. The above-mentioned documents in 2 Mac 11 may be evidence that in 164 BC there were exploratory negotiations about peace, but that these were fruitless.

There are, however, features of 2 Maccabees which suggest that we should use its testimony with caution. Some of its stories have an air of unreality about them, particularly those that incorporate visions or apparitions (3:22–30,33–4; 5:2–4; 10:29–30; 11:6–8; 15:11–16); such supernatural events usually tend to obscure the actual facts of the matter. Again, the use of numbers in 2 Maccabees is typical of many Jewish writers (as seen throughout the OT) insofar as accuracy was not a desideratum. On occasion 2 Maccabees can be modest in its numerical statements, as when Jason is said to have had 1,000 supporters (5:5) and Judas 6,000 (8:1), but generally its figures about armies and battle casualties are incredibly high (5:14; 8:24,30; 10:17,31; 11:4,11; etc). Its most extravagant claims are of the 120,000 Galatians killed in Babylonia (8:20), and the 110,000 infantry, 5,300 cavalry, 22 elephants, and 300 scythed chariots making up the army of Antiochus V and Lysias (13:1–2; cf 1 Mac 6:30).

In certain specific matters 2 Maccabees appears to be in error. In 10:3 the Jerusalem temple is said to have been out of Jewish control for two years, whereas the evidence of 1 Mac 1:54; 4:52–4 suggests three years. As examples of internal contradictions we may cite the following: the statement in 5:21 that after pillaging the Jerusalem temple Antiochus IV went to Antioch, never to return to Judea, while the legendary tale of the martyrdom of the seven brothers and their mother in 7:1–42, presumably in Judea, is set in the presence of Antiochus (vs 24); the statements about the Seleucid general Timothy, who in 10:24–38 was defeated and killed at Gazara, but who in 12:24–5, after being defeated by Judas, was captured by two Jewish captains and subsequently released. As examples of what appear to be deviations from the facts we may note: that the death of Antiochus IV is placed before Judas's recovery of the temple (9:1–29), whereas the correct sequence appears to be the recovery of the temple in 164 BC, followed by the death of Antiochus in 163 BC (so 1 Mac 4:36–59; 6:1–16); that the account of the siege and capture of Beth-zur in

13:18–22 is quite different from the more convincing one in 1 Mac 6:48–50; that the credit for taking Gazara is given in 10:32–8 to Judas, whereas 1 Mac 13:43–8 (reading Gazara instead of Gaza in vs 43) informs us that it was taken by Simon c 142 BC (cf *War* I, 50; *Ant* XIII, 215); that Judas's exploit at Jamnia, 12:8–9, involving the burning of the harbour and the fleet (Jamnia, four miles inland, may have been served by a roadstead), may have been only disciplinary, but it is hard to reconcile this story with the account of the Jewish repulse at Jamnia when Judas was engaged elsewhere (1 Mac 5:55–62), or with 1 Mac 15:40 to 16:10, which implies that Jamnia was taken by John Hyrcanus, encouraged by his father Simon, c 138 BC (cf *War* I, 50; *Ant* XIII, 215).

2 MACCABEES AS A RELIGIOUS DOCUMENT

2 Maccabees is important as a witness to a type of Pharisaic piety of about 100 BC. The chief constituents of its religious outlook are noted below.

1 / The Torah is the basic religious authority (3:15; 4:11; 6:1; etc). In 15:9 we have the phrase 'The Law and the Prophets' (cf the prologue to Ben Sira), but there is no reference to anything that might be called the oral tradition explicative of the Scriptures.

2 / The Lord, who made the world out of nothing (7:28), is the source of strength for the godly, and the constant Ally of Judas and his fighting men (8:18,24,36; 10:1,28,38; etc). While his retributive justice and corrective punishment can never be gainsaid (5:17; 6:12–13,18–19; 7:35–6; etc), prayer to this sovereign God is a frequent feature of the narrative (8:2,14,29; 10:4; 16; etc). Prayer on behalf of the dead is mentioned once (12:41–5), as is the intercession of the saints, in this case, the intercession of the prophet Jeremiah (15:11–6).

3 / The Jerusalem temple, 'the most holy temple in all the world' (5:15), receives much attention (3:2–3,24–40; 8:17; 9:16; etc). Its pollution by Antiochus IV was the great disaster of the age (6:1–5), although partly the result of Israel's sins (5:17; 7:18,32).

4 / While keeping the Sabbath is the religious practice most frequently referred to (5:25; 6:6,11; 8:26–7; etc), circumcision (6:10) and the dietary laws (6:7,9,18; 7:1; etc) also appear. The feasts of Weeks (12:31) and Purim (15:36) are the only festivals mentioned, but the

institution of Hanukkah (10:5–8, but not so-called) and Nicanor's Day (15:36) are found in their appropriate places in the narrative.

5 / The concern which 2 Maccabees manifests for the day-to-day problems of this world might be thought to preclude any great interest in what lies beyond death. Nevertheless 2 Maccabees holds firmly to a belief in the resurrection of the dead (7:9,11,14,23,29; 12:43–5; 14:46). No details of such a resurrection are furnished, although 7:14 asserts that the wicked will not share in it. Verses 7:36 and 14:15 seem to imply that God's people (presumably many in resurrected form) will endure on the earth forever, but no Messianic figure appears in connection with the age to come.

DATE

The letter now found in 1:1–10a is dated 124 BC, but this throws little light on the date of either Jason or the epitomist, unless the latter placed the letter where it now stands. The epitomist's statement in 15:37 that 'from that time the city [i.e., Jerusalem] has been in possession of the Hebrews,' would seem to fix 63 BC as the latest date for his work. There are no convincing data to suggest when it was begun. Since, as has been noted, 2 Maccabees appears in places to be less reliable than 1 Maccabees, and since it also introduces supernatural events unknown to 1 Maccabees, it can be urged that 2 Maccabees is later than 1 Maccabees. This would place its date after 125 BC, but before the time of Pompey.

XI

THE DEAD SEA SCROLLS AND THE COMPLETION OF THE CANON

The Dead Sea Scrolls (hereafter DSS) is the common designation for a quantity of manuscripts, written mostly in Hebrew, some well preserved, the majority in a fragmentary state, found from 1947 onwards in caves in the Judean desert near the western coast of the Dead Sea. Quite close to the spot where the first finds were made is an old ruin, Khirbet Qumran, and excavations carried on here, 1951–6, made it clear that it had been the centre of a settlement from c 130 BC to 68 AD. In view of the dates assigned to the scrolls (to be discussed later), it is a reasonable assumption that the DSS found in the caves near Qumran were in fact the library of this community, and that they had been hidden in these almost inaccessible places shortly before the Romans came in 68 AD.

Historical background

QUMRAN

The ruin Khirbet Qumran had long been known to Palestinian archaeologists, but the discovery of the DSS made a thorough examination of it necessary, and this was carried out in 1951 and 1953–6.

Khirbet Qumran can now be identified with the City of Salt mentioned in Josh 15:62. It was one of Judah's frontier fortresses and was probably built by Jehoshaphat in the ninth century BC (cf 2 Chr 17:12).[1] The site was deserted in the sixth century BC, presumably after the Babylonian wars, and was reoccupied in the second century BC by the people who built the structures whose ruins we see today. On the basis of the archaeological data (here coins are of prime importance) we can affirm that the site was inhabited by this group from c 130 to 31 BC. In the latter year an earthquake, to which Josephus refers (*War* I, 370–2), severely damaged the buildings, and the group left, only to return about a generation later. This time they stayed on until the forces of Vespasian attacked them in 68 AD (*War* IV, 450–1; cf II, 151–3), an attack which ended the life of the settlement. The later occupations by Romans and Jewish rebels do not concern us here.

Although Qumran was a fortified area, within its walls a complete community life was lived. There is evidence of cisterns, a pottery, a bakery, an assembly hall (also used as a refectory), a scriptorium, etc. It is probable that only some of the two hundred or so people (whom we name Qumranis) slept within the walls. The rest used the nearby caves. South of the walled area was the cemetery with more than a thousand graves. As the neighbourhood of Qumran has extremely sparse natural resources, it is supposed that ʿAin Feshka, a few miles to the south, with water and better soil, served as Qumran's economic auxiliary.

THE ESSENES

Of the three first-century AD writers who tell us about the Essenes, Philo, Pliny, and Josephus, the last-named gives us the fullest account (*War* II, 119–61; *Ant* XIII, 171–2; XVIII, 11, 18–22; *Life* 10). The Essenes, we learn, were a very pious sect within the Jewish community. As Josephus first mentions them in his discussion of second-century BC events in Judea (*Ant* XIII, 171–2), it has long been thought that they were either an offshoot of the Pharisees, or represented an independent protest against the growing secularism of the Hasmonean rulers. Their members lived in Palestine, and apparently nowhere else in the Jewish world, although the Therapeutae of Egypt, of whom Philo speaks in *The Contemplative Life*, must in some way have been related to them. Both Philo and Josephus say that there were altogether about 4,000 Essenes, living in small groups in or near various towns and villages. Each of these Essene communities was apparently independent of the others. What most impressed the outside world about the Essenes was their community of goods and property, and their disdain for women and marriage. Josephus, however, records that some Essenes did marry (*War* II, 160–1). He also has a good deal to say about their admission procedures, the pattern of their daily life, and the internal discipline of the group, and in addition he notes their studious habits centring in 'the writings of the ancients' (*War* II, 136). It is Pliny who locates the Essenes (he probably ought to have said 'an important Essene settlement') on the west side of the Dead Sea north of Engedi (*Natural History* V, XV, 73).

THE QUMRANIS AS ESSENES

It is now generally agreed that Qumran was an Essene community, and that the DSS were the property of this community. The main reasons for this consensus are listed below.

Various archaeological data tie the Qumran settlement and the DSS together. For instance, the dates assigned to the scrolls coincide roughly with those given to the Qumran site.

The jars holding the DSS in the caves are of the same age and type as some found at Qumran.

Josephus's references to the internal life of the Essene communities (*War* II, 137–50) clearly form a variant of the rules of the Manual of Discipline (1:16 to 9:11) found at Qumran.

Josephus's allusion to Essene studies (*War* II, 136, 159) is congruent with the existence of a scriptorium at Qumran and with the discovery in the nearby caves of so many scrolls.

Pliny's reference to an Essene settlement on the west side of the Dead Sea supports the association of Qumran with Essenes.

If this identification of the Qumranis and the Essenes is accepted, it means that we no longer have to rely exclusively upon ancient literary sources for our knowledge of the Essenes.

The scrolls

DATE

The question of the date of the DSS is a highly complicated one and cannot be presented here in any detail. The chief points that must be considered are as follows: (1) It is unlikely that any of the DSS are later than the destruction of the Qumran settlement in 68 AD. (2) The jars in which some of the DSS were stored belong to the Hellenistic age. (3) Radio-carbon dating of the linen wrappings of the DSS puts the origin of the linen in the period 168 BC to 233 AD. (4) The references in some scrolls (e.g., the Habakkuk commentary) to the wicked priest and the righteous teacher, and to the defilement of the temple in Jerusalem, point to a period of tension within the Jewish community. The only historical situation that takes account of these four points is the Hasmonean period, when there was strife between various religious and political groups. Many scholars identify the wicked priest with Jonathan or Simon, while others favour Alexander Jannaeus. Either supposition lends support to the view that many of the DSS belong to the second or first centuries BC. (5) The palaeographical evidence from the Hebrew scripts in which the DSS are written attests to dates from the late third century BC to the middle of the first century AD for the writing of the scrolls. Some, for example the great Isaiah scroll, may in fact be copies of scrolls written at an earlier date.

DESCRIPTION OF THE SCROLLS

Some of the DSS are in a good state of preservation and these have now been published, but most of the fragments still await publication. The scrolls that we know about fall into three main groups, as indicated below.

Biblical texts / MSS from all the biblical books save Esther have been found at Qumran.[2] It is evident from the distribution of this material that the favourite books were Genesis, Deuteronomy, Isaiah, and the Psalms. The largest and best preserved of the MSS, published in 1950, presents the complete text of the book of Isaiah (1 Q Is^a), and probably dates from c 100 BC. Another of the better preserved MSS is *The Psalms Scroll of Qumran Cave 11* (11 Q Ps^a), published in 1965 by J.A. Sanders (Oxford), which supplies parts of 37 of the canonical Psalms (from Ps 93 to Ps 150), as well as 9 apocryphal psalms and a small bit of Ben Sira; its date is the first half of the first century AD. These and other biblical texts are important because of the light they throw on the development of the Hebrew canon and because of the data they furnish to textual critics. They seem to offer a substantial basis for recovering, at least in part, a comparatively early text of the OT. The fragments of the Hebrew text of Samuel (commented on in chapter 5, p 94) and a MS of Jeremiah (4 Q Jer^b), both of which supply a Hebrew text approximating that used by the Septuagint translator, indicate that in specific cases the Septuagint may reflect, not the whimsy of the translator, but a current Hebrew MS, and the usefulness of the Greek version of the OT is thus enhanced for establishing the primary Hebrew text.

Extra-biblical texts / In this category we must place the Hebrew and Aramaic fragments of various books of the Apocrypha and Pseudepigrapha, such as Tobit, Ben Sira, Testament of Levi (or something like it), Testament of Naphtali, Enoch, Jubilees, Book of Noah. Enoch, which appears to lack the second section (chapters 37–71), is thought by some to derive from the Qumran settlement.[3] The above known works, as well as fragments from otherwise unknown writings (one has been titled the 'Book of Secrets'),[4] give support to the view that apocalyptic thought was of considerable interest to the Qumranis.

The sectarian texts / This term covers texts produced or used exclusively by the Qumranis.

1 / There are fragments of biblical commentaries on passages from Isaiah, Hosea, Micah, Nahum,[5] Habakkuk (most of chaps 1–2), Zephaniah, and Pss 37, 57, 68, and 107.[6] The usual procedure in these texts is to cite a biblical verse and then to give the interpretation (*pesher*). Predictably there is a general tendency to find allusions in the biblical text to the experiences of the community, and/or the imminent end of the age.

2 / While the unpublished fragments of the DSS may yet reveal more Targumic texts, the one important Targumic text so far published is

the Targum of Job (11Q tg Job).[7] Its 38 fragmentary columns present passages from Job 17:14 to 42:11. It probably dates from the first half of the first century AD, and it is therefore the earliest extant MS of any Aramaic Targum.

3 / The Genesis Apocryphon (1Q ap Gen) is one of the seven DSS which came to light in 1948, but it was so badly preserved and compacted that its unrolling presented serious problems. The preliminary publication of part of it by N. Avigad and Y. Yadin appeared in 1956 (when the title 'The Genesis Apocryphon' was used). J.A. Fitzmyer brought out a definitive treatment of the scroll, with commentary, in 1966 (Rome: Pontifical Biblical Institute).

The Apocryphon, written in Aramaic, is difficult to classify. The basic text is a kind of Targum on certain chapters in Genesis, but the biblical material is freely reworked and embellished with haggadic additions, and to that extent the work is a midrash. Columns 1–5 (of which only column 2 is reasonably intact) deal with the birth of Noah, being an elaboration of Gen 5:28–9 (cf Enoch 106–7). Columns 6ff appear to have treated Noah and the flood, and columns 19–22 are a paraphrase of Gen 12–15. The date of the scroll, on palaeographic grounds, is thought to be the first century BC, or the early first century AD. As is displays none of the theology or other characteristics of the Qumran community, there is no positive indication that the scroll was composed by Qumranis.

4 / The Manual of Discipline (1QS) is one of the seven original DSS, and was first published in 1951 by M. Burrows who gave it its title (called by some 'The Community Rule'). It is an outline of some of the group's basic practices and statutes, combined with a short religious code which stipulates the punishment for certain offences. It would seem to have arisen out of some experience with community living, and, while it may have been intended primarily for the leaders, it could only be a practical social instrument if its main provisions were understood and endorsed by the whole membership.

Columns 1–4 lay down the rules for entry into the community (the Covenant of Grace), and provide for the annual renewal of the covenant. In column 3, lines 13f, there is a homily on the theme of the spirit of light versus the spirit of darkness, or of the spirit of truth versus the spirit of falsehood. Columns 5–9 relate to the council of the community (the entire membership). The most important single group in this council is made up of the Zadokite priests. It is in this section that provision is made for the reception of neophytes and for the discipline of erring members. Column 9 (lines 9f) gives the rules for the master of the community, followed by the master's hymn of praise to God.

The Manual is a unique document in pre-Christian Judaism insofar as it reflects a kind of closed religious society, subject to rules and devoted to a form of asceticism. Qumran has given us various other versions of the Manual, but these cannot be treated here.

5 / In 1896–7 among some discarded MSS in an old Cairo synagogue two mediaeval copies of what was apparently an ancient Jewish document were found; these were published by S. Schechter in 1910 under the title *Fragments of a Zadokite Work*. Various interpretations of this material were offered by scholars, one of the more balanced being that of R.H. Charles in 1913.[8] His view that the Zadokite documents (hereafter Z Docs) belonged to a group of reform-minded priests in Judea and that they were written late in the first century BC was to prove to be not too far off the mark. Here the matter rested until the publication of the first DSS, and the discovery in caves 4, 5, and 6 of at least eight fragments of the Z Docs. It now became clear that the latter belong to the same tradition that we have at Qumran.

The Z Docs consist of two different writings, the Admonition (or Exhortation), and the Laws. The former is nearly complete, but the Laws lacks both a beginning and an end. These are found in two MSS, A (16 pp) and B (2 pp), but the relations between these MSS are too involved to be commented on here. The Admonition[9] offers a retrospective view of the origin of the congregation of the new covenant, to which is attached a survey of Israel's history and some isolated legal maxims. In 6:5 there is a reference to 'those who went out from the land of Judah and sojourned in the land of Damascus.' The allusion to Damascus (cf Amos 5:27) has been the subject of debate. Probably it is being used figuratively, and may denote any Essene settlement, including Qumran. The second writing, the Laws,[10] covers a wide field: capital punishment, taking vengeance, oaths, witnesses, the office of judge, sabbath observance, social intercourse with Gentiles, uncleanness, almsgiving. In 16:2–4 there is a reference to the book of Jubilees, seemingly in connection with the community's calendar.

The relation between the Z Docs and the Manual is a moot question. As many of the injunctions in the former imply close association with Gentiles, and as more than one settlement ('camp') of those who are members of the covenant is envisaged (14:3, 9), it is conceivable that the Z Docs were meant primarily for those Covenanters (or Essenes) who did not live at Qumran. No mention is made in the Laws of a community of property, and the references to a pedagogue carrying a child (11:11) and to a married woman's oath (16:10–12) suggest that the members led normal family lives.

6 / The Rule of the Congregation (Vermes, 'The Messianic Rule') exists in a short and badly preserved MS in two columns (1 Q S^a), which was purchased in 1950. It was recognized as belonging to the end of the scroll containing the Manual, although the two works differ considerably in content. For instance, it is clear from column 1, with its references to marriage, wives, and children (not mentioned in the Manual), that the Rule is intended for non-ascetic Essenes.

The Rule presents numerous problems in translation,[11] but the following points seem reasonably clear. The document is intended for Israel in the last days (col 1), and this is confirmed by the later reference to 'the war ... to vanquish the nations.' Despite this formal purpose there are allusions to the education of youth, participation in the administration of justice, and the variety of services members render to the congregation. The whole life of the community is under the supervision of the priests, the sons of Aaron.

Column 2 deals with a meeting of the council of the community, but the interpretation of the text is uncertain. The assembly, here described, may be purely eschatological, for the Messiah of Israel is present. Another figure, a priest (possibly the Messiah of Aaron), is mentioned first, and is evidently more important than the Messiah of Israel. The text then proceeds to speak of a meal around a table (for the whole council this would demand a gargantuan set-up), at which the priest blesses the food, and after him the Messiah of Israel shall likewise bless it. Some scholars argue that the text does not deal with an eschatological event but with a liturgical rite anticipatory of the Messianic age, in which case a member of the community would have to impersonate the Messiah of Israel. The obscurity of the Rule is not lessened by the rubric at the end to the effect that every meal at which ten men gather is to follow this statute.

7 / The Thanksgiving Psalms (1 Q H) (hereafter Thank Pss) were one of the finds of 1948, and, when the English translation of Sukenik's earlier Hebrew edition came out in 1955, there were eighteen plates of texts, in addition to those recording the fragments. Of the eighteen main plates, not one is free from extensive lacunae, and this problem not only makes the translation and interpretation of each plate difficult, but often prevents the identification of a psalm's beginning and/or end. There is therefore a disparity in the number of psalms which scholars identify.[12]

The Thank Pss are a collection of hymns of thanksgiving, although some verge on the threshold of laments in their recital of the speaker's troubles. The commonest beginning for a psalm is 'I praise (or 'thank') you, O Lord,' but 'Blessed are you, O Lord' is also found. The diction of the psalms is that of the canonical prophets and psalmists, enriched, as the occasion demands, by the distinctive vocabulary of the Qumran community. From their similarity in tone and structure it is thought that these poems come from a single author. Who he was is quite unknown, although we might expect him to be a leader of the group. In column 4, lines 9–10, he is opposed by 'expounders of lies and seers of deceit,' and from this and numerous other similar references it is clear that these poems reflect a period of tension and even conflict within the Jewish community. How these hymns were used by the Qumranis we do not know. Individuals would doubtless find comfort and strength by reading them privately, but it is conceivable that these poems were employed in some act of common worship.

8 / The War Scroll (1 Q M), the full title of which is 'The Scroll of the War of the Sons of Light against the Sons of Darkness,' is one of the seven original DSS. It is badly mutilated, all of its nineteen columns being eaten away at the bottom. Column 19 is on a separate sheet of parchment, and it is impossible to say what originally came between it and column 18. Yadin's critical edition of the text offers numerous excellent suggestions for filling in some of the lacunae.[13] The date of the scroll, mostly on the basis of the alleged references to Roman military equipment, is thought to be after 63 BC.

An internal problem in the scroll should be mentioned here. In column 1 'the Kittim of Asshur,' 'the Kittim in Egypt,' and 'the Kittim' (lines 2,4,6) appear as antagonists of the sons of light, and their dominion is brought to an end in line 6. Yet in columns 15–19 the Kittim, who are the object of Israel's enmity, are soundly defeated (col 18, lines 2–5; col 19, lines 10, 13 – with some textual restoration). The relationship between column 1 and columns 15–19 therefore poses a problem.

The War Scroll is an eschatological treatise insofar as it recognizes a basic conflict between the sons of light and the sons of darkness, and, further, it describes the final physical struggle between the two forces, with the ultimate defeat of the sons of darkness, the army of Belial. All this is presented without any claim to divine revelation. The author states his views with a quiet assurance. This, he says in effect, is the way it is going to be.

The contents of the scroll can be summarized as follows.

1:1–15, an introduction, describes how the sons of light (Levi, Judah, and Benjamin) are to fight and defeat the sons of darkness, specified as the army of Belial, the forces of Edom, Moab, Ammon, Philistia, and the Kittim of Asshur, reprobate Jews, the kings of the north, and the sons of Japheth. Seven engagements are to be fought, each side winning alternately until the seventh battle, when the sons of light emerge as the final victors.

2:1–14 tells us, after some details about services in the temple apparently during the war years, that the war is to last forty years, but owing to five sabbatical years, only thirty-five will be marked by actual fighting. In lines 10–4 the specific nations whom Israel (line 7) will be fighting are enumerated.

2:15 to 9:16 is concerned with the qualifications and equipment of the soldiers in the various units of Israel's army. Much attention is here paid to the trumpets and to the standards or banners. 7:8 to 9:16 describes the battle operations of the 28,000 infantry and the 6,000 cavalry. The weapons and protective armour of the fighting men are treated in great detail, almost with pedantry. It is maintained by Yadin and others that some of the armour and tactics betray an acquaintance with Roman military practices, and this argument is then used to date the scroll in the late first century BC.[14]

9:17 to 14:15 comprises various exhortations, hymns, and prayers for different stages of the war.

15:1 to 19:13 is a description of the war against the Kittim. Israelite and Kittim victories here alternate. In 19:10 Israel's foes are described as 'the mighty men of the Kittim, the multitude of Asshur, and the army of all the nations.'

The most obvious sources which the writer of the War Scroll utilized were Israel's Scriptures. Much of his basic thought and imagery is dependent on such passages as Num 31; Deut 20; 1 Chr 27:1–15; 2 Chr 20; Ps 83; Isa 11:11–16; Ezek 38–9; Dan 11:40–5. We suspect that various non-Biblical traditions also helped to shape his presentation, although the only specific allusion to such a source is in 15:5: 'as it is written in the book *Serekh 'Itto* (lit 'the order of his time').

While the Law is apparently assumed to be the community's basic religious document, the only direct reference to it is in 10:6, where Num 10:9 is said to have been 'spoken through Moses.' Various prescriptions in the scroll derive their authority tacitly from the law (e.g., 3:15–18; cf Ex 18:17–27; 7:4; cf Lev 13; 7:7; cf Deut 23:12–14; 10:5; cf Deut 20:5–8).

The scroll speaks of 'a time of mighty trouble for the people to be redeemed by God' (1:11–12; cf 15:1), but whether this affliction is being experienced during the writer's time, or whether it is something in the future, is not clear. In either case the author's conviction is that there 'shall be a time of deliverance for the people of God' (1:5). He very shrewdly gives no indication of the proximity of this age of salvation.

Although Belial, or his army, is often represented as Israel's and God's enemy (1:1; 13:2,4,11; 14:9; 15:2–3; 17:15), and, although Belial assists the sons of darkness (16:9), the fact remains that in the scroll Israel's enemies are such that they must be dealt with by fighting a war. These adversaries are people of flesh and blood, and to defeat them in battle is the only way to cope with them. If, therefore, we detect a form of dualism in the scroll, with Yahweh on one side and Belial on the other, it is evident that it is only an incipient dualism, whose full implications are nowhere worked out.

While the Israelite soldiers had to do the actual fighting and doubtless contributed their share to 'the slain' of 9:8, they did have the great moral advantage of knowing that God was with them (12:7–8). In some undescribed way God fights on Israel's side (1:4). The Israelites are also strengthened by angelic help (1:10; 7:6; 12:7–8), but whether the archangels assist is not clear (9:15–16; cf 17:6–7). In view of the references to the Messiah in other DSS, it is surprising that in this scroll the Messiah nowhere appears.

In contrast to the Manual, which reveals friction within the Jewish community (Manual 5:1–20), the War Scroll appears to ignore such differences. There is only one reference to 'the offenders against the Covenant' (1:2), which may designate apostate Jews. Our scroll assumes that the people of God are a unity. Further, despite the restrictive nature of the sons of light in 1:3 (Levi, Judah, and Benjamin), the author later moves away from this position, so that Israel's army is in fact to be drawn from 'all tribes of Israel' (2:7; cf 3:13; 5:1).

Since most Jewish eschatological forecasts envisage a return of the Diaspora to the homeland, it is of interest that the War Scroll is not concerned with exiles in the usual sense of the term. 'Exiles' appears twice in 1:2–3, but it is evident that the reference is to those Jews who withdrew from the ordinary life of Judea to adopt the discipline of the Essenes. When the great war starts, they will return 'to encamp in the wilderness of Jerusalem.'

We note, finally, that the Gentiles are cast in the role of the opponents of Israel (1:1–2,4,6,12; 11:13; 12:10; 15:1–2,13), and there is no indication that they are to share in any positive way in the salvation which the war is to bring to Israel.

9 / The latest DSS to come to light is what has been called the Temple Scroll, which came into Jewish hands in 1967 during the Arab-Israeli War, and which Y. Yadin described in a preliminary report in BA XXX, 4, (Dec. 1967), 135–9. This scroll, over 28 feet long, and written in 66 columns, is thought to date from about the late first century BC. Its extraordinary contents are summarily described by Yadin as follows: '1) a large collection of *Halakhoth* (religious rules) on various subjects, among them ritual cleanness ...; 2) enumeration of the sacrifices and offerings according to the festivals; 3) a detailed description of the temple [which differs from all known data re Israel's three temples, and seems to imply that Herod's temple, or its predecessor, was not built according to the divine instructions]; 4) the statutes of the king

and the army [these pertain to the king's bodyguard, and to mobilization plans in the event that Israel was faced by a Gentile force bent on its extermination].' If these first impressions of the scroll are borne out by a thorough study of it, then it may turn out to be one of the most important of all the DSS. Unfortunately its damaged condition is likely to delay its definitive publication.

10 / In 1952 two strips of rolled copper were found in cave 3 of Qumran, but it was not until 1955–6 that the rolls were successfully cut open. It was then evident that they were two parts of a single document, which we shall refer to as the Copper Document. This document, engraved in a first-century AD Hebrew script, lists about sixty treasures, totalling a fabulous amount, and describes their hiding places. It is thought that the document is a piece of folk-lore, and that it has little or nothing to do with the Qumran community (see BA XIX, 3 (Sept. 1956), 60–4).

THE RELIGIOUS IDEAS OF THE DSS

The vocabulary and ideology of the DSS are basically biblical, which is what we should expect in scrolls from a community which recognized that God had spoken 'through Moses and through all his servants, the prophets' (Manual 1:3). There is therefore no criticism of, or theoretical opposition to, the temple cultus as such. The refusal of the Essenes to participate in the sacrificial system in Jerusalem was the result of their conviction that it was under the control of wicked priests (cf *Ant* XVIII, 18–19). The acceptance of the Torah and the Prophets did not exclude the use of other material. As was earlier mentioned, the War Scroll refers to the book *Serekh 'Itto* (15:5), and in the Z Docs the book of *the Hagu* is referred to in 10:6; 13:2, and probably in 14:8 (cf also col 1 of the Rule). The survival at Qumran of fragments of various apocryphal and pseudepigraphic works is further indication that the Qumranis did not restrict their interests to the biblical traditions.

The DSS come from a community that believed itself to be an assembly of the sons of light, the true keepers of the covenant, who carry out God's ordinances and who love one another, but who hate the sons of darkness (Manual 1:1–10).

The keeping of the Law involved the Qumranis in a calendar, and it may be assumed that at one time they used only the lunar calendar of their fellow Jews. There is a limited amount of evidence, however, such as the reference to the book of Jubilees in Z Docs 16:1–4, that the Qumranis were familiar with a solar calendar of 364 days, which is referred to in Jub 6:29–38; Enoch 74:12; 82:4–6. Thank Pss 12:4–9, which recognizes the importance of the sun, War Scroll 2:2, which divides the priests into 26 courses (cf 24 in 1 Chr 24:1–19), and Z Docs 6:18–19, which suggests that the members of the New Covenant had their own calendar, have been thought to point to a solar calendar, although at best it was only a 364-day year. Whether the old lunar calendar lingered on beside the solar one we do not know.

The angelology of the scrolls goes beyond the biblical traditions but is not as elaborate as in Enoch. Angels are referred to by sundry familiar terms: 'Holy Ones,' 'Spirits' (with various adjectives), 'Sons of Heaven,' 'angels of the Presence,' etc. Four archangels appear to be recognized: Michael, Gabriel, Sariel, and Raphael (War Scroll 9:15–16; cf Michael in 17:6–7). The Prince of Lights (Manual 3:20; Z Docs 5:17) is probably Michael, although some take him to be Uriel.

Evil / The Qumrani view of God, which is that of a sovereign Power who in some sense predestines everything that happens (Manual 3:15–18; Thank Pss 1:1–20), led them to affirm that God had designated two spirits (*ruḥoth*) in which man is to walk, the spirit of truth and the spirit of deceit (or injustice, wrong). 'Spirit,' which has various meanings in the DSS, seems here to be almost a metaphysical principle. This spirit of deceit is under the control of 'the angel of darkness' (Manual 3:20–1), who most commonly is called Belial (Manual 1:23–4; Thank Pss 2:16; War Scroll 1:1; etc). 'Prince of the dominion of wickedness' is another designation (War Scroll 17:5–6). At present the world is largely ruled by Belial (Manual 1:18; 2:19), who is assisted by spirits, the angels of destruction (War Scroll 13:12), but in the end his power will be broken (War Scroll 18:1).

Eschatology / It has been suggested on the basis of the opening verse of the Rule that at the end of the days there will be an accession to the membership of the Essene community, so that the latter will truly represent the whole congregation of Israel.

As we have seen earlier, there is to be a war which will eventually destroy Belial. The 'prince of the whole congregation' (War Scroll 5:1) in this war is probably the secular head of all Israel (in contradistinction to the religious head).

The references to a coming final judgment (as in Manual 4:20; Thank Pss 6:29) are not elaborated. Although the Manual speaks of 'everlasting joy in the life of eternity' (4:7), the DSS display almost no interest in the resurrection of the dead. The few passages that have been thought to point to a resurrection (Thank Pss 4:21; 6:29,34; 11:12; Z Docs 7:5–6) lend the idea very flimsy support. It is possible that the Qumranis, like the Essenes of whom Josephus wrote (*War* II, 154–8), believed in the immortality of the soul, and they may have been indifferent to what happened to the body.

At the end of the days there is to arise a righteous teacher (Z Docs 6:11). This, possibly, is the same figure whom the Manual refers to as 'the prophet' (9:11). The well-known biblical references (Deut 18:15,18–19; Mal 4:5) must lie behind this hope of a future teacher-prophet.

The use in the DSS of the term 'Messiah' as applied to a future leader had led to considerable discussion. The Manual refers to 'the coming of ... the Messiahs from Aaron and Israel' (9:11), whereas the Z Docs refer to 'the Messiah of Aaron and Israel' (12:23 to 13:1; 14:19; 19:10). In the Rule (col 2) the Messiah of Israel appears in an assembly where he is of lower status than the officiating Zadokite priest (the latter may be the Messiah of Aaron). While this looseness in the use of the term 'anointed' reflects biblical usage, it is also a recognition that there were two areas of importance in Israel's life, the cultic and the political (cf T Sim 7:2; T Iss 5:7; T Jos 19:11). As a further example of Jewish inexactness in the use of 'Messiah,' there is the allusion by R. Dosa (second century AD) to an Ephraimite Messiah, the son of Joseph, in distinction from the Judean Messiah, the son of David.[15] In the DSS there is no indication of what precisely the Messiah(s) of the future is(are) to do.

The final goal, towards which the Qumranis are moving, is described succinctly in the Manual 4:6–8:

These are the counsels of the spirit of the sons of truth in this world, and the gracious visitation [by God?] of all who walk in it [i.e., the truth] will be healing, and abundance of peace [or well-being] in a long life, and fruitfulness in offspring, along with all eternal blessings, and everlasting joy in an endless life, and a crown of glory together with resplendent raiment in eternal light.

The same vein of thought appears in Thank Pss 7:29–31. A somewhat more mundane view of the future is held out in the War Scroll 12:11–14.

CONCLUSION

The DSS are important for a variety of reasons, but only two of them, which are relevant to the present volume, are dealt with here.

The DSS are clearly of great value to the textual critic. All textual criticism, including the textual criticism of the Bible, aims to recover the text of a writing in the form in which it left the author's or editor's hands. In the case of the OT the critic has had to use basically such Hebrew MSS as are available (and they are mostly medieval) to establish the original text of the Scriptures. It is at this point that the DSS render an invaluable service to scholarship. For the scrolls bring us documents or fragments of documents which are about a thousand years earlier than the best of the extant MSS, and the textual experts are thus provided with improved resources for the accomplishment of their task.

The major contribution of the scrolls to scholarship relates to the history and religion of the Palestinian Jews from 150 BC to 70 AD. These sectarian writings (the non-biblical material found at Qumran) have added greatly to our understanding of the Judaism of this age. It had been surmised long before the discovery of the scrolls, partly because of the Essene traditions and partly because of the existence of such works as Enoch, Jubilees, etc, that there were varieties of Jewish life and thought outside of what has been called normative Judaism. But with the finding and publication of the DSS solid literary evidence became available to throw invaluable light upon these rather murky two centuries in the history and development of Judaism. This expansion of our knowledge of the Jews, primarily a matter of interest to Jewish scholars, is also of great concern to students of early Christianity. Anything related to Jewish life and thought in the first century AD is grist for the mill of the historian of the NT Church. It is here that the

DSS pose certain fundamental questions, such as: Did the Qumrani community in any way influence the practice and theology of the primitive Church? Any attempt to answer this and related questions, however, lies beyond the purpose of this volume.

THE COMPLETION OF THE CANON OF ISRAEL'S SCRIPTURES

To Jamnia, 90–100 AD

We have earlier seen (chapter 4, pp 51–3; chapter 5, pp 91–3) that by c 250 BC the Jewish community had a collection of books which was acknowledged to be religiously authoritative, and which comprised two parts, the Law and the Prophets. It is a fact, however, that presently other writings became associated with the Law and the Prophets (in some instances the association with prophetic books may predate 250 BC), so that by the beginning of the Christian era, and probably as early as 100 BC, the corpus of Israel's sacred literature was expanded by a third division, the Hagiographa. The term 'Writings' is used of the third part of the Scriptures by R. Akiba in the early second century AD (M *Yadaim* 3.5). The Writings include, in the order of Kittel's *Biblia Hebraica* 3rd edition (1937), Psalms, Job, Proverbs, the Five Scrolls (Ruth, Song of Songs, Qoheleth, Lamentations, Esther), Daniel, Ezra-Nehemiah, 1 and 2 Chronicles.

There is no precise information about how or when the Writings came to be grouped with the Law and the Prophets. The Prologue to Ben Sira (c 132 BC) refers to 'the law and the prophets and others who followed after them'; the last phrase also appears as 'and the books of our forefathers' and 'the rest of the books.' Clearly in the late second century BC there were some books (not described) that could legitimately be classed with the Law and the Prophets. Philo, writing two centuries later, reports that the Therapeutae of Egyptian Jewry took into their cells 'laws and oracles delivered through the mouth of prophets, and psalms and anything else [Gk *ta alla*] which fosters and perfects knowledge and piety.'[16] We must, I think, conclude that, before the Christian era opened, there were various books which by reason of their intrinsic merits, and in some cases, as with the Psalms, because of their cultic use, had survived in the Jewish community, and which by reason of their reputed authorship (the Psalms by David, Proverbs, Ecclesiastes, and the Song of Songs by Solomon) had established a special position for themselves. To associate such books with the Law and the Prophets was very natural. 1 Mac 2:59–60 not only knows of Dan 3 and 6, but Daniel and his friends are mentioned in the same breath with Abraham, Joseph, Phinehas, Joshua, Caleb, David, and Elijah, and 1 Mac 7:17 quotes Ps 79:2–3, introducing it with 'in accordance with the word which was written.' 2 Mac 15:36 seems to treat the story of Esther as a familiar tale. Since Philo, not later than 40 AD, refers not only to the Torah and the Prophets, but also to Ruth, 1 and 2 Chronicles, Ezra, Job, Psalms, Proverbs, Ecclesiastes, and the Song of Songs,[17] it is clear that the Scriptures in his time included the books just named.

While the limits of the Law and the Prophets were clearly established, without dissent as far as we know, by 250 BC, Jews found some difficulty in determining what books should be included in the third division of the Scriptures. The theory which was eventually worked out, and which finds expression in Josephus (*Apion* I, 38–42), was that after the death of Moses prophets wrote books down to the time of Artaxerxes (?I, 465–424 BC), and that anything written after Artaxerxes was not from a prophet, and could not be reckoned as Scripture. Josephus further states that there were twenty-two such books, a figure which can be obtained only by counting Ruth with Judges, and Lamentations with Jeremiah. Josephus's discussion indicates that he was following the arrangement of books in some current Greek version. Origen (died c 254 AD) stated that 'there are 22 canonical books according to the Hebrew tradition' (Eusebius, *Ecclesiastical History* VI, 25). Other sources, however, refer to twenty-four, as in 2 Esdras 14:37–48.

While the theory mentioned above that the Scriptures were written by prophets may seem to be a generally serviceable formula, it did not prevent debate about the rights of certain books to be included in the canon. There were, at one time, reservations about Esther.[18] We know from the Mishnah (*Yadaim* 3.3–5) that the claims of both the Song of Songs and Ecclesiastes were challenged, and that both were finally approved by the majority. These and other questions related to the third division of the Scriptures were settled at a rabbinical council (of which our knowledge is imperfect) held at Jamnia (Jabneh) in Palestine c 90–100 AD.

Although the limits of the Scriptures were not formally agreed upon until the end of the first century AD, we must allow, largely on the evidence of Ben Sira and Philo, that by c 100 BC the Scriptures of ancient Israel had reached the form they were to retain from that day to this. These Scriptures were not merely literature from pre-Christian Israel. They were looked upon as a closed collection of writings, different from all others in possessing the quality of inspiration. As Josephus put it: 'It is an instinct with every Jew ... to regard them (the Scriptures) as the decrees of God' *Apion* I, 42). The early Christian community inherited this Jewish estimate of the Scriptures, and so we find Paul speaking of the Jews as having been 'entrusted with the oracles of God' (Rom 3:2). In the period we are considering neither the Jews nor the Christians ever worked out a satisfactory theory of what 'decrees [or "oracles"] of God' really meant or implied.

However we may assess ancient Israel's legacy both to later Judaism and to early Christianity, it is clear that nearly everything we can say is related in one way or another to the Hebrew Scriptures. For these writings are the literary record of a unique religious experience stretching over a thousand years in the pre-Christian era. Such writings necessarily reflect the culture of the age from which they come, and as such they contain a fair amount of chaff, of little value to later generations. But their glory is that they also contain daring affirmations about the nature of God, as well as invaluable insights into the nature of man and his problems. They offer a religious interpretation of the world centring in the concept of a Power that is holy, just, and compassionate. As long as man continues to believe in such a Power, in a God, as Josephus expresses it, 'under whose eye and direction is everything in the whole universe' (*Apion* II, 294), he will find in the Jewish Scriptures 'a lamp to my feet and a light to my path' (Ps 119:105).

The outside books

The discussions both in this chapter and in chapters 5 and 9 have indicated that the Jews had and used many books which, as matters turned out, were not included in the canon of Scripture. The community at Qumran is a case in point, for the DSS indicate a lively interest by the Qumranis in a considerable body of non-canonical writings. The Alexandrine Septuagint, which initially reflected the life and needs of the Jews of Alexandria, also gives evidence of the place which non-canonical books had among the Jews of Egypt.

All this seems to have changed after the disastrous rebellion in Palestine, 66–70 AD. This war called for a thorough reexamination of Judaism's premises. Apocalypticism, with its hopes of a new age to be ushered in dramatically, appears to have lost ground in Jewish thought. With the temple gone there was nothing left to guide Israel but God's revelation in his Scriptures, and hence, as we have seen, an effort was made, 90–100 AD, to establish the limits of Holy Writ. Those writings that could not qualify for scriptural status were simply to be ignored in the future. There is no evidence that any effort was made to destroy those in Jewish hands. From now on they simply had no standing in the Jewish tradition: they were termed 'the outside (ḥîṣônîm) books.' The fact that many of them were now being used by members of the growing Christian movement was an additional reason for the Jews to leave them alone. Thus we have the later Jewish saying: 'He who brings into his house more than twenty-four books [of the accepted Canon] brings confusion' (*Midrash Qoheleth* 12:12).[19]

The 'outside books' were in fact preserved for posterity by the Christian Church. Some were saved by reason of being included in the Septuagint, and others because they were treasured by isolated Christian groups. It is modern scholars who have brought the latter together to form the Pseudepigrapha of the Old Testament.

NOTES

CHAPTER I

1 All Achaemenid dates are taken from R.N. Frye, *The Heritage of Persia* (London 1962), p 293.

2 ANET, pp 315–16; DOTT, p 82

3 See P.R. Ackroyd, *Exile and Restoration* (Philadelphia 1968), pp 22–3, n 24. For a short treatment of the Babylonian exiles see pp 12–16.

4 Tell el-Fûl; BA XXVIII, 1 (Feb. 1965), 6 (the 1964 campaign)

5 El-Jîb; AOTS, p 239; J.B. Pritchard, *Where the Sun Stood Still* (Princeton 1962), p 163

6 Tell en-Naṣbeh, probably Mizpah; AOTS, pp 330, 332; BA X, 4, (Dec. 1947), 69–77

7 Khirbet et-Tubeiqah; BA XXI, 3 (Sept. 1958), 74 (the 1957 campaign)

8 Ramat Raḥel, probably Beth-haccherem; AOTS, p 172

9 AOTS, p 226

10 AOTS, pp 394, 397–8

11 AOTS, p 274

12 Tell er-Rumeileh; AOTS, p 204

13 Tell Beit Mirsim; AOTS, pp 209, 218

14 Texts 5 and 6 in Cowley, pp 11, 16

15 *History of Israel*, 2nd ed (London 1960), p 292

16 DOTT, pp 84–6

CHAPTER II

1 R.C. Zaehner, *The Dawn and Twilight of Zoroastrianism* (London, 1961), p 33

2 For a translation of the Gathas see J.H. Moulton, *Early Zoroastrianism* (London, 1913), pp 343–90.

3 On Josephus as a writer and historian see H.St. J. Thackeray's introductions to vols I, II, and IV of Loeb; CAH X (1934; 1952), pp 884–7.

4 For accounts of the Elephantine Jews see A.E. Cowley, *Aramaic Papyri of the Fifth Century B.C.* (Oxford 1923); E.G. Kraeling, *The Brooklyn Museum Aramaic Papyri* (New Haven 1953); P. Porten, *Archives from Elephantine* (Berkeley 1968).

5 Josephus saw the difficulty of putting Artaxerxes between Cyrus and Darius, and he therefore placed 1 Esd 2:16–30 in the time of Cambyses (*Ant* XI, 21, 26, 30).

6 See R.A. Bowman on Ezra 4:13, IB III, 603.

7 On grain storage in the Persian period see L.E. Stager, BA XXXIV, 3 (Sept. 1971), 86–8.

8 See B. Kanael, BA XXVI, 2 (May 1963), 38–42.

9 For a brief discussion of eschatology and apocalyptic see 'The beginnings of apocalyptic' in chapter 5, pp 100–1.

CHAPTER III

1 On the office of cup-bearer (Gk *oinochoos*) see Xenophon, *Cyropaedia* I, iii, 8–9, 11; Herodotus III, 34.

2 On Herod the Great's eunuchs see *Ant* XVI, 229–31.

3 Cowley, text 30, line 29

4 See R.A. Bowman in IB III, 764. This is the half-shekel temple tax (Gk *didrachma*, 'double drachma') of Matt 17:24, which was collected annually from all male Jews of twenty years and older for the maintenance of the temple cultus (cf *Ant* XVIII, 312). On the Mishnah's refinements of this tax see the tractate *Shekalim*.

5 Cf *War* II, 425; M *Taanith* 4.5.

6 M *Aboth* 1.1; G.F. Moore, *Judaism* (Cambridge 1927), I, 31–3

CHAPTER IV

1 Judah's involvement in the Phoenician rebellion is not mentioned in Diodorus XVI.40–5, as W.O.E. Oesterley seems to imply, *History of Israel* (Oxford 1932), II, 69.

2 Cowley, text 30, line 1

3 Y. Aharoni, BA XXIV, 4 (Dec. 1961), 110–11

4 Aharoni, pp 111–12. It should be noted however that in the *Antiquities* (XI, 347) Josephus gives the name of the high priest in the late fourth century as Onias, son of Jaddus (Jaddua).

5 As one example of dissent from the theory just elaborated see Y. Kaufmann, *The Religion of Israel*, trans M. Greenberg (Chicago 1960), who argues that the P document is earlier than Deuteronomy.

6 Cowley, text 30, lines 1, 18

7 For a useful discussion of the book of Ruth see D.R. Ap-Thomas in *The Expository Times*, Sept. 1968, pp 369–73.

8 On Egyptian influence on Israel see R.J. Williams in *The Legacy of Egypt*, 2nd ed, ed J.R. Harris (Oxford 1969), pp 257–90. On wisdom in Babylonia see W.G. Lambert, *Babylonian Wisdom Literature* (Oxford 1960).

9 Ecclesiastes (Qoheleth) belongs in this category, but for chronological reasons it is being treated in chapter 5. The Wisdom of Solomon, found in the Apocrypha, is another widsom product, but because of its origin in Alexandria it is not included in the present study.

10 ANET, pp 421–4

11 Some commentators have suggested that chapter 42 originally ended either at verse 9 or verse 11. This conjecture has now received support from the recently published Targum of Job (one of the Dead Sea Scrolls), in which chapter 42 ends with verse 11. See *Le Targum de Job de la Grotte XI de Qumran*, ed J.P.M. van der Ploeg and A.S. van der Woude (Leiden 1971), pp 86–7.

12 See T.J. Meek, IB V, 91.

13 M *Yadaim* 3.5

14 Id

15 References in Eissfeldt, p 485, n 3

16 The phrase 'A Psalm of David' occurs in the titles of 73 psalms: the second word in the Hebrew means 'belonging to David,' 'for David,' 'by David,' and most take this to mean 'dedicated to David.' It is them theorized that there was a collection of psalms to which, for one reason or another, David's name had become attached. It is not beyond the range of possibility that some of these so-called Davidic psalms go back to David himself, although there is no way of identifying such psalms in our present Psalter.

17 A convenient summary of this is found in J. Macdonald, *The Theology of the Samaritans* (London 1964), pp 15–21.

18 Cowley, text 30, lines 1, 29

19 See R.J. Bull, BASOR 190 (April 1968), 4–18; BA XXXI, 2 (May 1968), 58–72.

20 See F.M. Cross, BA XXVI, 4 (Dec. 1963), 110–21.

CHAPTER V

1 For a publication of those papyri at Columbia University see *Zenon Papyri*, ed W.L. Westermann and E.S. Hasenoehrl (New York vol 1/1934, vol 2/1940). For a useful summary of the relation of the Zenon documents to Palestine see V. Tcherikover, *Hellenistic Civilization and the Jews*, trans S. Appelbaum (Philadelphia 1959), pp 60–73.

2 On these wars see CAH VII, chapter 22.

3 The Hebrew name 'Judah' will henceforth be replaced by the Greek form 'Judea.'

4 U. Wilcken claims that, when Alexander was at Tyre in 331 BC, he created an office of finance for Cicilia, Phoenicia, and Syria: *Alexander the Great* (London 1932), p 131.

5 See R. Marcus, Loeb VII, 92–3, note (c).

6 Marcus, Loeb VII, 732–6, summarizes Josephus's data on the high priests in Ptolemaic times. The sequence he favours is Jaddua, Onias I, Simon I, Eleazar, Manasses, Onias II, Simon II.

7 W.F. Albright, BASOR 85 (Feb 1942), 18–27; Tcherikover, pp 104, 451, n 109, 453, n 128

8 See P.W. Skehan, 'The Biblical Scrolls from Qumran and the Text of the Old Testament,' BA XXVIII, 3 (Sept 1965), 87–100.

9 J. Gray, DOTT, pp 124–8

10 *Old Testament Apocalyptic* (London 1952), p 33

11 See W.S. McCullough, 'Israel's Eschatology from Amos to Daniel,' *Studies in the Ancient Palestinian World*, ed J.W. Wevers and D.B. Redford (Toronto 1972), pp 86–101.

12 So Charles II, 168; cf II, 221.

13 For a detailed discussion of this see J.D. Purvis, *The Samaritan Pentateuch and the Origin of the Samaritan Sect* (Cambridge, Mass. 1968), pp 119–29.

14 This account of the fortunes of the cities of Samaria and Shechem is based mostly on chapter 10 in G.E. Wright, *Schechem* (New York 1965); the ancient literary sources, Q. Curtius Rufus, Josephus, and Eusebius, are cited by Wright. On the Samaria papyri see F.M. Cross, BA XXVI, 4 (Dec. 1963), 110–21.

15 J. Macdonald, *The Theology of the Samaritans* (London 1964), p 16

16 Purvis, pp 36–52, 116–18. Purvis contends that the sectarian changes in the received text of the Pentateuch were not made until the first century BC.

17 BA XXVIII, 3 (Sept. 1965), 99

CHAPTER VI

1 On the treaty of Apamea see CAH VIII, 222, 225–6.

2 CAH VIII, 498

3 J.C. Dancy, *A Commentary on I Maccabees* (Oxford 1954), p 46

4 So J. Moffatt, in Charles I, 142

5 That Antiochus IV should have attempted to change the customs of all his subjects, as 1 Mac 1:41–2,51 suggests is highly unlikely. This matter is dealt with on pp 114–16 in the discussion of Antiochus IV.

6 See J. Neusner, *A History of the Jews in Babylonia*, I *The Parthian Period*, 2nd rev ed (Leiden 1969), pp 12–13, 22.

7 CAH VII, 162–3

8 Palestine's history for this period presents a number of problems, principally because of the nature of the literary sources. For a succinct discussion of the latter see Dancy, pp 1–36. On 1 and 2 Maccabees see chapter 10, pp 207–14, in this volume.

9 On the Greek cities of Palestine see chapter 5, p 85, in this volume; also V. Tcherikover, *Hellenistic Civilization and the Jews*, trans S. Applebaum (Philadelphia 1959), pp 90–116.

10 See J. Morgenstern, 'The Ḥasîdîm – Who Were They?' *Hebrew Union College Annual* XXXVIII (1967), 59–73.

11 On the historicity of these documents preserved by Josephus see R. Marcus, Loeb VII, 743–61.

12 An excellent treatment of Antiochus and the Jews is found in chapter 5 of Tcherikover, pp 175–203.

13 The location of the Acra is uncertain. One view is that it was on the western hill, opposite the temple area, overlooking the Tyropoen valley; another places it on the southeast hill. See W.A. Shotwell, BASOR, 176 (Dec. 1964), 10–19.

14 See Dancy, pp 75–6.

15 2 Mac 6:7 tells of Jews, probably of Jerusalem only, being forced to take part in a Dionysiac festival, the precise nature of which is not described.

16 E. Bickerman claims, on what basis is not stated, that the pig was the animal offering both in the Jerusalem temple and elsewhere (*From Ezra to the Last of the Maccabees*, p 93).

17 According to 1 Mac 2:1 and *Ant* XII, 265, Mattathias, an Aaronite, belonged to the descendants of Joarib (cf Jehoiarib of 1 Chr 24:7).

18 Judas, who succeeded his father in the leadership of the dissident Jews, had the nickname 'Maccabeus.'

19 Dancy, pp 18–21, 97–9

20 For Tcherikover's discussion of these letters see pp 213–20, 225–6.

21 The appointment of Alcimus indicated to Onias IV, son of Onias III, that he was unlikely ever to become high priest in Jerusalem, and he therefore fled to Egypt. Ptolemy VI (181–145 BC) gave him shelter and granted him some land at Leontopolis, where Onias built a Jewish temple, which stood until 73 AD (*Ant* XII, 387–8; XIII, 62–73; M *Menahoth* 13.10).

CHAPTER VII

1 Josephus is the principal source for this period (*War* I, 50–158; *Ant* XIII, 194 to XIV, 79).

2 The Roman decree, now found in 1 Mac 15:15–24, should probably follow 1 Mac 14:16–24, and it may be related to the one in *Ant* XIV, 144–8, which is out of place in its existing context.

3 See B. Kanael, 'Ancient Jewish Coins and their Historical Importance,'
   BA XXVI, 2 (May 1963), 43–4.
4 See R. Marcus, Loeb VII, 148, note (a).
5 Kanael, p 44
6 Strabo, *Geography* 753 (XVI, ii, 10)
7 Over against the Jewish Levirate marriage custom (Deut 25:5–10) we have
   to set Lev 21:10–15, which forbids the high priest to marry a widow.
8 Some of the coins refer to Jannaeus as king, others do not. See Kanael,
   pp 44–5.
9 J. Neusner, *A History of the Jews in Babylonia*: I *The Parthian Period*,
   2nd rev ed (Leiden 1969), p xix
10 Neusner, pp 25–7
11 On the Sanhedrin see chapter 8, pp 159–60.
12 There is some confusion in the sources about the sequence of events in the
   Roman occupation of Syria and Palestine; CAH IX, 381–3, is here being
   followed.

CHAPTER VIII

1 Josephus remains the chief source of our information about Herod. He
   once refers to Herod's *Memoirs* (*Ant* XV, 174), although he himself probably
   never saw or used them. His principal source for Herod was Nicolaus of
   Damascus, the friend and biographer of Herod, whose work, *Histories*, is
   referred to in *Ant* I, 159. Josephus is occasionally critical of Nicolaus's
   partiality to Herod (*Ant* XIV, 9; XVI, 184–6). For a full list of the sources on
   Herod see CAH X, 932–5.
2 The sources in Josephus are *War* I, 159–247; *Ant* XIV, 80–184; 268–329;
   various decrees and letters favorable to the Jews are preserved in *Ant* XIV,
   185–267.
3 The sources in Josephus are: *War* I, 248–358; *Ant* XIV, 330–491.
4 On the coins which Antigonus issued see B. Kanael, 'Ancient Jewish Coins
   and their Historical Importance,' BA XXVI, 2 (May 1963), 46–7.
5 Mariamme: this (not Mariamne) is how Josephus writes Miriam (*Ant* III,
   54, 105; IV, 78; cf Mariame, II, 221); in the narrative about Herod it is
   uniformly Mariamme (*War* I, 241, 262, 432, etc).
6 On this date see R. Marcus, Loeb VII, 694–5, note (a) and 700–1, note (d).
7 The sources in Josephus are *War* I, 359–673; *Ant* XV, 1 to XVII, 199.
8 J. Neusner, *A History of the Jews of Babylonia*. I *The Parthian Period*,
   2nd rev ed (Leiden 1969), pp 34–7.
9 The month is uncertain, but it is likely to have been after Cleopatra's death

in August 30 BC. A. Wikgren, Loeb VIII, 89 note (e), and CAH X, 325 support a date in the spring of 30 BC, before Octavian reached Egypt.

10 On Herod's coins see Kanael, pp 48–50.

11 This was part of the general reduction in the number of Roman legions brought about by Octavian (CAH X, 280).

12 The earlier conclusion of C.N. Johns that the so-called 'Tower of David' is in fact Herod's Tower of Phasael (War I, 418; V, 166–9) is now confirmed by R. Amiran and A. Eitan ASOR, Newsletter no. 6 (Jan. 1971), p 4.

13 In 1971–2 Caesarea Maritima, which had earlier been investigated only sporadically, was the object of a joint archaeological expedition (a group from several schools), directed by R.J. Bull. See ASOR, Newsletter no. 1 (July 1971), pp 1–4; BA XXXIV, 3 (Sept. 1971), 88–91; ASOR, Newsletter no. 5 (Jan. 1973), pp 1–4.

14 The cities or districts that Herod befriended included Tripolis, Damascus, Ptolemais, Byblus, Tyre, Sidon, Laodicea, Ascalon, Cos, Rhodes, Lycia, Samos, Ionia, Athens, Sparta, Nicopolis, Pergamum, Antioch, Cilicia, and Elis, where he endowed the Olympic games (War I, 422–8).

15 Cf the instances where the high priest was either appointed by the king or acted under his orders (1 Kgs 2:26–7,35; 2 Kgs 12:7; 16:10–1,15).

16 Neusner has a good discussion of the reasons for Herod's choice of a Babylonian Jew, p 37. Some have thought that Ananel may be Hanamel the Egyptian, referred to in M Parah 3.5.

17 The high priests who followed the second term of Ananel were Jesus, Simon, Matthias, and Joazar, who survived Herod (Ant XV, 320, 322; XVII, 78, 164).

18 War I, 401 gives the date as 23–22 BC, which may be an error.

19 A useful account of the temple is to be found in IDB IV (R–Z), 550–60.

20 On recent excavations of the temple precincts see B. Mazar, BA XXXIII, 2 (May 1970), 47–60; ASOR, Newsletter no. 6 (Jan. 1971), pp 1–4.

21 On Herod's wives see War I, 562–3; Ant XVII, 19–22.

22 So C.A. McRae, MD, of Toronto, in a private communication, on the basis of Josephus's account of Herod's last illness.

23 The sources in Josephus are War I, 665–73; II, 1–100; Ant XVII, 188–323.

24 Herod seems to have made at least four wills: (1) in a speech in Ant XVI, 133, he designated Antipater, son by Doris, to succeed him, and after him, the sons by Mariamme I, Alexander and Aristobulus; (2) in War I, 573; Ant XVII, 53, Antipater is to be king, and after him, Herod, son by Mariamme II; (3) in War I, 646; Ant XVII, 146, Antipas, son by Malthace, is to be king; (4) in War I, 664; Ant XVII, 188–9, Archelaus, son by Malthace, is to be king, Antipas, son by Malthace, to be tetrarch of Galilee and Perea, and Philip, son by Cleopatra of Jerusalem, to be tetrarch of Gaulanitis and neighboring regions. It was this last will that was read publicly by Ptolemy.

CHAPTER IX

1 On the Hebrew fragments of Ben Sira found at Qumran see Eissfeldt, p 599; on those found at Masada (39:27 to 43:30), see Y. Yadin, *The Ben Sira Scroll from Masada* (Jerusalem 1965).

2 An exhaustive study of these traditions is now available in J. Neusner, *The Rabbinic Traditions about the Pharisees before 70*, 3 vols (Leiden 1971).

3 G.F. Moore believed that Samaias was Shammai, Hillel's contemporary: *Judaism* (Cambridge, Mass. 1927), I, 313, n 4.

4 See M *Megillah* 3.4–6 for an early list of appointed lessons from the Law.

5 *The Contemplative Life*, 30–3. Actually this passage relates to the practice of the monastic group, the Therapeutae, who met together in their sanctuary on the Sabbath. What Egyptian Jews did who were not Therapeutae is not stated.

6 For a second-century AD opinion about what scholars of different ages should study see M *Aboth* 5.21.

7 See Moore, pp 244–5.

8 The one possible reference is in 4:14 where 'from another quarter' may be an oblique reference to God.

9 See 'The Additions to the Book of Esther' in the RSV Apocrypha; see also pp 179–80 in this chapter.

10 It should be noted that in the fifth century BC the Jews of Elephantine in Egypt were the object of Gentile hostility.

11 See A. Rahlfs, *Septuaginta* (Stuttgart 1935), II, 180–1.

12 A Targum was a translation, frequently paraphrastic, of a Hebrew text into Aramaic. A Midrash (lit 'study,' 'exposition') varied somewhat in its signification. Most commonly it meant either the exegesis of a biblical passage or sermonic material intended to teach or edify.

13 C.C. Torrey favours a date about a century later: *The Apocryphal Literature* (New Haven 1945), p 128.

14 Haggadah (lit 'telling'), when applied to the Scriptures, designated material that was essentially didactic or inspirational. In contradistinction to it, Halakah, which has a strong juristic overtone, meant a legal interpretation of the Law or of the tradition.

15 So Eissfeldt, pp 633, 635

16 See M. Burrows, *More Light on the Dead Sea Scrolls* (New York 1958), p 179.

17 Charles II, 310

18 M. de Jonge, *The Testaments of the Twelve Patriarchs* (Assen 1953); D.S. Russell, *The Method and Message of Jewish Apocalyptic* (Philadelphia 1964), p 57

19 R.H. Charles, *The Greek Versions of the Testaments of the Twelve Patriarchs* (Oxford 1908), p xliv

20 Charles II, 341
21 Charles II, 294

CHAPTER X

1 The critical view of the origin of Daniel is here assumed. For a summary of the main arguments in support of this position see *Daniel*, IDB, vol A–D, pp 761–8; Eissfeldt, pp 516–29.
2 See A. Rahlfs, *Septuaginta* (Stuttgart 1935), II, 174–7.
3 Portions of ten MSS written in Aramaic: M. Burrows, *More Light on the Dead Sea Scrolls* (New York 1958), p 407
4 An extreme view, adopted by Milik, is that chapters 37–71 come from a Jewish Christian of the second century AD (Eissfeldt, p 620).
5 Cf C.C. Torrey's view that no part of Enoch is earlier than 95 BC: *The Apocryphal Literature* (New Haven 1945), pp 112–14.
6 E.g., Eusebius, *Ecclesiastical History* VI, xxv, quoting Origen's list of the Scriptures, which gives 1 Maccabees a title pointing to a Hebrew original
7 For examples see J.C. Dancy, *A Commentary on I Maccabees* (Oxford 1954), p 9.

CHAPTER XI

1 F.M. Cross and J.T. Milik, BASOR 142 (April 1956), 5–17.
2 Of the almost 400 MSS found in cave 4 about one-quarter are biblical. See F.M. Cross, *The Ancient Library of Qumran and Modern Biblical Studies* (New York 1958), pp 30–1.
3 Eissfeldt, pp 619, 621, 661
4 Eissfeldt, p 662
5 See pp 231–2 of G. Vermes, *The Dead Sea Scrolls in English* (Middlesex 1962). The reference in this fragment to 'Demetrius king of Greece' is probably to the Seleucid king, Demetrius III (96–88 BC), the contemporary of Alexander Jannaeus.
6 On Ps 107 see I. Rabinowitz in BA XIV, 2 (May 1951), pp 50–2.
7 *Le targum de Job de la grotte XI de Qumran*, ed J.P.M. van der Ploeg and A.S. van der Woude (Leiden 1971)
8 Charles II, pp 785–834
9 Pp 2–43 in C. Rabin, *The Zadokite Documents* (Oxford 1958)
10 Rabin, pp 44–77
11 A serviceable translation in Vermes, pp 118–21
12 See, for instance, M. Mansoor, *The Thanksgiving Hymns* (Leiden 1961), pp 97–193; Vermes, pp 149–201.

13 Y. Yadin, *The Scroll of the War of the Sons of Light against the Sons of Darkness*, English trans B. Rabin and C. Rabin (Oxford 1962)
14 Yadin, pp 243–6
15 G.F. Moore, *Judaism* (Cambridge, Mass. 1927), II, 370
16 *The Contemplative Life*, trans F.H. Colson, vol IX of Philo in the Loeb Classical Library, section 25, p 127
17 See the Scripture Index in vol X of Philo in the Loeb Classical Library, pp 259–63.
18 Moore, II, 238, 244
19 Quoted by C.C. Torrey, *The Apocryphal Literature* (New Haven 1945), pp 14–15

BIBLIOGRAPHY

The major literary sources for this study, as well as two (out of many) useful works for the biblical material, are noted below:

The Holy Bible, Revised Standard Version, Toronto, New York, Edinburgh, 1952

The Apocrypha, Revised Standard Version, Toronto, New York, Edinburgh, 1957

The Apocrypha and Pseudepigrapha of the Old Testament in English, edited by R.H. Charles, 2 volumes, Oxford 1913; volume I, *the Apocrypha*; volume II, *the Pseudepigrapha*. Many of the books contained in these two volumes were published separately in a series Translations of Early Documents, edited by W.O.E. Oesterley and G.H. Box, London and New York.

Josephus, 9 volumes in the Loeb Classical Library, edited by H.St.J. Thackeray, et al., London 1926–65

The Dead Sea Scrolls in English, edited by G. Vermes, Harmondsworth, 1962

Cambridge Ancient History, edited by J.B. Bury, et al., Cambridge volume IV/1926; 1930 to volume X/1934; 1952

The Interpreter's Dictionary of the Bible, edited by G.A. Buttrick, et al., 4 volumes, New York and Nashville 1962

O. Eissfeldt, *The Old Testament, an Introduction*, translated by P.R. Ackroyd, New York 1965. This volume, despite its title, treats all the literature discussed in the present study.

The Mishnah, translated by H. Danby, Oxford, 1933

Listed below are some modern studies dealing with various aspects of our subject.

P.R. Ackroyd, *Israel under Babylon and Persia*, Oxford 1970

J.M. Allegro, *The Chosen People: Jewish History from the Exile to 135 A.D.*, London 1971

D. Baly and A.D. Tushingham, *Atlas of the Biblical World*, New York 1971

S.W. Baron, *A Social and Religious History of the Jews*, volume 1, New York 1952

E. Bickerman, *From Ezra to the Last of the Maccabees*, New York 1962

G. Cornfeld, *Daniel to Paul*, New York 1962

R. de Vaux, *Ancient Israel*, translated by J. McHugh, London 1961

M. Noth, *The History of Israel*, second edition, London 1960

D.S. Russell, *The Jews from Alexander to Herod*, Oxford 1967

N.H. Snaith, *The Jews from Cyrus to Herod*, Wallington 1949

INDEX

Index